THE NATURE OF THE OPERATIONS OF MODERN ARMIES

CASS SERIES ON THE SOVIET STUDY OF WAR

(Selected Translations)

Series Editor: David M. Glantz

Fort Leavenworth, Kansas

This series examines what Soviet military theorists and commanders have learned from the study of their own military operations. Separate volumes contain annotated translations of Soviet works analysing their own experiences, as well as the works of important Soviet military theorists and collections of Soviet articles concerning specific campaigns, operation or military techniques.

1. Harold S. Orenstein, translator and editor, *Soviet Documents on the Use of War Experience*, Volume I, *The Initial Period of War 1941*, with an Introduction by David M. Glantz
2. Harold S. Orenstein, translator and editor, *Soviet Documents on the Use of War Experience*, Volume II, *The Winter Campaign 1941–1942*, with an Introduction by David M. Glantz
3. Joseph G. Welsh, translator, *Red Armor Combat Orders: Combat Regulations for Tank and Mechanized Forces 1944*, edited and with an Introduction by Richard N. Armstrong
4. Harold S. Orenstein, translator and editor, *Soviet Documents on the Use of War Experience*, Volume III, *Military Operations 1941 and 1942*, with an Introduction by David M. Glantz
5. William A. Burhans, translator, *The Nature of the Operations of Modern Armies* by V.K. Triandafillov, edited by Jacob W. Kipp, with an Introduction by James J. Schneider

THE NATURE OF THE OPERATIONS OF MODERN ARMIES

V. K. Triandafillov

Translated by William A. Burhans

Edited and with a foreword by Jacob W. Kipp

Introduction by Professor James J. Schneider

FRANK CASS

First published in 1994 in Great Britain by
FRANK CASS & CO. LTD
Newbury House, 900 Eastern Avenue,
Newbury Park, Ilford
Essex IG2 7HH

and in the United States of America by
FRANK CASS
c/o International Specialized Book Services, Inc.
5804 N.E. Hassalo Street, Portland, Oregon 97213–3644

British Library Cataloguing in Publication Data

Triandafillov, V. K.
Nature of the Operations of Modern Armies.—(Cass Series on the Soviet Study of War)
I. Title II. Kipp, Jacob W.
III. Burhans, W. A. IV. Series
355.001

ISBN 0-7146-4501-X (cloth)
ISBN 0-7146-4118-9 (paper)

Library of Congress Cataloging in Publication Data

Triandafillov, V. (Vladimir), 1894–1931.
[Kharakter operatsii sovremennykh armii. English]
The nature of the operations of modern armies / by V. K. Triandafillov ; translated by William A. Burhans; edited and with a foreword by Jacob W. Kipp; introduction by James J. Schneider.
p. cm. — — (Cass series on the Soviet study of war; 5)
Includes index.
ISBN 0-7146-4501-X (cloth); 0-7146-4118-9 (paper)
1. Military art and science. I. Kipp, Jacob W. II. Title.
III. Series: Cass series on the Soviet study of war; no. 5.
U102.T8413 1994
355--dc20 92–28919
CIP

The views expressed here are those of the authors and should not be construed to represent those of the US Department of Defense or the US Department of the Army.

Typeset by Datix International, Bungay, Suffolk
Printed in Great Britain by Bookcraft (Bath) Ltd

Contents

Foreword

This edition of V.K. Triandafillov's *The Nature of the Operations of Contemporary Armies* makes accessible to Western military historians and analysts one of the most important works in the development of Soviet military theory from the inter-war period. Triandafillov's volume became both a basic work in the development of Soviet theory of operational art and a model for the method of engaging in foresight in military affairs.[1] His work is noteworthy as an early attempt to come to grips with the military-technical characteristics of modern operations as they would shape the character of future war [*budushchaia voina*]. His approach explicitly acknowledges the reality that future war will be different from past combat experience, but stresses the need to study those trends affecting the character of armed conflict to understand the evolution of military art. It is a method conducive to the examination of radical breaks or "revolutions" in military affairs.

Triandafillov's *The Nature of the Operations of Contemporary Armies* belongs to such an era in military theory. A Janus-like work, this volume, built upon the accomplishments of tsarist military theorists, conditioned by Marxist-Leninist ideology, and informed by the systematic reflections on the experience of the First World War and the Civil War, became a keystone in the development of Soviet operational art. Triandafillov was credited with making a major contribution to the theories of deep battle, successive operations, and deep operations, and to the study of "future war."[2] First published in 1929 at the very beginning of Stalin's revolution from above, the volume provides key insights into the professional military's assessment of the need for the industrialization and militarization of the Soviet economy and society in light of the then-dominant assumptions about the Soviet Union's probable opponents in a future war.

Following Triandafillov's death in an airplane crash in July 1931, the work went through three posthumous editions in 1932, 1936 and 1937. In a bibliographic guide to the most important Soviet and foreign literature on various aspects of operational art and the study of future war, which appeared in 1933, I. Ivanov listed the volume as the basic work in four out of twelve categories relating to operational art. These included modern operational means, the conduct of operations, meeting operations, and offensive operations. Ivanov also featured Triandafillov's book as crucial to the study of three specific aspects of the conduct of operations: command and control, transport, and rear services.[3] P.I. Vakulich likewise acknowledged the debt Soviet military science owed to Triandafillov's work, calling it "most serious and original, in the full sense progressive."[4]

Triandafillov's volume exemplified the contribution of Soviet military theory's application of a scientific approach to foresight in military affairs during one of its most dynamic and innovative periods, when the military leadership struggled to absorb the changes in modern warfare which had been emerging with mechanization. Sixty years after the author's death, his method still retains its value for military analysts and theorists, especially in another era of radical changes in military art.

Over the last decade Western military historians and analysts have come to appreciate the enduring contributions of Soviet officers to the study and conduct of war at the operational level, that is, at echelons above corps and on the scale of theater-strategic campaigns. This appreciation stands in stark contrast to the situation two decades ago when the very term "operational art" (*operativnoe iskusstvo*) was dismissed in the West as mere pretention, an artificial creation imposed between tactics and strategy without content, rigor or merit.[5] Such an evaluation of operational art was, however, not surprising, because Soviet theorists and practitioners were scarcely known to Western military historians, who dismissed Soviet theory as irrelevant ideological eyewash or categorized the theorists as crude epigones of the German military theorists who conceived and put into practice blitzkrieg. Owing to the distortions imposed upon military history by Stalinism and the continuing dictates of Party-guided history, the Red Army even in the early 1960s lacked a clear appreciation of the origins of operational art.[6] As Professor James J. Schneider points out in the introduction to this volume, that situation has changed significantly over the last decade. Much more is known about the origins of operational art and its significance for modern military theory.

FOREWORD

THE MAN

V.K. Triandafillov (1894–1931) drew upon what were the most healthy and dynamic elements among the old military intelligentsia, that is, *genshtabisty/voenspetsy*, in Soviet service, and the young Red Commanders. He was one of the first products of the Soviet system of military education. His was a generation which for a little more than a decade managed to combine pen and sword, "knowledge" (*znanie*) with "know-how" (*umenie*), to the mutual advantage of both military science and military art.[7] Like many other young officers of the Red Army, his military career was the result of war, revolution and civil war, not family tradition or youthful dreams. Born on 14 March 1894 (N.S.), to a Greek peasant family in the village of Magaratszhik, near Kars on the Turkish border, he studied at the Trans-Caucasian Pedagogical Seminary. Upon completion of the seminary, Triandafillov was conscripted into the tsarist army at the outbreak of the First World War.[8]

A conscript and combat veteran, he was selected for officer training in 1915, one of those thrust into command by the heavy losses inflicted upon the tsarist army in the first year of the war. Upon commissioning Triandafillov returned to the front and rose to the rank of Staff Captain, commanding a battalion on the Southwestern Front. As a soldier-revolutionary he was popular enough with his fellow soldiers in the turbulent days of 1917 to be elected to command the 7th Army. Like many other soldiers, Triandafillov was radicalized by the revolutionary events of 1917 and joined the SRs. By the October Revolution he was a Left SR supporting the seizure of power by the soviets in the name of bread, land and peace. Both Kerensky's Provisional Government and that of Petlura in the Ukraine condemned him for this radicalism.[9]

When the Left SRs broke with the Bolsheviks over peace with Germany Triandafillov supported Lenin and Soviet Power. At the outbreak of the Civil War he joined the Red Army as a military specialist (*voenspets*), and thereafter commanded a company, battalion, regiment and brigade. He fought on the Ural Front against Dutov and on the South Front against Denikin. Joining the Communist Party in 1919, he was a natural choice for education as a Red *genshtabist* posted to the Military Academy of the RKKA in the same year.[10] He graduated with honors in 1923.

This extended tenure at the Academy was a result of the Soviet government's decision out of necessity to combine formal education with practical experience. From 1919–23 Triandafillov, like many of his fellow students, combined classroom study with short-term, staff assignments and tactical command on the various fronts of the Civil War. This gave him a solid basis for various professional studies of the most important operations of the Civil War.[11]

As General-Major A.A. Svechin, one of the Academy's most eminent professors, noted, these students were soldier-revolutionaries and not traditional student-officers. Young men, just arriving from the fronts of a bloody and bitter civil war, were already hardened veterans, having seen combat in the First World War as well as the Civil War. Full of enthusiasm for a cause but distrustful of professors from the tsarist Nikolaevsky Academy of the General Staff, who were suspected of being "class enemies," they refused to be intimidated by classical authorities or to accept the "school" solutions. Their test of instruction was its relevance to their own practical experience in the field. Svechin could see in the face of each man ". . . an idea which is blasphemous to the temple of science, that is, to bring in something of his own – to criticize thoroughly the ideas presented to them. Their enthusiasm merged with a scorn for the old forms of military science."[12] These extraordinary circumstances created a unique climate for the serious study of military art. Vigorous debate and sharp polemics were the order of the day.

General A.I. Verkhovsky (1886–1938), Professor of Tactics at the Military Academy and former Minister of War of the Provisional Government, saw the *voenspets*-professors, like himself, as military "realists," engaged in "a war on two fronts." The realists had to contend with conservatives, who wanted to maintain past views because they were sanctioned by history and the unchanging laws of military science, and the futurists, who, on the basis of their experience in the Revolution and Civil War, put their faith in crude military means and political agitation and trusted in class struggle to ignite revolution behind the enemy's lines. In assessing this struggle during the Academy's first decade, 1918–28, Verkhovsky concluded that it had been one full of vitality. The Red Army had made significant progress in the study of military science and military art.[13]

In such heady times a rough and tumble theory, conditioned by practical experience and guided by a militant ideology, became the basis for a new military science. Its demand for a unity of theory and praxis was fulfilled in the "scientific" analysis of their own combat experience as reflected in the activites of the Military Academy's Military–Scientific Society.[14] Triandafillov delivered his first lecture to that body on 24 December 1919, when he discussed the recent offensive operations of the Southern Front against Denikin's Army.[15]

In the great debate over the approach to the study of military science and the articulation of a unified military doctrine, Triandafillov belonged to those in the center who resisted past authority, even as they studied military history, and rejected the myth of the world revolution advancing on the bayonets of the Red Army. In seeking a mature military theory to encompass the reality of modern war he stressed the role of critical insight as the chief vehicle for securing the unity of theory and praxis. He brought this approach to his studies of Frunze's final offensive against Baron Wrangel. As a brigade commander with the 41st Rifle Division, Triandafillov had taken an active part in these operations. At the same time, in his studies he persisted in showing their deficiencies in his contributions to the activities of the Academy's Military–Scientific Society.[16]

In 1921 he took part in the suppression of the Tambov Insurrection, when he served under M.N. Tukhachevsky. Triandafillov was closely associated with Tukhachevsky for the next decade. For Tukhachevsky, the "March Beyond the Vistula" in 1920 was the campaign most relevant to the development of Soviet military art in keeping with the class-nature of the Soviet state and the possibility of using the Red Army to bring about "revolution from without." Like many other Soviet officers, Triandafillov also wrote on the Polish–Soviet war; his first study on a tactical engagement during the final phase of the campaign appeared in 1922.[17]

In his major study of troop control during the 1920 campaign, Triandafillov accepted Lenin's self-critique of the Soviet leadership's mis-assessment of the revolutionary situation in Poland. This had led to a strategic disjuncture between the military means available and the political objectives sought, and doomed the operation to failure. An insufficient mobilization base in the shattered economy of War Communism and an inadequate logistical system connecting front and rear meant that during initial operations the Red Army was unable to achieve a favorable correlation of forces on the main axis of attack, and during the pursuit of a disorganized but undefeated Polish Army to the Vistula the Red Army suffered an attrition of combat power so that at the culmination of the campaign its divisions had exhausted their combat power and were vulnerable to the Polish counteroffensive.[18]

In his study Triandafillov focused on the problem of operational troop control. He identified the failure of troop control at front and supreme high command levels as the key factor in undermining the coherent development of successive operations by multiple fronts throughout the theater campaign. An already risky campaign in these circumstances with the breakdown of cooperation led to defeat. The advance of S. Budenny's First Cavalry Army against Lvov in place of a coordinated blow towards Lublin in support of Tukhachevsky's Western Front's effort to envelop Warsaw from the north in late July was for him primarily a problem of ineffective control in which each front fought its own campaign without unifying direction to a common, decisive goal, in this case the destruction of the Polish forces before Warsaw. Triandafillov noted the failings of the RKKA high command in Moscow and both front commands, and singled out the overextended commitments of Southwestern Front, which in the summer of 1920 simultaneously had to control operations against Wrangel in the Crimea, keep a keen eye on the Romanian border, and provide direction for operations of 1st Cavalry Army, 12th Army and 14th Army south of the Pripyat Marshes. Southwestern Front Commander A.I. Egorov, in the words of Triandafillov, found himself caught trying to direct operations on two axes without staff support and did not feel "the beating pulse of the operations."[19]

Following his graduation from the Military Academy in 1923, Frunze chose his former subordinate to join the Main Staff of the RKKA, where he took over as Chief of the Operations Section in 1924. From there he moved on to command a rifle corps and then returned to Moscow as Deputy Chief of Staff for RKKA in 1928.

Charged with putting operational art into practice, Triandafillov began working on a major study on the nature of the operations of modern armies. The first part of this effort, which appeared in 1926, echoed Mikhail Frunze's injunction to study and prepare for total war by assessing the military potential of the state and its probable opponents. For Frunze, under the then existing conditions, any future war for the Soviet state would be a protracted struggle and not be decided by a single battle or even one campaign.[20] This attention to the economic and industrial foundations of military power led to assessing the role of the rear in determining the scale of operations which modern armies could conduct. The throughput capacity of railroads, as the artery tying an attacking army to its rear, became the chief determinant of the depth of an operational advance, since an attacking force with severely limited motor transport to support its advance could not maintain a rate of resupply to sustain the tempo of advance against an opponent falling back on his own rail network. His subsequent studies built upon this foundation to lay out in detail the military context of the theory of successive, deep operations. In such deep operations he envisioned a reorganized system of road transport, which would make it possible to shift operational scale from 190–240 km to 320–400 km and, thereby, an army might achieve the destruction of an opposing army throughout the depths of its dispositions.[21]

The scale of operations in good measure also depended upon the density of forces in a particular theater of military actions, which, in turn, depended upon the nature of a given state's mobilization system. The hard realities of mobilization precluded any state from making use of its maximium mobilization potential into the initial period of war. Smaller states might approach such a potential rapidly but large states, especially agrarian ones like the Soviet Union or Poland, could not. Indeed, looking at the military situation in post-war Europe, Triandafillov concluded that the overall mobilization capacity of most states was substantially less than in the pre-1914 period for a complex set of reasons. The only unknown of true consequence was Weimar Germany, as Triandafillov noted: "The mobilization capabilities of Germany are difficult to foresee because at the present time it is difficult to foresee the circumstances of its mobilization."[22]

Triandafillov called attention to the process of technological development which was making possible the "mechanization" of warfare, but noted its limited impact upon the economically backward regions of Eastern Europe with their peasant rear. New automatic weapons, armor, aviation and gas would affect such a war, but would not become decisive. He also treated the problem of manpower mobilization and the reality of mass war quickly becoming a war of conscripts and reservists. This brought him to the problem of addressing the means of achieving breakthrough and sustaining pursuit in successive deep operations. Here he drew upon Frunze's use of shock armies against Wrangel for the breakthrough and the employment of echeloned strategic cavalry forces to facilitate exploitation and pursuit. Deep operations would employ operational maneuver to encircle and destroy the opposing force. Success in such operations turned upon two related problems: the organization of an effective command and control system to coordinate the operations of several armies and the establishment of realistic logistical norms in keeping with the geographic-economic realities of the theater of military action.[23]

As Deputy Chief of Staff to the RKKA Triandafillov's views reflected some basic assumptions regarding the sort of war the Red Army would fight in the future. The Field Regulations of 1929 in its treatment of the offensive touched on many of the same themes developed by Triandafillov in greater detail.[24] While the new regulations did provide for successive, deep operations based upon a combined-arms offensive, the armies described by Triandafillov and the regulations were modernized versions of the Red Army from the Civil War.

THE SUBJECT

Although long in incubation, operational art by the mid-1920s had emerged as an intermediary category of military art between strategy and tactics. Strategy by this time had a new content in keeping with the realities of World War and Civil War. It embodied Lenin's redefinition of Clausewitz's formulation of war as a continuation of politics and stressed economic mobilization for total war: "The mobilization of all the resources of the country and the directing of the country's armed forces toward the achievement of the political objectives of the war have become the affair of strategy, that is, of the high command."[25] Tactics remained the conduct of combat in direct contact with the enemy. Between these two domains lay the "employment of the armed forces in the theater of military actions, the domain of operational art."[26]

The term "operational art" had first been used by A.A. Svechin in a series of lectures at the Academy devoted to strategy in 1923–24.[27] Svechin developed the concept of operational art within the context of a critique of existing strategic concepts and under the influence of the German military historian and analyst, Hans Delbrueck. Svechin's major points can be summarized as an explicit attack upon the old strategy-tactics dichotomy and the articulation of a new and very different approach in which operational art assumed central importance. His main points can be summarized as the following: (1) the establishment of a political-economic foundation beneath strategy; (2) a division of strategy into two ideal types: attrition (*izmor*) and destruction (*sokrushenie*); (3) the delineation of operational art and the assertion of radically new understanding of the concept of operations; (4) a reduction of the role of combat; (5) denial of the importance of the single decisive engagement and the transformation of combat into an on-going, episodic process; (6) radical reduction of the role of march-maneuver as a major strategic factor; (7) emphasizing the role of transportation and communications in strategy and the significance of military-technical superiority.[28]

Svechin described operational art as the bridge between tactics and strategy, that is, the means by which the senior commander transformed a series of tactical successes into operational "bounds" linked together by the commander's intent and plan and contributing to strategic success in a given theater of military actions.[29] As Svechin formulated the relationship among tactics, operational art, and strategy, operational art emerged as the critical conceptual linkage for the conduct of theater war.

> Then, battle is the means of the operation. Tactics are the material of operational art. The operation is the means of strategy, and operational art is the material of strategy. This is the essence of the three-part formula given above.[30]

This domain of military art became the focus of Triandafillov's study.

Svechin's conceptualization of operational art coincided with Frunze's appointment as Chief of Staff of the RKKA and Chief of the Military Academy. At Frunze's initiative, a Chair of Army Operations was established at the Academy of the RKKA in 1924, but did not survive for long.[31] The content of that part of the Academy's curriculum was directed at the techniques required to conduct operations. The emphasis was more upon general commentary rather than practical preparation to conduct operations. Typical of this literature was M. Bonch-Bruevich's essay on principles of operational leadership in modern war. This laid out the content of an operational plan, outlining its features: mission statement, intelligence on enemy forces and their probable courses of action, information on the status of one's own forces, the specific missions of subordinated units, the structure of rear services, the organization of supply, and the support of the operation.

Bonch-Bruevich emphasized the role of troop control organs in turning the commander's intent to an operational plan, and outlined the various areas where the staff had to assess the situation. His list of such activities was extensive and encompassed all aspects of operational planning. Bonch-Bruevich emphasized the art of troop control and the role of staff calculations as critical to operational leadership and pointed out the role of the struggle for time in "all preparatory actions and during execution." [32]

THE METHOD

Triandafillov's method of studying operational art deserves attention because of both its content and impact. This is not the reflective work of the retired soldier-scholar looking back on past campaigns. The focus is upon future battles in future wars. The objective is to use past experience, current capabilities and trends to foresee the nature of future operations. Triandafillov's abiding concerns are those of a chief of staff entrusted with the dual tasks of training an army and planning operations.[33] In this regard Triandafillov followed in the footsteps of Svechin, who defined the role of military science in practical terms: "The conclusions of military theory do not represent incontrovertible exactitudes. . . . We are inclined to understand military theory as referring to any system of knowledge which aids us in understanding life and practice." [34]

Triandafillov devotes the first part of the study to those economic developments, socio-political shifts, and technological changes which are shaping the evolution of military art. They guarantee that future war will be different from past war. He treats technological developments in the post-First World War decade, beginning with infantry weapons and moving on to artillery, chemical weapons, tanks, communications and engineering support, and aviation. He examines not only the status of such weapons but also the probable trends in their further development, making effective use of the works of foreign military specialists in his assessment of these trends. Triandafillov then confronts the most burning question of his day: whether future armies would be small, professional, mechanized forces or million-man, mass armies. On the basis of an analysis of capitalist societies, he concludes that mass, mechanized armies will dominate future battlefields.

Writing in the late 1920s, he divides Europe into two military spheres, that is, the Western advanced capitalist zone and the Eastern underdeveloped zone, in which he includes the Soviet Union. In the West, mass, mechanized warfare has already become possible, but in the East economic underdevelopment means that these armies are based on a "peasant rear." Given the then-dominant Soviet assumptions about "threat," that is, concept of attack by the various successor states of Eastern Europe with the support of Britain, France, and other Allied powers, his categorization of Eastern Europe set the material-technical characteristics of that theater of military actions.[35] Mechanization, therefore, would for the immediate future only be an addendum in this theater to traditional, that is, infantry and cavalry, armies, so long as the national economies remain underdeveloped.[36] Experiments with small mechanized units to enhance the capabilities of the various combat arms are foreseen, as in the case of adding light tanks and armored cars to strategic cavalry.[37] Based on these assumptions, Triandafillov addresses the problems of mobilization and sustainment. He concludes the first section of his book by turning his attention to force structure and addressing the problems of combined arms and the logistical support of a modern army in the field.

Having set the context, he shifts his focus to the conduct of operations by modern armies. He defines the densities of various forces during deployment and the initial phase of an operation. Herein lay the "art" or skill portion of operational art. The key to success in this new art lies in the application of "scientific methods" to the problem of planning operations. He stresses the role of "calculations" in determining the feasibility of various courses of action in support of an operational concept. Such calculations will not predict the outcome of the operation, but they do serve the commander and his staff in planning operations.

Frunze played a leading role in promoting such an approach by invigorating the Military Academy's Higher Military-Academic Courses (*VVAK*) for senior Red Army commanders, which focused on the further education of brigade and higher commanders.[38] Frunze's commitment to this program brought more attention to the Chair of Strategy and its further development. He emphasized the need to change the content of the course on the conduct of operations by shifting from general observations to working out the practical details and techniques for the conduct of operations.[39] Over the next several years this led to the development of a program of operational war-gaming in which students were expected to do the necessary calculations and estimates necessary to prepare for an army operation. This "applied" approach to training future commanders and staff officers was a major break with past Russian tradition and placed primary stress upon finding means in the educational process of unifying theory and practice. The leaders in the development of operational war-gaming at the Academy were Triandafillov, K. Berends, and N. Varfolomeev, the Deputy Chief of the Department of Strategy.[40] The summer campaign of 1920 served as both a model and a case study for such operational gaming, since it embraced a major operational axis in a war aganst one of the most probable future opponents of the Soviet state.

While Triandafillov recognized a wide range of army operations, he chose to present to his readers the offensive of a shock army. He emphasized the need to achieve sufficient force to secure a breakthrough of a prepared defense and to advance into the depths of the enemy position. He applied various norms, that is, optimal numerical densities of men and fire, to calculate the necessary correlations of forces needed to accomplish these tasks, that is, penetration, breakthrough, exploitation, and pursuit, and identified the objective limitations which proscribe the temporal and spatial limits of such deep operations and, therefore, affect the course and outcome of such operations. He concluded that in a major war among large states no single operation could be decisive, and that final victory would go to the force which could conduct a series of successive and coherent operations. The question of integrating tactical engagements into operational successes and operational successes into strategic victory led him to examine in detail two other problems associated with the operational level of war – troop control and logistic capabilities.[41]

These elements set the very tone of the Red Army's new field regulations of 1929.[42] Slow mobilization potential, the scale of theater operations in Eastern Europe, and technological backwardness in these circumstances dictated a strategic posture during the initial period of a future war that would stress the attrition of successive operations, rather than decisive operations in the initial period of war. At the same time Triandafillov noted that the class nature of the Soviet state dictated a policy of socio-political transformation in areas liberated by the Red Army, that is, the extension of Soviet power into these conquered areas to bring about their effective mobilization and to disarm the forces of the counterrevolution.

THE IMPLICATIONS

By the late 1920s, M.N. Tukhachevsky had emerged as the most important opponent of such views. In their place he advocated a strategy of "destruction" (*sokrushenie*), that is, decisive offensive operations in the initial period of war with the intent of seizing the initiative and destroying the enemy force by means of deep operations and envelopment. This he deemed possible on the basis of the mass mechanization of the Soviet armed forces. Tukhachevsky promoted the idea of linking economic development to the requirements of a total war economy under the slogan of "militarization" (*voennizatsiia*).[43] Tukhachevsky, ever the young Red Commander, postulated a total war in defense of socialism in which the combination of a mass, mechanized Red Army and class struggle in the enemy rear would smash the opposing capitalist coalition and set in motion the revolution from without.[44] He stood the basic assumptions of Soviet strategic planning during the NEP on their head, rather than relying upon the proletariat to weaken the rear of attacking East European successor states supported by France and Britain and thereby give the USSR time to mobilize for protracted war.

For Tukhachevsky the vision of future war, a combination of mass, mechanized warfare and revolutionary upheaval, made a strategy of "destruction" the appropriate one for the Soviet state. He specifically criticized those military theorists, especially Svechin, whom he accused of underestimating the transformations being brought about by the First Five-Year Plan and, therefore, assuming that the Red Army in future wars would have to rely upon a "low economic-technological base" and, therefore, employ a strategy of "attrition" (*izmor*).[45] For Tukhachevsky, "attrition" and partial victory in a protracted struggle as strategic principles robbed the Soviet state of the possibility of putting into practice a new form of war, combining total war with revolutionary upheaval. He not only endorsed the Stalinist program of industrialization and collectivization as the necessary prerequisite for a strategy of "destruction," but also sought to stigmatize those favoring a strategy of "attrition" as class enemies, bourgeois theorists, and idealists. In seeking to establish his own credibility by invoking ideological purity and Party loyalty, Tukhachevsky contributed to the end of professional debate within the Red Army.[46]

Tukhachevsky juxtaposed the views of the old specialists/military theorists with those of the Red Army's "practical workers," among whom he included Triandafillov. Tukhachevsky was critical of those who saw *Blitzkreig* and lightning operations by elite professional armies as a way of avoiding a protracted war. His critics within the Red Army, however, detected just such a flight from reality in his own writings and accused him of writing science fiction, rather than forecasting the nature of future war. As one commentator stated his "strategy of destruction" had too much in common with the novels of H.G. Wells.[47]

Tukhachevsky naturally rejected this assessment. Foresight in military affairs required that the theorist assess precisely those tendencies of development which would bring about qualitative changes in military art. As he asserted in a study that went unpublished during his lifetime, projections of future capabilities required more than an extrapolation on past combat experience:

> Thus, the study of the experience of the imperialist war (First World War) from the point of view of employment of the basic combat types of armaments is a necessary first step toward correct preparation for future conflicts. But the study of that experience alone is not sufficient. One must be able to follow up just how newly appearing means of combat and operations will modify operational forms and how it is necessary to develop our own armaments in order to achieve the most effective use of military-technological resources, which the country's growing technology and industry could provide for war.[48]

By 1931 Triandafillov, whose career had been closely tied with Frunze, Svechin and Tukhachevsky, was revising his work on operations to postulate a mass, mechanized Red Army. He died before this process could be completed. However, his outline of topics and problems assumed a major shift in tactics and operational art based upon the threat environment, Soviet economic capabilities, and specific force structure changes in keeping with a mass, mechanized army. The threat assessment assumed an increased likelihood of conflict with major capitalist powers as a result of the Great Depression, increased instability in the capitalist system, and their opponents' more overtly anti-Soviet policies.[49] Writing at a time when Left Communists in the military were echoing M.N. Pokrovsky's call for a "certain monopoly" for their views in "scientific-methodological work" in order to ensure their victory over "bourgeois objectivism", Triandafillov now accepted the possibility of creating a mass, mechanized army in the USSR through the Stalinist drive for heavy industrialization and sided with those who saw these changes as revolutionary, a "new stage of development of tactics and operational art."[50] His comments are, at best, a sketch without details. Soviet officers have been willing to assert that these few remarks anticipate the mechanization of successive deep operations as presented in the 1936 Field Regulations.[51]

The final edition of Triandafillov's book appeared in 1937 and coincided with Stalin's blood purge of the Red Army's officer corps. The climate of open discussion and debate gave way to totalitarian control. Thereafter, in light of the Stalinization of military science it became a work without context or roots. Even after a decade of de-Stalinization the contributions of Soviet military theorists, including Triandafillov, to the development of operational art in the 1920s were unappreciated.[52] Until *glasnost* and *perestroyka*, an appreciation of the contributions of that period to military theory, as General-Colonel V.N. Lobov noted in 1989, were little known and poorly appreciated even within the Soviet Armed Forces.[53]

THE EDITION

The translation by William A. Burhans is faithful to the original in style and meaning. Triandafillov's idiom and jargon have been preserved within the dictates of a modern military lexicon. This foreword seeks to place the author and his work in its Soviet context. Professor Schneider's introduction addresses *The Nature of Operations of Modern Armies* in the larger context of twentieth-century military thought and thereby underscores this work's contribution to the evolution of military art and the emergence of operational art. The editor hopes that other readers will find Triandafillov's work insightful and thought-provoking.

Jacob W. Kipp

NOTES

1. V.K. Triandafillov, *Kharakter operatsii sovremennykh armii* (Moscow: Gosvoenizdat, 1929), p. 3 ff.

2. *Sovetskaia voennaia entsklopediia*, 2 vols. incomplete (Moscow: Gosudarstvennoe Slovarno-Entsiklopedicheskoe Izdatel'stvo, 1933), II, cols. 843–4.
3. I. Ivanov, "Voenno-tekhnicheskaia literatura po voprosam kharaktera budushchei voiny i operativnogo iskusstva," *Voina i revoliutsiia*, No. 2 (March–April 1934), pp. 13–30. Ivanov explicitly linked future war [*budushchaia voina*] and operational art [*operativnoe iskusstvo*] in this bibliographic guide. The posthumous second (1933) edition of Triandafillov's book was cited as the basic work in four out of twelve major categories, that is, contemporary operational means, the conduct of operations, meeting operations, and offensive operations. Under the subtopics listed for conduct of operations, *Kharakter operatsii sovremennykh armii* was listed as the basic work for studying general questions, control of operations, and transport and rear.
4. P.I. Vakulich, "Predislovie k 3-mu izdaniiu," in V.K. Triandavillov, *Kharakter operatsii sovremennykh armii*, 3rd edition (Moscow: Gosvoenizdat, 1936), pp. 5–7.
5. J. Walter Jacobs, "The Art of Operations," *Army*, No. 11 (November 1961), p. 64.
6. V.A. Semenov, *Kratkii ocherk razvitiia sovetskogo operativnogo iskusstva* (Moscow: Voenizdat, 1960), pp. 118–22.
7. E. Smyslovskii, "Voennaia nauka i voennoe iskusstvo," *Voennaia mysl' i revoliutsiia*, No. 3 (1922), pp. 11–20.
8. Vakulich, "Predislovie k 3-mu izdaniiu," in Triandafillov, *Kharakter*, pp. 7–8.
9. Ibid., and A. Golubev, "Vydaiushchiisia sovetskii voyennyi teoretik," *Voenno-istoricheskii zhurnal*, No. 3 (March 1968), p. 108.
10. Ibid., pp. 8–9.
11. Golubev, "Vydaiushchiisia," p. 108.
12. A.I. Reznichenko (ed.), *Akademiia imeni M.V. Frunze: Istoriia Voennoi ordena Lenina, Krasnoznamennoi ordena Suvorova Akademii* (Moscow: Voenizdat, 1972), p. 40.
13. A. Verkhovskii, "Evoliutsiia prepodavaniia taktiki v 1918–1928 gg.," *Voina i revoliutsiia*, No. 11 (November 1928), pp. 50–52. On Verkhovsky's background and career see *Voennyi entsiklopedicheskii slovar'* (Moscow: Voenizdat, 1983), p. 126.
14. *Voennaia akademiia imeni M.V. Frunze: Istoriia voennoi ordenov Lenina i Oktiabr'skoi Revoliutsii Krasnoznamennoi Ordena Suvorova Akademii* (Moscow: Voenizdat, 1980), p. 41, citing Voennaia akademiia za piat' let, p. 168.
15. Ibid., pp. 42–4.
16. Vakulich, "Predislovie k 3-mu izdaniiu," Triandafillov, *Kharakter*, 3rd edition, pp. 7–9, 255. Triandafillov's study of the Perekop Operation was later reworked and published as part of the three-volume history of the Civil War. This essay is noteworthy for its attention to the problem of combined arms, especially the coordination of infantry and artillery in the attack, and the analysis of the role of the higher density of machine guns in this breakthrough operation. See N. Triandafillov, "Perekopskaia operatsiia Krasnoi armii (takticheskii etiud)," in Bubnov *et al.*, *Grazhdanskaia voina 1918–1921: Boevaia zhizn' Krasnoi armii*, I, pp. 339–57.
17. V. Triandafillov, "O Volkovysskoi operatsii," *Krasnaia Armiia: Vestnik Voenno-Nauchnogo obshchestva pri Voennoi Akakemii*, Nos. 10–11 (January–February 1922), pp. 34–43.
18. V.K. Triandafillov, "Vzaimodeistvie mezhdu zapadnym i iugo-zapadnym frontami vo vremia letnego nastupleniia Krasnoi armii na Vislu v 1920 g.," *Voina i revoliutsiia*, No. 2 (February 1925), pp. 21–2.
19. Ibid., 26–7.

20. A. Golubev, "Obrashchena li byla v proshloe nasha voennaia teoriia v 20-e gody?," *Voenno-istoricheskii zhurnal*, No. 10 (October 1965), pp. 35–8.
21. V.K. Triandafillov, *Razmakh operatsii sovremennykh armii* (Moscow: Gosvoenizdat, 1926), pp. 16–17.
22. V. Triandafillov, "Vozmozhnaia chislennost' budushchikh armii," *Voina i revoliutsiia*, No. 3 (March 1927), p. 14, 37.
23. Triandafillov, *Kharakter*, 1st edition, pp. 1 ff.
24. *Field Regulations of the Red Army 1929* (Washington, DC: Foreign Broadcast Information Service, 1985), pp. 63–93.
25. P.I. Vakulich, "Sovremennaia operatsiia," in V.N. Levichev (ed.), *Voina i voennoe delo* (Moscow: Gosvoenizdat., 1933), p. 550.
26. Ibid.
27. N. Varfolomeev, "Strategiia v akademicheskoi postanovke," *Voina i revoliutsiia*, No. 11 (November 1928), p. 84.
28. A.A. Svechin, *Strategiia*, 2nd edition (Moscow: Voennyi Vestnik, 1927), pp. 14 ff.
29. Svechin, *Strategiia*, 1st edn (Moscow: Gosvoenizdat, 1926), pp.18–19.
30. Varfolomeev, "Strategiia v akademicheskoi postanovke," *Voina i revoliutsiia*, No. 11 (1928), p. 84.
31. *Akademiia im. M.V. Frunze* (1972), p. 98.
32. M. Bonch-Bruevich, "Nekotorye osnovy operativnogo rukovodstva v sovremennoi voine," *Voina i revoliutsiia*, No. 12 (December 1927), pp. 46–63.
33. V. Triandafillov, "K voprosu o polevykh poezdkakh nyneshnego goda," *Voina i revoliutsiia*, No 4 (April 1946), pp. 5–18; *Krasnaia zvezda* (4 April 1926); and V. Triandafillov, "K voprosu ob ocherednykh zadachakh po usovershenstvovaniiu boevoi podgotovki vysshego komandnogo sostava," *Voina i revoliutsiia*, No. 1 (January 1927), pp. 31–43.
34. V.V. Larionov and A.A. Kokoshin, "Introduction," in A.A. Svechin, *Strategy* (Minneapolis: East–West Publications, forthcoming).
35. R.A. Savushkin, *Razvitie sovetskikh vooruzhennykh sil i voennogo iskusstva v mezhvoennyi period (1921–1941 gg.)* (Moscow: VPA imini V.I. Lenina, 1989), pp. 9–11.
36. Triandafillov, *Kharakter*, 1st edition, p. 54.
37. Ibid., pp. 70–72.
38. *Akademiia General'nogo Shtaba: Istoriia Voennoi ordenov Lenina i Suvorova I stepeni akademii General'nogo shtaba Vooruzhennykh Sil SSSR imeni K.E. Voroshilova*, 2nd edition (Moscow: Voenizdat, 1987), pp. 22–4.
39. Frunze, *Izbrannye proizvedenniia* (Moscow: Voenizdat, 1957), II, p. 35.
40. Varfolomeev, "Strategiia v akademicheskoi postanovke," *Voina i revoliutsiia*, No. 11 (November 1928), pp. 92–3; Varfolomeev, "Operativnaia voennaia igra," *Voina i revoliutsiia*, No. 6 (1928), pp. 18–35; K. Berends, "Shtabnye voennye igry," *Voina i revoliutsiia*, No. 6 (1928) pp. 36–55; and V. Triandafillov, "Materialy dlia zadachi na shtabnuiu voennuiu igru," *Voina i revoliutsiia*, No. 12 (December 1927), pp. 31–45.
41. Triandafillov, *kharakter*, 1st edition, pp. 95 ff.
42. *Field Regulations of the Red Army 1929*, pp. 1 ff.
43. M.N. Tukhachevskii, "K voprosu o sovremennoi strategii," in *Voina i voennoe iskusstvo v svete istoricheskogo materializma* (Moscow: Gosvoenizdat, 1927), pp. 129–33.
44. M.N. Tukhachevskii, "O kharaktere sovremennoi voiny v svete reshenii VI kongressa kominterna," in Kommunisticheskaia Akademiia, Sektsiia po izucheniiu problem voiny, *Zapiski*, I (1930), pp. 15–17.
45. Ibid., p. 21.
46. M.N. Tukhachevskii, "Predislovie k knige Del'briuka 'Istoriia voennogo iskusstva v ramkakh politicheskoi istorii'," in M.N. Tukhachevskii, *Izbrannye sochineniia*, 2 vols. (Moscow: Voenizdat, 1964), II, pp. 116–46.

47. Tukhachevskii, "O kharaktere sovremennoi voiny," in *Izbrannye sochineniia*, II, p. 30.
48. M.N. Tukhachevskii, "Novye voprosy voiny," in *Izbrannye sochineniia*, II, p. 181.
49. Triandafillov, *Kharakter*, 3rd edition (1937), pp. 235–6.
50. Ibid., p. 235.
51. Ibid., pp. 235–54.
52. G. Isserson, "Razvitie teorii sovetskogo operativnogo iskusstva v 30-e gody," *Voenno-istoricheskii zhurnal*, No. 1 (January 1965), p. 36; and Golubev, "Obrashchena . . .," p. 35.
53. V.N. Lobov, "Aktual'nye voprosy razvitiia teorii sovetskoi voennoi strategii 20-kh-seredeny 30-kh godov," *Voenno-istoricheskii zhurnal*, No. 2 (February 1989), pp. 41–2.

Introduction

THE LEGACY OF V.K. TRIANDAFILLOV

On 27 February 1991 in his final briefing before the Gulf War cease-fire, General H. Norman Schwartzkopf stressed the importance of being "schooled in the operational art." The comment by the allied commander underscored a significant aspect of the coalition success over Iraqi forces. The victory in the Gulf War was a triumph for military education as much as anything else. Many of the staff planners, standing at the levers of command, had indeed been schooled in the operational art. This schooling included the writings of V.K. Triandafillov, whose work in some small but substantive measure contributed to the Allied design for victory.

Following in the wake of the Vietnam débâcle, the United States Army passed through a period of deep and profound introspection. This period of introspection was also a period of intellectual renewal in which the primacy of military education was reaffirmed: in the last analysis, the mind was the real key to victory. As if to underscore the importance of this, in 1983 the Army founded the School of Advanced Military Studies in the Command and General Staff College with the charter to school officers in the theory and practice of operational art. One of the first challenges to confront the School's founder, Brigadier General Huba Wass de Czege, was to identify core readings that would support a graduate-level curriculum in operation art. This turned out to be no easy task.

Although the Army had recognized at least informally the operational level of war by 1983, much of the institutional dialogue then going on was flawed owing to a tangle of ideas that continued to emerge from the German experience in the Second World War. This was further conflated with the relatively new lessons derived from the Yom Kippur War of 1973. Despite the intensity of the discussion, the debate failed to coalesce into a canonical statement about the nature of operational art. Those who thought much about the issue generally equated operational art with something called "maneuver warfare," a favorite shibboleth of the Defense Reform Caucus.

By 1985 the SAMS curriculum reached some level of maturation, driven in part by its responsibility to revise Field Manual 100–5 *Operations.* The revision of the manual created a dynamic within the School that pressed further the question concerning the nature of operational art. Many of the curriculum developers began to turn increasingly toward Soviet authors for meaningful writings on operational art. One of the most fruitful areas of inquiry was found among the works of early Soviet military theorists. These writings included M.N. Tukhachevsky's *New Problems of War.* A translation of this work had been previously provided to the School by the US Army War College. It immediately became a course reading in the theory portion of the SAMS curriculum.

During May 1986 the Army published its revised FM 100–5 *Operations.* In the new manual the Army officially recognized operational art and the operational level of war. Also by this time SAMS had established a close professional association with the Soviet Army Studies Office (SASO) which had been founded in early 1985 by Dr Bruce W. Menning. SASO provided substantial support to the SAMS curriculum, most notably in the theory block by presenting specially prepared lectures and providing critical reading materials. The most important of the latter was Triandafillov's *Character of the Operations of Modern Armies.*

Although Tukhachevsky's *New Problems of War* was an important addition to the SAMS theory curriculum, it failed, as an essentially incomplete work, to provide a full and coherent statement on operational art. Fortunately, SASO's commissioned translation of Triandafillov provided a significant and timely contribution to the core body of theoretical writings supporting the SAMS curriculum. For the first time the students had a major work on operation art of sufficient depth and resonance to stand as a theoretical touchstone beside Clausewitz's *On War.* Unlike Clausewitz's study of classical strategy, Triandafillov's work could be read with immediate understanding and direct comprehension by the serving officer. Because of its accessibility and insight, *The Character of Operations of Modern Armies* forms an intellectual bridge from classical strategy to modern operational art. It is no exaggeration to say, therefore, that any understanding of operational art must necessarily begin with V.K. Triandafillov and his chief work.

At the time of writing (March 1991) there were more than 70 SAMS students serving in the Gulf region. Every one of these students read Triandafillov. Many of these same students helped design and execute plans at the tactical and operational levels of war. In large or small measure these students were influenced by the ideas of V.K. Triandafillov, ideas that were formulated more than 60 years ago. It is difficult, then, to imagine a more appropriate meaning for the term military classic; or a more enduring testimony to a soldier and his contribution to military knowledge.

We now turn and examine in greater detail the nature of this unique contribution.

REVOLUTIONS IN WARFARE

The collapse of the tsarist regime in 1917 profoundly affected virtually all traditional Russian institutions, including the military. In many ways, the two revolutions of 1917 merely completed the disintegration of the military that had already begun with the start of the First World War. Along with the physical destruction of the old Imperial Army, war and revolution also destroyed much of the former intellectual fabric which had provided motivation, purpose and direction to the military. As the Russo-Japanese War of 1904–05 had begun to suggest, and as the First World War had clearly demonstrated, this fabric was woven around fundamentally flawed premises, many of which had become totally irrelevant to the new conditions of warfare emerging even by the end of the nineteenth century.[1] Many of the same forces that had swept away the old military order also fueled the impulse to challenge outmoded and discredited ideas of warfare. Following the Bolshevik coup, a handful of Soviet military theorists set aside old concepts to work towards a new understanding of contemporary war and military art. One of them was Vladimir Kiriakovich Triandafillov (1894–1931). The purpose of the following discussion is to provide a modern interpretation of his theoretical treatise, *The Nature of Operations of Modern Armies.*

Revolutions often cast aside not only old regimes but also old and seemingly outmoded ideas.[2] In the military realm, the Russian Revolutions of 1917 provided the impetus for theorists to attack old shibboleths on the basis of fresh insight and experience. With the First World War in the recent past and even as the Russian Civil War raged, they began to subject traditional military verities to intense scrutiny and criticism and gradually developed a new vision of land warfare appropriate to the changing means and methods of the twentieth century. By the late 1920s and early 1930s the cumulative work of these new theorists – in which Triandafillov figured prominently – added up to a revolution in military thought.

Their revolution traced its remote roots to another age of revolutionary military change, that of the French Revolution and Napoleon. For nearly two thousand years before 1789, military strategy had consisted of the maneuver of a single densely-packed army.[3] Towards the end of the eighteenth century, following hard on the heels of revolutionary political upheaval in France, Napoleon Bonaparte brought to fruition a corresponding revolution in military affairs.[4] Mobilizing the entire military manpower of the state in a continuing *levée en masse*, Napoleon formed large numbers of troops into a relatively new combat formation called the *corps d'armée.* Under the command of a marshal, each corps maneuvered independently before beginning the decisive battle.

Following the end of the Napoleonic Wars the pace of the military revolution quickened dramatically. It was hastened by advances in technology and changes in organization. The technological changes were most evident in their application to tactics.[5] The most important technological advancement in this regard was the development of the rifled musket. Its lethal impact led directly to expansion of the battlefield.

In the realm of strategy, a continuing increase in national population led to the employment of masses of troops arrayed in multiple field armies. By the mid-nineteenth century, with the development of the telegraph and the railroad, these field armies could be controlled and maneuvered over vast distances prior to concentration for decisive battle.

While the use of field armies underwent refinement, several improvements to the rifled musket were also being made. An effective breechloading mechanism was developed by the Prussians in 1840. A vertical magazine was added in the 1870s, and in the 1880s a smokeless-powder cartridge was developed. The convergence of these technological advancements into the modern rifle continued the dramatic increase in battlefield expansion and lethality.

By the end of the nineteenth century the field army could control a much broader expanse of frontage than previously.

Thanks to the final development of the modern rifle and improvements in artillery, it became virtually impossible to compress enemy formations onto one dense battlefield. These conditions led to a style of strategy characterized by the Soviet military writer G.S. Isserson as a strategy of the discontinuous front.

During the First World War a further complication evolved with the employment of barbed wire and entrenchments. This, together with higher troop densities and rapid-fire artillery, led to a "linear strategy of the continuous front" and a subsequent military stalemate lasting four years.[6] The stalemate arose, at least in part, out of a failure to recognize that underlying incremental changes added up to a fundamentally changed military reality. When the war began, most parties to the conflict believed in the possibility of a quick decisive military victory in the Napoleonic manner. Instead a long war of exhaustion ensued.

It is easy to describe contending generals and their civilian counterparts as simple incompetents or dunderheads. But this explanation misses the point. In fact, First World War generals were often highly competent – by Napoleonic standards. By this time, however, Napoleon's style of war – even as expanded and embellished by his heirs – had become irrelevant. In the East, it was left to a group of Soviet theorists to analyse carefully the nature of the Russian defeat in the First World War and Bolshevik operations during the Russian Civil War. Among them was an obscure former brigade commander named V.K. Triandafillov.

THE EARLY WORK OF TRIANDAFILLOV

Triandafillov was born on 26 March 1894, in the village of Magaradzlie, Kars district, in what is now Turkey. He served in the Imperial Russian Army during the First World War, rising to the rank of staff captain. He joined the Red Army in July 1918, being promoted successively to battalion, regiment and brigade command. During the Russian Civil War, Triandafillov took an active part in operations against A.I. Dutov on the Ural Front. He was later transferred to the Southern and Southwest Fronts in operations against Denikin and Wrangel. It was as brigade commander in the crack 51st Rifle Division that Triandafillov came to the attention of M.V. Frunze. Frunze commanded the Southwest Front in a successful offensive operation at the Perekop Isthmus against White Russian forces under Wrangel. Based largely upon

Frunze's strong recommendation, Triandafillov was accepted for the four-year course of instruction at the Military Academy of the Workers' and Peasants' Red Army (RKKA). In 1921 Triandafillov, while still a student, took part under M.N. Tukhachevsky in the suppression of the Tambov insurrection.

It was during this period that Triandafillov came under the intellectual tutelage of Tukhachevsky. In this regard it is important to note that the British military theorist, B.H. Liddell Hart, had stressed the fundamental importance of the impact of "thought on thought." This intellectual dynamic was especially evident throughout the early formulation of a Soviet theory of operational art. As far as the work of Triandafillov is concerned, the genesis of his major work, *The Nature of Operations of Modern Armies*, can be traced to 1923 and to a series of lectures presented by Tukhachevsky at the Academy. Tukhachevsky had been appointed to head the Military Academy in Moscow in 1922. From 7 to 10 February 1923, Tukhachevsky delivered a series of lectures to the Advanced Class of the Academy assessing the recent military operations of the Civil War. Tukhachevsky concluded:

> Since it is impossible, with the extended fronts of modern times, to destroy the enemy's army at a single blow, we are obliged to try to do this gradually by operations which will be more costly to the enemy than to ourselves. The more rapidly we pursue him, the less time we give him to organize his retreat after the battle, and the more we hasten the disintegration of his armed forces and make it impossible, or at all events difficult, for him to enter upon another general engagement. In short, a series of destructive operations conducted on logical principles and linked together by an uninterrupted pursuit may take the place of the decisive battle that was the form of engagement in the armies of the past, which fought on shorter fronts.[7]

In 1924, the year following Triandafillov's graduation from the Academy and his subsequent appointment by Frunze to become Deputy Chief of Staff, a professorial chair to teach the "conduct of the operation" was established. This position was first occupied by N.E. Varfolomeev, who had served with the Western Front during the campaign on the Vistula. During his three-year occupation of the chair, Varfolomeev sought to establish a coherent theory to guide the conduct of successive operations. He derived two main principles as the foundation of his theory. The first was to conduct simultaneously a tactical penetration and pursuit into and through the depths of the enemy deployment. This was to be accomplished by the "zigzags of a whole series of operations successively developed one upon the other, logically connected, and linked together by the common final objective." The second principle was based upon the recognition of the importance of logistical sustainment. The success of a series of integrated operations depended upon the "successful struggle against the consequences of attendant operational exhaustion."[8]

Triandafillov's work as Deputy Chief of Staff coincided with some of his early writing efforts. In 1925 he published a paper in *Voina i Revoliutsiia* analysing the operations in Poland in 1920.[9] Triandafillov concluded that the Warsaw operation failed because of insufficient concentration of force at the decisive point. This failure was due to the faulty command relationship between the Soviet High Command (GLAVKOM) and the Southwestern Front commander. In 1926 Triandafillov was appointed to head the Operations Section of the Soviet General Staff. That year brought the publication of his first major work, *The Scope of Operations of Modern Armies.* This book was significant because it formed the theoretical basis for his later and more important effort, *The Nature of Operations of Modern Armies.* In the former he began an early elaboration of his theory of successive operations. He wrote that

> the center of gravity of a series of successive operations lies not at their beginning, but rather at their end. The theory of a series of successive operations anticipates a decisive clash with all the enemy's main forces at the end or ahead of the very end of the operation.[10]

The following year Triandafillov wrote his second paper for *Voina i Revoliutsiia.*[11] In this paper he thoroughly analysed the open literature to determine the organization of armies in future war, especially with respect to potential enemies of the Soviet Union. In 1928 Triandafillov took leave of his staff duties to assume command of a rifle corps. That same year he published a paper in the first volume of *The Civil War, 1918–1921* entitled "The Perekop Operation of the Red Army."[12] This paper was a tactical study of the operations against Wrangel in the Perekop Isthmus.

Also in 1928 another Soviet military theorist, N.N. Movchin, published a critical study of the Marne (1914) and Vistula (1920) operations. In many ways this work was a continuation of the careful study of successive operations begun by Varfolomeev at the Military Academy in 1923. Movchin's study concluded that "it was impossible under present-day conditions to rout the *entire* enemy army in a single operation." Movchin was the first to elaborate formally the structure of an entire operational campaign. The campaign, according to Movchin would consist of three distinct phases of operations. The first phase would comprise a series of initial border operations. The second, pursuit, phase would consist of a series of exploitation operations. The third and final phase would consist of a series of operations aimed at the decisive destruction of the enemy.[13] At the same time as Movchin was writing, a group had been established in the Fourth Directorate of the General Staff to study future war. This staff group, consisting of M.N Tukhachevsky, Ya. K. Berzin, A.N. Nikonov, and Ya. M. Zhigur, concluded that

> it is essential to conduct a series of successive operations which are appropriately distributed in space and time. By a combination of a series of operations, it is essential to force the enemy to exhaust its material and human resources or to cause the enemy to accept battle by its main mass of troops under disadvantageous conditions and eliminate them.[14]

It was thus upon the shoulders of these contemporary theorists that Triandafillov stood to catch a glimpse of the nature of future war. In 1929 he published his vision under the title of *The Nature of the Operations of Modern Armies.*

THE STATE OF MODERN ARMIES

This work is divided into two major parts. The first is entitled "The State of Modern Armies" and is largely a reworking of Triandafillov's *Scope of Operations of Modern Armies.* The second part, "Operations of Modern Armies," is the most original and significant part of the entire book. It is divided into two major subsections.

The author begins the section on "The State of Modern Armies" with a review of the current state of technology as it existed among the various modern armies. Triandafillov's purpose is clear: he seeks to identify patterns of technology that will evolve in the near future and thus determine the operational employment of combat forces in a future conflict, especially with respect to the initial period of the war. Triandafillov believes that it is very difficult and perhaps dangerous to project the conduct of operations beyond the initial period of war. But in any case, "one absolutely must be aware both of contemporary achievements in military equipment and trends in the further development of every type of weapon. Otherwise, one cannot understand those changes that may occur in the organization of armies in the near years."[15]

The author begins with an analysis of contemporary infantry weapons technology. He sees a clear trend toward the lightening of infantry weapons and an increase in their mobility, range and rate of fire. He expects, for example, that the range of fire of the machine gun will be extended three to five kilometers. All these and related advancements will greatly increase the effectiveness of infantry in the defense.[16]

Triandafillov's discussion of artillery technology proceeds along similar lines. He is quick to point out that the range of post-1918 artillery has increased 25 to 80 per cent. At the same time, more powerful artillery shells have also appeared. In addition to improvements in technological performance, the greatest challenge facing modern artillery is the question of mechanization. As the author sees it, there is a growing divergence between the rapid mechanization of infantry and tanks on the one hand, and the problem of the transition to mechanical traction for the bulk of the artillery on the other. Without a resolution to this problem, the writer fears that the movement of tanks and mechanized infantry will outpace supporting artillery.[17]

According to Triandafillov, "chemical weapons promise the most surprises in a future war."[18] Like Liddell Hart and other contemporary theorists, Triandafillov's most serious concern is the employment of chemical weapons from aircraft. The author observes that the range of aircraft now defines the practical scope for the employment of chemical weapons, which may reach from 500 to 600 kilometers into the depths of the enemy's interior. Clearly the armies of the day were ill-prepared to conduct chemical defensive operations on the magnitude envisioned by Triandafillov. According to the writer "the ominous possibility cannot be excluded that, in the future, there will be a requirement to be able to live and work not only in a gas mask, but in protective clothing as well."[19]

With regard to the employment of tanks, Triandafillov readily acknowledges that "the tank problem occupies a significant place in the organizational development of all armies."[20] The author is one of the earliest theorists to recognize that the significance of tanks extended beyond the tactical confines of the battlefield. Triandafillov saw the tanks as working closely with strategic cavalry to pursue retreating enemy formations from the battlefield. He was also careful to note that the subsequent development of armed combat formations would depend heavily upon the economic capabilities of the employing nation. He speculated that nations like the United States, Great Britain and France would be able to field a series of independent motorized formations. The implications of this view on Soviet capabilities are obvious and constitute an underlying theme which the author develops throughout the work.

The rapid movement of mechanized forces across vast expanses of terrain gives rise to a requirement for an appropriate system of command and control. Here Triandafillov is wide of the mark. The solution to this problem, of course, was the radio. The author concludes that because of the requirement to encode transmissions, the radio, "despite all its advantages, . . . still remains an auxiliary signal device."[21] Interestingly, evolution of German blitzkrieg doctrine somewhat later hinged directly on the successful integration of the radio as the primary means of controlling the operations of rapidly exploiting armored formations. Failure to consider the importance of the radio, even at this relatively early stage in the evolution of modern Soviet military theory, may also explain the failure to consider the integration of aviation assets with mechanized formations, a relationship impossible without appropriate signal and communications equipment. Triandafillov's main interest in aviation, however, was in the realm of reconnaissance and level bombing.[22]

Following his tactical survey, Triandafillov turns to the question of likely numerical strengths of mobilized armies. Here he is critical of such Western military theorists as J.F.C. Fuller who advocated the fielding of small professional armies, rather than large armies based upon mass conscription.[23] Triandafillov attributes this western inclination to a "distrust of the masses" and a "fear of the inevitable proletarian revolution."[24] Actually the real reasons were chiefly economic stemming from the high costs associated with fielding and maintaining large armies. These were largely the same reasons that had led to the rapid demobilization of the Red Army in 1922 following the war with Poland.[25]

Despite these reservations, Triandafillov is quite correct in asserting that when confronted with the specter of total war,

> *the best conditions for free maneuver, for extensive tactical and operational art, will be achieved* not through a return to the small armies of armchair warriors, but by the corresponding *increase* in the *mobility of modern million-man armies by improving the technology of transportation assets* [emphasis in the original].[26]

In his analysis, therefore, the author assumes that modern nations in time of total war will exercise their "maximum mobilization capabilities."

In assessing the logistical sustainment capabilities of nations at the strategic level, Triandafillov is concerned with two fundamental constraints. The first concerns the problem of force quality. According to the author, "million-man armies are . . . an enormous incrustation on the body politic." The mobilization of millions of troops will put the severest burden on the capitalist nations, whereas "the Soviet state . . . has every reason to rely upon the broad toiling masses."[27] The increased complexity of weapons technology and the conduct of highly dispersed mobile operations placed a greater burden on the effectiveness, cohesion and initiative of tactical subunits than previously. According to Triandafillov, the short one-year term of reserve service common among the capitalist nations was inadequate to prepare properly reserve cadres for extensive combat actions. Thus during the initial stages of war the quality of newly mobilized combat formations would decline rapidly and commanders would be able to conduct only the simplest of defensive operations.[28]

The second primary constraint concerns the introduction of forces into a theater of operations. While mechanization may have been evolving rapidly at the tactical level, only the same modes of strategic transport were available to most nations as had existed before the First World War. The introduction of such large forces into theaters of operations would probably take place at an even slower rate than previously. This was because while the numerical size of field armies had slightly declined since the First World War, their logistical tail had greatly increased. Triandafillov notes, for example, that the old First World War division of 20,000 men had been supported by 3,920 horses and 910 wagons. The modern division of 12,000–15,000 men, even with reduced artillery, required 7,000–8,000 horses, 2,000 wagons and 400 motor vehicles. The old field army had been supported by 6,500 wagons and 15,000 horses. A contemporary Soviet rifle corps required

10,000 wagons and 25,000 horses. Nearly 550–600 double wagons were necessary to haul a full day's load of food and forage. This same corps with reduced artillery required 1,500–2,000 double wagons to carry one unit of fire. Yet despite this increase in strategic bulk shipping requirements, the actual amount of rolling stock available to introduce newly mobilized forces into the theater of operations, and sustain them, had remained the same, if not actually declined. At the same time, there was little effort among most nations, especially the new Soviet state, to increase the number of rail lines and railheads.

These logistical considerations led Triandafillov to distinguish between Western and Eastern European armies in terms of a mechanized front and a peasant rear (*krest'ianskii tyl*). Relative to the Soviet Union, and despite shortcomings with respect to strategic transport assets, the Soviet Union and other Eastern European nations had a "peasant rear." These nations were only just beginning to develop a mechanized front. Most Western nations had at least the industrial potential to develop both a mechanized front and rear. The remainder of Triandafillov's work would repeatedly address the issue of operational and strategic sustainment.

THE OPERATION

Through the middle of the nineteenth century the campaign formed the primary basis for strategic planning. At the core of the campaign plan was the decisive battle of annihilation. The maneuver of forces, organized as corps during the time of Napoleon and somewhat later as field armies, brought the opposing armies into a state of great compression in space and time on a relatively small field of battle. This particular aspect of nineteenth-century warfare moved some military theorists, among them G.S. Isserson, to characterize this phenomemon as the "strategy of a single point" (*strategiia odnoy tochki*).[29]

Typically the decisive battle decided the campaign and often the outcome of the war as well. As we noted earlier, because of the impact of military technology and organization, the linear distribution of field armies made it much more difficult for forces to compress themselves upon a small battlefield. As a result it became harder to achieve a decisive battle of annihilation. Consequently campaigns became protracted. As field forces began to deploy in depth, as well as breadth, the planning and conduct of campaigns began to be based upon "chunks" or portions of the whole campaign. These portions came to be known as *operations* and eventually gave rise to *operational art.* According to Triandafillov the core problem of modern strategy was the conduct of the individual operation.

The second major portion of Triandafillov's work is concerned with the conduct of the modern operation. In order to gain insight into the conduct of future operations, the author develops some analytical assumptions, the most important of which concerns the density of fire generated by the defense. In his analysis the author concludes that the current (1929) density of fire has increased by a magnitude of six to eight times over the corresponding factor for 1914. Here the author strikes at the fundamental essence of the conduct of the offensive operation. Firepower has made the defense, the stronger form of war, even stronger. How does one, then, overcome the overwhelming superiority of fire now inherent in the defense?

The solution to the problem lay in the *suppression*, not necessarily the destruction, of the defender. For Triandafillov suppression is virtual attrition. A suppressed defender is for all practical purposes destroyed – at least for a perhaps decisive time. The mechanism of the solution is artillery in close support of attacking infantry.[30]

As Triandafillov envisions it, the operation will be conducted by one or more shock armies (*udarnye armii*) and will have strong artillery assets. The organization that the writer proposes will consist of 4–5 rifle corps with their own organic artillery, up to 4–5 artillery divisions (16–20 artillery regiments of army artillery and 8–12 tank battalions). Clearly such a force is beyond the present (1929) means of the Soviet Union. As part of his hidden agenda Triandafillov is merely serving notice that such a force is absolutely essential if a nation is to prosecute successfully an operational campaign. According to the author, "countries lacking sufficient suppressive assets and other hardware will be constrained by the greatest degree when forming those armies that will have to accomplish assault missions."[31]

As noted earlier, an operation is a clearly defined phase of a campaign. The definition of an operation is made most explicit by a plan of operations. An operation consists of a series of battles and maneuvers that evolve over space and time toward some end-state. The accomplishment of the end-state usually marks the termination of the operation and the end of a phase of the overall unifying campaign plan. With the dispersion of troops in depth and breadth, the battlefield took on greater dimensions. Battles were fought, as a result, over expanded ground. Because of the increase in the scope of battle, its very nature began to change: it lasted longer and, although it had become more lethal, casualty rates over time actually declined.[32] The twentieth-century battle, therefore, no longer resembled its Napoleonic ancestor, and semantics sought to accommodate changes. Throughout the nineteenth century the Russian word *srazheniye* meant "battle." Increasingly, after the Russian Civil War and with the formulation of operational art theory, the word took on a broader meaning to reflect the expansion of battle and came to mean "operational engagement."

Operational engagements and maneuvers in any combination comprise operations. Triandafillov provides a clear discussion on the conduct of such engagements. Because of the great size and dispersion of forces, the commander must make his decision to commit forces to combat as early as two days' march from the enemy. The shock army must send cavalry forces 3–4 days' march from the enemy to obtain his location and projected route. This intelligence is updated continuously by aviation elements. In planning to conduct an operational meeting engagement the shock army commander

> must insure that sufficient forces, both infantry and artillery, are committed immediately. One division will be required for every 2–3 kilometers of front in the sector of the main blow. A sector of up to 8–10 kilometers may be assigned for division auxiliary actions. This is the case even if the main attack frontage will only be 25 kilometers and eight rifle divisions will be required for auxiliary actions on a front of 20–25 kilometers, i.e., from 10 to 11 infantry divisions must be committed immediately. The remaining four to five infantry divisions must receive directions as to which area to go and to whom they are to be subordinate. Shock corps usually have to retain their third and fourth divisions. The third divisions from those corps accomplishing auxiliary missions will be removed and transferred to the area of the main attack. A minimum of 30 pieces [of artillery] per kilometer of front must be committed in the sector of the main blow on the first day of combat, so it is mandatory that one regiment

> of additional artillery be attached to each first-echelon division in that sector. Divisions acting in an auxiliary sector retain just enough of their own artillery. The main thing is that some of them will be reinforced from corps artillery.[33]

If the attack has begun successfully, by the second and third day the enemy will be forced onto the defense. At this stage it is important for the commander to prevent the defense from solidifying. He does this by committing his tanks and shifting his artillery fire from other sectors to increase densities to 45–60 pieces per kilometer of front.

During these combat operations, aviation elements are employed in reconnaissance and rear area bombardment roles. Triandafillov has not yet developed a means to employ aviation in a direct ground support role. Bomber aviation is employed against enemy columns immediately prior to contact.

The operational engagement may last as many as ten or more days. Because the opposing forces are echeloned so deeply, by as much as 75 kilometers, the deployment alone may take 2–3 days. The depth of the operational battlefield will probably be 25–35 kilometers, taking 5–6 days just to penetrate this depth.

Given the 1929 force structure of eastern European armies, Triandafillov concludes that combat would likely take place at a pace reminiscent of the German offensives in the spring of 1918. "Only as a result of increased suppressive assets, commitment of a greater number of tanks, and widespread force motorization can the rate of development of an operation be elevated to the [August] 1914 level."[34]

The force structure displayed by the shock army was simply a logical development driven by the demands of offensive action in its search to regain dominance over the defense. For its operational redemption the offense paid a heavy price. The shock army, forerunner of virtually every field army employed in the Second World War, presented logistical planners with a nightmare. The *daily* food and forage requirements for a shock army of five rifle corps and four artillery divisions, by Triandafillov's own estimate, required rail assets of 142 boxcars. In terms of rail transport this meant four trains for food and forage and one train for fuel. More staggering was the ammunition requirement. One day's unit of fire required an additional 18 trains comprised of 540 boxcars. These estimates did not consider medical and communications requirements. To account for these elements the total transport requirements for a shock army would be 25–28 (650–840 boxcars) trains per day.[35] Needless to say, these requirements were well beyond the capabilities of the Soviet economy in the 1920s.

SUCCESSIVE OPERATIONS

Having dealt with the single operation of a shock army, Triandafillov next considers the question of linking these separate operations successively according to some coherent whole. Here the author continues his analysis along purely empirical grounds. Triandafillov, and in keeping with virtually all Soviet military theorists, rejects "drunken speculation." Indeed, the question of successive operations had been empirically explored the year previously (1928). That year Triandafillov, as Chief of Operations of the Red Army staff, ordered the conduct of wargames to develop practical solutions to the problem of successive operations.[36]

The purpose of successive operations was to achieve the decisive strategic goal set forth in the campaign plan. Such decision meant the total destruction of the enemy army throughout the depths of his deployment, and also meant the deep penetration of several hundred kilometers into enemy territory. Triandafillov saw first

> a significant penetration into the [tactical] depth of the enemy disposition; [then] immediate infliction of a second, third, and subsequent blows on the heels of the first [in order] to bring the enemy to complete defeat. The ideal would have to be to plan the actions of friendly army forces in such a way that, employing a series of crushing blows carried to their conclusion, they would lead to complete defeat of the enemy, to his complete capitulation.[37]

According to the ideal the operations would commence along at least two separate but converging axes. This whole operational campaign would last 30 days. The initial operation, the breakthrough, would consist of an operational engagement of 30–36 kilometers in depth. The tempo of advance would be perhaps 5–6 kilometers a day. This initial breakthrough operation would last 5–6 days. A second series of operations aimed at pursuit and exploitation of the retreating enemy. It was hoped that the bulk of the enemy formations would be annihilated during this phase. These intermediate operations would be conducted to depths of

150–200 kilometers at a tempo of 8–10 kilometers per day. The duration of the intermediate operations would last 18–20 days. The final and decisive operation would drive to a depth of 30–50 kilometers. The rate of advance would be 6–7 kilometers a day and last 5–6 days.[38]

The ideal operational campaign, comprising a mosaic of successive operations was, however, limited by several real world constraints. The first concerned the mobility differential between the attacker and the defender. The First World War had demonstrated time and again that a defender could withdraw faster than an attacker could advance. This meant that the attacker could never get positional advantage over the defender so as to envelop and annihilate him. Consequently the defender, supported by strong reserves, could reestablish a coherent defense and force the attacker to reposition his forces and gather his logistical assets for another major breakthrough operation. The second constraint was strategic logistics. As the defender withdrew he typically destroyed railroad and bridge structures. The ball-and-chain effect of logistics could shut down an operation even in the face of limited resistance. As it was, Triandafillov admitted, the Soviet rail network then in existence was woefully inadequate to support the logistical requirements of his scheme of successive operations in the best of circumstances.

To offset the first constraint the "Future War" cell of the Fourth Directorate of the General Staff advocated the development of: "(1) motorized rifle-machine gun units reinforced by high-speed tanks and motorized artillery; (2) large cavalry units reinforced with armor (armored cars and high speed tanks) and guns prepared for conducting dismounted and combined arms combat; (3) large airborne assault units."[39]

The second constraint regarding strategic logistics was never properly solved. The variance between the peasant and mechanized rear was so great that as late as the end of the Second World War the Soviet Union still could not assign two railroad lines to support the operations of one shock army, as required by Triandafillov's model. Indeed, the peasant rear may have been the greatest single contributor to Germany's defeat in its invasion of the Soviet Union in 1941.[40] Certainly the logistical problem of sustaining successive operations continues to dog armies today.

There was another, third, constraint that existed within the geographic context. With the "Balkanization" of parts of Northeastern Europe, countries like Latvia, Estonia and Lithuania were never more than 250 kilometers deep at any point. It seems that the operational campaign envisioned by Triandafillov was to some degree at least predicated upon the defeat of nations with geographical depths not greater than 250 kilometers and in a time not to exceed 30 days. Poland, however, presented a depth greater than 500 kilometers in many places. Thus the operational scheme presented by Triandafillov does not appear to address the geographic reality of the Soviet Union's main potential enemy, Poland. What would happen if the Polish Army was not defeated within the first 250 kilometers of the Polish border? Triandafillov stands mute on this question.

A fourth constraint concerned the question of command and control. Triandafillov is fairly vague on this issue until the very end of his work. As early as the last year of the American Civil War (1864–65), it was understood that a superior headquarters was required to coordinate and control the successive operations of several armies. On the Atlanta front, for example, the Division of the Mississippi was created under the command of William T. Sherman to command and control three subordinate field armies. On the Richmond front a less formal command structure under Ulysses S. Grant was used to control the three Federal armies operating against Robert E. Lee. These early American lessons in the practice of what later became known as operational art were since lost to the mists of time. During the Russo-Japanese War, however, Russian forces suffered a series of defeats partly as a result of the inadequacy of their command and control structure. The Germans suffered a similar débâcle during the opening months of the First World War as their command system broke down while they were conducting a wide enveloping maneuver through France.

After addressing many of these same examples, Triandafillov concludes:

> In major operations, direction of all army formations accomplishing the main blow can be entrusted to one *front* [army group] command element . . . . In this case, as far as major operations are concerned, [Supreme] Headquarters defines their [fronts'] immediate and subsequent targets, allocates the requisite resources for their conduct, but operational direction itself, in the exact sense of the word, entirely is the task of the commander of a given *front*.[41]

Typically each major axis of advance is commanded by a *front* headquarters. With regard to the question when a *front* commander should intervene in operations, the author suggests that it will probably be necessary for direct *front* intervention after the completion of each successive operation. In instances where defeat occurs during an operation, intervention may become mandatory as commanders will be forced to give new guidance and conduct major regroupings of forces.

Triandafillov ends his book with a discussion of one of the more difficult command and control problems that would be likely to present itself to a *front* commander, and stemming from an aspect unique to the Soviet style of war. Fresh from its success in the Russian Civil War, the Red Army during the 1920s prided itself as the military arm of world revolution. Any military operation conducted by the Red Army would conform to strict world revolutionary guidance: "The Soviet state will never assign [operational] goals and missions that will contradict the interests of the working and the broad toiling masses. The war of the Soviet state against any capitalist power will have a class, a revolutionary, nature."[42] The Red Army, therefore, would be involved with several political tasks. The most important task would be the conduct of propaganda and agitation operations before and during the actual conduct of military actions. According to Triandafillov the

> successful conduct of this political work among enemy troops can, along with other situational data, create conditions favorable for deep crushing blows. Major offensives with relatively small forces, with lower suppressive asset norms, also can be undertaken against morally unstable and politically vacillating enemy troops.

This additional burden to the *front* and army command and control system arises when commanders

> must use the results of [their] successful operations to the maximum possible extent for the purposes of political work among enemy forces. . . . Only in this way, properly using political agitation to prepare the prerequisites of a military blow . . . is it possible to achieve the successive physical and moral rout of the enemy, gradually to create an internal front [a "fifth column"] in the rear area, to convert the war into a civil war.[43]

THE STRUCTURE OF REVOLUTION IN SOVIET MILITARY THOUGHT

In the spring of 1930, one year after the publication of Triandafillov's book, Tukhachevsky published a review of the book emphasizing the impact that industrialization could have in transforming the peasant rear into a mechanized rear. The success of the First Five-Year Plan for military construction was only beginning to bear fruit.[44] For Triandafillov the apparent success of these and other economic measures led him to begin a revision of his work. But before he had developed more than a brief sketch, the theorist was killed in a plane crash near Moscow on 12 July 1931.

Even before his death Triandafillov's book was regarded by many as a classic. Its most significant impact on the subsequent development of Soviet thought was to provide the basis for the theory of the *deep campaign*. Triandafillov himself had recognized that it might be possible "to merge the initial and subsequent operations into one continuous, protracted operation."[45] Such an operation would coincide in time and space with the duration of the campaign. The campaign and the operation would be one. Development of this theory would continue into the 1930s. Its chief architect would be M.N. Tukhachevsky.

In a sense, then, we have come full circle. The influence of thought on thought guided the evolution of Soviet theory along the strictly empirical lines of military science. Triandafillov himself had written: "Tactics, operational art, and strategy as a whole stem from the materiel and personnel that a state allocates for the conduct of war. Military art torn from this foundation, inevitably is converted into adventurism and fantasy and can lead to nothing good."[46] The impact of a handful of thoughtful individuals in an institution largely set free of its intellectual past can be profound. These few theorists, beginning with Tukhachevsky, Frunze, Triandafillov, Svechin and others, at last recognized the revolution that had taken place in the conditions of empirical military reality. This knowledge was so rapidly infused into the small body of collective professional wisdom then existing in the Red Army that a military–intellectual revolution in its own right had taken place.

JAMES J. SCHNEIDER
Professor of Military Theory, School of Advanced Military Studies, USACGSC, Fort Leavenworth, Kansas

NOTES

1. Ivan S. Bliokh, *Budushchaia voina v tekhnicheskom, ekonomicheskom i politicheskom otnosheniiakh*, 5 vols. (St. Petersburg, 1898).
2. Jonathan R. Adelman, *Revolution, Armies, and War* (Boulder, CO.: Lynne Rienner Publishers, Inc., 1985), *passim.*
3. Arthur Ferrill, *The Origins of War* (London: Thames & Hudson, 1985), pp. 187–223.
4. Robert S. Quimby, *The Background of Napoleonic Warfare* (New York: Columbia University Press, 1957), pp. 300–44.
5. James J. Schneider, "The Theory of the Empty Battlefield," *Journal of the Royal United Service Institute*, September 1987, pp. 37–44.
6. G.S. Isserson, *Evoliutsiia operativnogo iskusstva*, reprinted in A.B. Kadishev, *Voprosy strategii i operativnogo isskustva v sovetskikh voennykh trudakh [1917–1940 gg.]* (Moskva: Voenizdat, 1965), p. 418.
7. M.N. Tukachevsky, "March to the Vistula," in Josef Pilsudski, *Year 1920* (Pilsudski Institute of America/London, 1972), p. 168. Wherever possible, English translations of the Soviet authors are provided.
8. Cited in Jacob W. Kipp, "Mass, Mobility and the Red Army's Road to Operational Art, 1918–1936," *Staff Study* (Ft. Leavenworth: Soviet Army Studies Office, February 1987), p. 36. This study is especially useful.
9. V.K. Triandafillov, "Vzaimodeistvie mezhdu zapadnym i iugo-zapadnym frontami vo vremia letnego nastupleniia krasnoi armiia na Vislu v. 1920 g.," *Voina i revoliutsiia*, No. 2 (1925), pp. 21–51.
10. Cited in R. Savushkin, "K voprosu zarozhdenii teorii posledovatel'nykh nastupatel'nikh operatsiy," *Voenno-istoricheski zhurnal*, May 1983 (No. 5), p. 12.
11. V.K. Triandafillov, "Vozmozhnaia chislennost' budushchikh armii," *Voina i revoliutsiia*, No. 3 (1927), pp. 14–43.
12. V.K. Triandafillov, "Perekopskaia operatsiia Krasnoi armii," in Bubno *et al.* (eds.), *Grazhdanskaia voina, 1918–1921, t. I* (Moskva: Voennyi vestnik, 1928), pp. 339–57.
13. Cited in Savushkin, op. cit., pp. 78–9.
14. Archives cited in Savushkin, op. cit., p. 79.
15. V.K. Triandafillov, *The Nature of Operations of Modern Armies*, translated by William A. Burhans under Department of the Army contract number DABT 19–86–M–1742/5231–0500 for the Soviet Army Studies Office. (Reproduced as student text by School of Advanced Military Studies, USACGCS, Ft. Leavenworth, KS.), 3 [6]. (Number in brackets refers to pagination from original Russian text published in 1929 by the State Publishing House [*Gosizdat*], Military Literature Section of Moscow–Leningrad.)
16. Ibid., pp. 3–10 [7–12].
17. Ibid., pp. 10–14 [13–16].
18. Ibid., p. 14 [17].
19. Ibid., p. 17 [18].
20. Ibid., p. 18 [19].
21. Ibid., p. 20 [21].
22. Ibid., pp. 20–24 [21–24].
23. For a view on Fuller's thinking in this regard, see the excellent interpretation of his work by Brian Holden Reid, *J.F.C. Fuller, Military Thinker* (New York: St. Martin's Press, 1987), especially pp. 81–106. A unique new interpretation of B.H. Liddell Hart's early writing is presented in Richard M. Swain, "B.H. Liddell Hart: Theorist for the 21st Century," *Advanced Operational Studies Fellowship Monograph* (Ft. Leavenworth: School of

Advanced Military Studies, USACGSC, 20 May 1986). Col. Swain develops the theme of the impact of "thought on thought" throughout his monograph.

24. Triandafillov, op. cit., p. 27 [27].
25. In this regard see Paul Kennedy, *The Rise and Fall of the Great Powers* (New York: Random House, 1987), pp. 285, 320–27.
26. Triandafillov, op. cit., p. 51 [48].
27. Ibid., pp. 51–9 [48–53].
28. Ibid., pp. 76–81 [*68–72*].
29. Isserson, op. cit., p. 418.
30. Triandafillov, op. cit., pp. 82–109 [73—95].
31. Ibid., p. 114 [99].
32. Schneider, op. cit., pp. 40–44.
33. Triandafillov, op. cit., pp. 126–7 [109].
34. Ibid., p. 137 [119].
35. Ibid., pp. 151–6 [132–5].
36. Savushkin, op. cit., p. 81.
37. Triandafillov, op. cit., p. 157 [136].
38. Ibid., pp. 156–79 [136–155].
39. Savushkin, op. cit., p. 81.
40. See Martin van Creveld, *Supplying War* (London: Cambridge University Press, 1977), pp. 142–180.
41. Triandafillov, op. cit., p. 207 [178].
42. Ibid., p. 197 [172].
43. Ibid., pp. 202–3 [175–6].
44. Kipp, op. cit., pp. 44–5. Savushkin, op. cit. p. 82.
45. For a different interpretation of the origins of the "deep operation" see Kurt S. Schultz, "Vladimir K. Triandafillov and the Development of Soviet 'Deep Operations'," David R. Jones (ed.), *Soviet Armed Forces Review Annual*, IX, 1984–85, pp. 232–44. See also Earl F. Ziemke, "The Soviet Theory of Deep Operations," *Parameters*, Vol. XIII, No. 2, pp. 23–33. In this regard it is important to bear in mind the theoretically distinct difference between "successive operations" and "deep operations." Some writers treat these two forms of operations as one and the same.
46. Triandafillov, op. cit., p. 211 [184].

Glossary of Selected Equivalent Terms

INTRODUCTION

People intimately familiar with Soviet military writings are often struck by how carefully the Soviets use military terminology. They have developed a precise set of terms to describe people, places, concepts and things, while generally adhering to strict usage consistent with the elements of Soviet military art. There appears to be a concerted desire to retain a separate set of terms for use when discussing affairs at the strategic, operational, and tactical levels and, in some instances, when discussing foreign practices. The Soviet demarcations referred to as operational-strategic and operational-tactical make the translator's task more difficult.

An additional impediment is the claim some would make that there is so much mystery attached to certain Soviet concepts or that some of these concepts are so vital and important that the associated terminology simply cannot be rendered properly in English. These people advocate that the English language adopt the pure Soviet Russian-language word or phrase, apparently thinking that this approach makes the supposedly untranslatable idea, concept or term somehow more understandable to the reader.

Either though ignorance, sloth or the desire to vary the English words and phrases selected for a translation, translators of Soviet military works often fail to retain important distinctions that the Soviets are always very careful to make. Wordiness often encountered seems to be a purely editorial desire to provide the reader with a more interesting text containing a variety of different so-called English equivalents for the same Soviet term or concept.

Great care was taken in this translation to differentiate and to retain Soviet distinctions. The following list identifies the English translation used for major terms encountered in this work on

Soviet operations, identifies the Russian term the author used, and provides a definition of the term or the rationale for selection of the English equivalent, citing a reputable source. The terms are listed alphabetically in English.

artillery support [*artilleriyskoye obespecheniye*] – common, but unofficial, name for artillery combat actions. (1, I, 270)

aviation [*aviatsionnyy*] – the word aviation was retained throughout to preserve the distinction the Soviets make between air/aerial and aviation. An exception is the preferred translation of aerial bomb for *aviabomba.*

combat [*boy*] – generally speaking, the designation implying events at the tactical level and defined as the basic forms of the tactical actions of ground, aviation, and naval forces. Combat is blows, fire, and the maneuver of formations, units, and subunits, coordinated in goal, place, and time, to destroy or rout the enemy. (2, 92)

combat actions [*boyevyye deystviya*] – military actions, organized employment of units, formations, and field forces of all services of the armed forces to accomplish assigned combat missions. The main types of combat actions are the offensive and the defense. Combat actions is a term applying to actions on a tactical and operational scale. (1, I, 539; 2, 89)

combat arm [*rod voysk*] – component element of a service of the armed forces, which includes military entities with basic weapons and military equipment inherent in that element, as well as inherent methods of employing these weapons and equipment. Examples include rifle forces, tank forces, and missile forces and artillery. (2, 638)

combat aviation [*boyevaya aviatsiya*] – aviation formations, units, and subunits intended for direct accomplishment of combat missions, generally at the operational-tactical and tactical levels. It was born in the First World War, when bomber and fighter aviation appeared alongside reconnaissance aviation. Combat aviation now includes bomber, fighter-bomber, ground-attack, fighter, and other aviation. (2, 85)

engagement [*boy*] – The term engagement was used in this translation instead of combat on those occasions when the context so dictated.

entity [*formirovaniye*] – newly organized (formed) or extant military unit, formation, or field force. Temporary military entities such as combined teams and march subunits may also exist. (2, 782)

envelopment [*okhvat*] – a maneuver by forces to break out to the flank(s) or to the rear of the enemy combat formation in tactical and fire coordination with forces acting from the front to achieve the most decisive results in combat. An envelopment may be combined with a turning movement (see) against the enemy forces. (1, VI, 177)

fighting efficiency [*boyesposobnost'*] – the ability of forces to conduct combat actions, to accomplish combat missions. It is the decisive element of combat readiness and a condition vital to achievement of victory. Fighting efficiency is dependent upon manning, the nature and intensity of combat actions, casualties and the potential for replacing them quickly, level of personnel training, logistic support, and other conditions. (1, I, 544; 3, 144–7)

formation [*soyedineniye*] – military entity comprising several units or formations of lesser composition, usually of different combat arms, combat support (services), and combat service support. Depending upon affiliation to a service of the armed forces, composition, and assigned missions, formations are categorized as operational (in the armed forces of certain foreign states), higher tactical (operational-tactical), and tactical. In Soviet usage, the term formation is generally taken to mean a corps, a division, or a brigade. (1, VII, 426, 427)

forms of combat actions [*formy boyevykh deystviy*] – historical term that encompasses the categories combat, engagement, operation, blow, and systematic combat actions. Combat is the basic tactical combat action, the operation is the basic form of combat action at the operational-tactical and operational-strategic level, and the strategic operation in a theater of military actions is the basic form at the strategic level. (1, VIII, 305)

front [*front*] – depending upon context, line of deployment of armed forces and their contact with the enemy in a theater of military actions, territory where combat actions are being conducted, or side of a combat or operational formation of troops that faces towards the enemy. (1, VIII, 333)

front – Russian or Soviet operational-strategic field force usually created at the onset of a war and intended to accomplish operational-strategic missions in several operational sectors (sometimes in one strategic sector) of a contintental theater of military actions. (1, VIII, 332)

headquarters [*stavka*] – this generic term was selected because the discussion in Triandafillov's book centered around command and control centralization in the Western European, Eastern European, and Russian armies during the First World War. Since the word was not capitalized in the text, the indication is that the author was not referring to the highest command and control organ of the Russian field army and the location of the Supreme Commander-in-Chief of the Russian Armed Forces, *Stavka Verkhovnogo Glavnokomanduyushchego*. The title of this and the later Soviet equivalent rarely, if ever, is uncapitalized in Soviet writings. (1, VII, 511, 512)

logistic units [*tyly*] – the resources providing logistical and maintenance support to the army and navy in peacetime and wartime. (1, VIII, 152)

military actions [*voyennyye deystviya*] – actions of armed forces to rout the enemy on the ground, in the air, and at sea. As opposed to combat actions, military actions usually refer to actions on a strategic scale. (1, II, 260)

mission capabilities [*boyevyye vozmozhnosti*] – quantitative and qualitative indicators that characterize the capabilities of subunits, units (or ships), formations, and field forces to perform specific combat missions in a set time in specific circumstances. They depend on personnel strength, the level of their combat training and moral-political state, availability and state of weapons and equipment, degree of training and skill of command personnel, and also the nature of enemy resistance, terrain conditions, weather, and other factors. Different indicators are used to express the mission capabilities of the military entities in the services of the armed forces. (2, 89; 3, 144–7)

operational engagement [*srazheniye*] – aggregate of blows and battles directed towards achievement of the goals of an operation or of its individual missions. A variety of an offensive operational engagement is the operational meeting engagement (see). Until the concept of the "operation" appeared in military art, the operational engagement was the basic form of the combat activities of armies. (1, VII, 502, 503)

operational meeting engagement [*vstrechnoye srazheniye*] – actions of operational field forces during which both sides strive to achieve the assigned goals with an offensive. A variety of offensive operational engagement. (2, 168; 1, VII, 503)

organic [*voyskovoy/aya/oye/yye*] – adjective from the word *voysko*, which is the aggregate of the armed forces of a state or a part of them. From the ancient Russian word *voya*, *voysko* historically was the term used to mean the army as a whole and its component parts. It was replaced in the seventeenth and eighteenth centuries by the term "army" in connection with creation of regular armies. The term "organic" is used in this translation to retain the distinction from the adjective *armeyskiy* and to avoid confusion when the army context is lacking. (4, I, 203; 2, 155)

piece [*orudiye artilleriyskoye*] – this generic term was retained throughout the translation to insure that the important differentiation between a gun and a howitzer is not lost. (1, VI, 121)

shock group [*udarnaya gruppa*] – historical term describing an element of an infantry combat formation carrying out the main blow in an offensive or counterattacks in a defense. It comprised at least two-thirds of the infantry plus a majority of the suppressive assets (see) in an offensive and at least one-third of the infantry reinforced by artillery in the defense. Shock groups are linked with development of the theory of combat in depth and generally refer to the tactical and operational-tactical level. (1, VIII, 172)

shock grouping [*udarnaya gruppirovka*] – resources of a field force intended to crush the enemy in the sector of the main blow in an offensive operation. Static warfare levied the requirement for creation of shock groupings to provide the requisite resource density in decisive sectors. Shock groupings generally refer to the operational level. Postwar views also envision the concentration of resources in the form of shock groupings. (1, VIII, 172)

suppressive assets [*sredstva podavleniya*] – fire support assets required to create the requisite density of forces in a given sector to achieve fire damage during a battle or operation. Suppressive assets in this particular book refer to artillery and tanks. (2, 507, 508)

tactical meeting engagement [*vstrechnyy boy*] – actions of subunits, units, and formations in which both sides strive to achieve the assigned goals with an offensive. A tactical meeting engagement may develop into an operational meeting engagement (see). (2, 168)

theater of military actions [*teatr voyennykh deystviy*] – part of the territory of a continent with the coastal waters of the ocean, internal seas, and air space (continental theater of military actions) or the area of water of one ocean encompassing the islands in this ocean, adjoining seas, coastal strips of mainland, and the air space above them (oceanic theater of military actions) within which strategic groupings of armed forces may deploy and conduct military actions. (2, 732)

turning movement [*obkhod*] – maneuver involving a deep advance by combined-arms formations, units, and subunits into the enemy disposition to occupy a position advantageous for a blow (blows) against one or both flanks and the rear area of the grouping. A turning movement is usually carried out in conjunction with an envelopment (see). (1, V, 675)

REFERENCES

1. *Sovetskaya voyennaya entsiklopediya* [Soviet Military Encyclopedia] (Moscow: Voenizdat, 1976–80), Volumes I–VIII.
2. *Voyennyy entsiklopedicheskiy slovar'* [Military Encyclopedic Dictionary] (Moscow: Voenizdat, 1983).
3. *Problemy voyennoy teorii v Sovetskikh nauchno-spravochnykh izdaniyakh* [Questions of Military Theory in Soviet Scientific Reference Editions] (Moscow: Nauka, 1985).
4. *Slovar' russkogo yazyka* [Dictionary of the Russian Language] (Moscow: Russkiy yazyk, 1981–84), Volumes I–IV.

Scientific Research Section of the Central Council of the USSR Society for Assistance to Defense, Aviation, and Chemical Construction

NATURE OF THE OPERATIONS OF MODERN ARMIES

V. Triandafillov

State Publishing House
Military Literature Section
Moscow–Leningrad, 1929

Contents

PART TWO

OPERATIONS OF MODERN ARMIES

CONTENTS

From the Author

The task of this particular work is to study the sum of those problems that define the nature of operations of modern armies.

Initially, the author examines the material base of these operations – the weapons of modern armies, their numerical strength and organization, and other vital situational data (in the broad sense of the word) impacting upon the nature of combat actions and, after that, on the basis of these data, studies the *core problems* of modern tactics, the individual operation, and a series of successive operations.

Since the material base examined in this book is in the main characteristic of the *beginning* of a future war, all of the author's tactical and operational premises and conclusions are mainly valid for the operations of the *first period of this war*. The nature of the operations of subsequent periods naturally will be subject to changes in accordance with those changes in the armaments, numerical strength, organization, and combat training of the forces, and other situational data that will unavoidably occur during a war.

At present, it is possible to establish only *tendencies* in the development of the material base relative to these subsequent periods of a war. It is impossible now to foresee the *precise dimensions* of the changes that will occur in the material base and in other conditions defining the nature of a war. Thus, opinions on operations in subsequent periods of a war cannot be as categorical as those on the forms and content of the operational art of the initial period of a war.

During the entire exposition, the author strove to avoid the general debate and all the premises that must characterize a particular problem, to discourse in the language of specific figures, of tactical and operational norms. He considers that this is the only way to demonstrate the difference between the present and the past, to show the *direction* in which military affairs *are heading*.

Nonetheless, it would be an egregious error to accept the numerical norms presented in this work unconditionally for all instances. All numerical material in this work is *approximate*. It provides those *initial data* as a starting point for any specific calculations. These norms may change for every specific situation. It is the job of the commander and practitioner to establish the nature and degree of such changes.

V.K. Triandafillov

PART ONE

The State of Modern Armies

Development of Military Equipment following the World War

Military equipment took a great step forward following the World War. Major new achievements are being made in all areas involving small arms, artillery, tank construction, aviation, chemical weapons, and signal equipment. The results of this development in materiel have been partially realized already (reequipping of the American Army, reequipping of aviation in all countries, introduction of new tanks into the inventory, and so forth). However, for the main part, they manifest themselves as prototypes and their mass production has yet to be initiated. Nonetheless, these achievements are so great that, even in their present form, they can be added to the army inventory and this certainly would occur during a war. Thus, one must be fully aware both of contemporary achievements in military equipment and trends in the further development of every type of weapon. Otherwise, one cannot understand those changes that may occur in the organization of armies in the near future.

INFANTRY WEAPONS

At present all European armies retain those weapons models that they had at the end of the World War. The small arms of European armies continue to be an old magazine rifle, old heavy machine gun (Maxim, Hotchkiss, Vickers, Colt, and others), famous 1918 light (hand-held) machine guns (light Maxim, Lewis, Chauchat, and others), and the same old infantry pieces (McLean and Rosenberg 37mm gun and Stokes 81mm mortar).

Only the United States of America completely reequipped its army after the war. The USA introduced into the army inventory new heavy machine guns and the Browning M1918 rifle-machine gun, which are lighter by a factor of about two than older models while retaining identical ballistic properties.[1]

Since the aforementioned models comprise the only small arms in peace-time, one must assume that, in the event of war, over the next three to five years, armies will go to war primarily with them. But it would be a mistake to think that these weapons will survive until the end of the war. All armies recognize that the infantry weapons in their inventory are quite obsolete.

The rate of fire of today's magazine rifle is considered completely insufficient. Those targets the infantry is called upon to take under fire will be of a fleeting nature. The infantry requires a weapon that would make it possible to destroy these targets with a short and intensive fire strike. This requires an automatic rifle with a greater rate of fire than that of the magazine rifle. Technology has offered an entire series of models of such rifles. American Thompson M1923 automatic rifles weighing 4.5 and 6.8kg, firing 50–60 rounds per minute, and as accurate (at close range) as the magazine rifle, deserve the most attention. At present, no army has an automatic rifle in its inventory due to reequipment costs. But just as a light machine gun entered the infantry inventory during the World War, during a future war one must anticipate that the infantry will be reequipped partially or completely with an automatic rifle. In peacetime, plants are no longer working on a magazine rifle. Its production has been reduced and even has ceased in some countries. Industry will manufacture a modern automatic rifle based upon the models manufactured in peacetime when war is declared, when military industry goes into action and armies require new weapons reserves. Since, during a war, virtually complete replacement of the hand-held weapon will be required over a period of one year, all or part of the infantry may have a new hand-held weapon by the end of the first year of a war.

Old light and heavy machine guns are also considered unsatisfactory. The World War demonstrated that the main shortcoming of the heavy machine gun is its great weight (64kg), making it barely mobile. The machine gun was an excellent weapon for the defense, but turned out to be too unwieldy for the offensive. It was unable to keep up with small forward infantry units. So, light (hand-held) machine guns (up to 36 per battalion) found wide usage during the World War. But due to the haste with which they were manufactured during combat actions they did not satisfy completely the requirements levied for that type of weapon. They

Models	*System Weight (With Tripod)*	*Rate of Fire (Rounds/Minute)*
Old Models		
Lewis	12.5kg	120
Chauchat, M1915	8.75kg	120
Brixia	16.30kg	400
Maxim, 1908–1918	13.6kg	400
Madsen	10.5kg	250–400
New Models		
French Hotchkiss, M1922	7.5kg	220
Italian Brixia, M1923	11kg	300–350
Italian Brixia, M.5	8.8kg	150
Dutch Madsen, M1922	–	–
French Chatellerault, M1924	9kg	450

too turned out to be too heavy. After the war, designers were tasked to provide lighter hand-held machine gun models. The United States of America not only invented such machine guns, but they completely reequipped with them. Reequipment occurred in the French Army as well.

The table on this page shows the characteristic elements of the old and new models of the weapons.

Thus we note in the new models not only a weight decrease, but a rate of fire increase. Since the accuracy of the new machine guns remains fully satisfactory, they are a more powerful and modern infantry weapon than their predecessors. Infantry maneuverability and mobility increase and the power of the smallest infantry units is strengthened thanks to the decreased weight.

The Italian Fiat M1924 machine gun weighing 11.5kg is deserving of attention among the new heavy machine guns, as is the Browning M1918 machine gun that has entered the American Army inventory.

The main development of heavy machine guns after the war trended towards improving their sights, supplying them with an optical sight and a clinometer for more accurate long range fire and for firing from indirect positions, and with special supports for firing at airborne targets. These improvements significantly strengthened the fire effectiveness of these machine guns to long ranges, made them less vulnerable to artillery, and provided the capability to change their positions more easily (to include a lateral move via approaches along the front). The heavy machine gun in armies liberally supplied with light machine guns again became an independent weapon with special missions. A requirement now exists to provide *prolonged* nonstop fire to a range of up to three and even five kilometers and the capability to fire over the head of the infantry, both from a direct and an indirect position. It is natural that this machine gun remains, as before, a powerful infantry weapon at medium and close ranges, especially on the defensive.

Development of tank affairs (appearance of heavy and medium tanks with stronger armor) and success in employing armor protection for aviation demonstrated that the heavy machine gun cannot cope with antitank and antiaircraft fire missions. Therefore, work is underway in all armies to invent a large-caliber machine gun. Technology has yet to provide a *completely* satisfactory model of such a weapon.

Finally, new models of a lighter infantry gun firing a more powerful projectile have also been invented.

This table characterizes the new models of infantry (rifle) pieces compared with old models.

Models	*System Weight (kg)*	*Projectile Weight*	*Range (meters)*
In the Inventory:			
37mm gun, M1916	157	0.5	2400
81mm mortar, Stokes	52.5	3	2000
New Models:			
45mm gun, Saint Chamond	190	1.2	5500
French:			
75mm gun, Saint Chamond	71	3	1000
75mm howitzer, Schneider, M1923	100	3.3	2500
American:			
37mm gun, M1923	135	0.57	4500
75mm gun, M1923	130	5.67	4690
57 mm howitzer, M1923	99.7	2.75	1700
75.2mm gun, Vickers-Maxim, M1920	168.8	6.8	6000

Thus, development of the regimental artillery piece has trends toward:

1. Lightening the system to make it more suitable for infantry accompaniment.
2. An increase in the power of the projectile so that the piece

will rate with the projectile of a light cannon, since only then will infantry artillery be able to liquidate *rapidly* those obstacles the infantry will encounter when surmounting the depth of the enemy position.

3. Some increase in range, up to 4–5, even 6, kilometers, which, to a significant degree expands the zone of actions of infantry artillery.

Simultaneously, an effort has been made to employ this piece both for flat trajectory and high angle fire, for which projectiles with variable charges will be introduced. This same piece must also serve as an antitank weapon.

In countries with developed industry, the desire to place the infantry piece on a tracked carriage and lightly armor it, essentially to convert this piece into a light and mobile tank, is already evident.

Thus, to date, the following is clearly noteworthy in the development of infantry weapons:

1. The desire to replace the extant magazine rifle with a new automatic rifle, which, having a maximum rate of fire and not an especially great range (up to 800 meters), would at the same time be lighter and less complex than the extant rifle. Technology has furnished only prototypes of such a weapon.
2. The desire to supply the infantry with a simpler, lighter automatic weapon with a higher rate of fire and range of up to 1,500 meters. Technology has already provided fully satisfactory new models of such a weapon.
3. The desire to *improve* the extant heavy machine gun, having simplified and lightened it as much as possible, increased its range, and supplied it with new sights, a mount for antiaircraft fire, and armor-piercing rounds so that it will be capable of firing from an indirect fire position, against aerial targets, and against armored units. Technology has coped significantly with this task.
4. The desire to provide the infantry with a large-caliber machine gun capable of placing effective fire at medium ranges against modern tanks and simultaneously capable of firing on aerial targets.
5. The desire to provide the infantry with a new infantry piece that would be sufficiently light to be moved manually and sufficiently powerful (firepower approximating that of a light gun). It would provide flat trajectory and high angle fire and,

if possible, be capable of being mounted on a tracked carriage.

But all of this is on the drawing board. In peacetime, depending on the duration of the breather, only individual models of this weapon will reach the army. In all probability, the economically powerful countries will have some reserve of this weapon at the beginning of a war. But *in the course of the war*, we must expect that this weapon will appear on the battlefields.

Combat conditions will change as this weapon appears in the army. The machine gun zone of fire will expand to 3–5 kilometers. Firepower will be much greater at medium ranges than during the World War, thanks to improved light machine gun systems. Fire at close ranges will be even more deadly since automatic rifle fire will be combined with light machine gun fire. The infantry will have its own powerful infantry pieces that can accompany it and rapidly organize sufficiently powerful fire against targets inaccessible to divisional artillery fire. The stability of the infantry defense will increase to a powerful degree thanks to numerous vehicle-mounted weapons and logistical conditions better than those in an advance.

At the same time, all infantry weapons will become lighter, more mobile, and more offensive than those now in the inventory.

ARTILLERY

In the artillery field, just as in the field of the infantry piece, we do not observe reequipping anywhere, with the exception of the United States of America, whose artillery consists exclusively of new artillery pieces. New pieces have also been designed in other states (in France, particularly), but reequipping has not yet occurred there.

The new models of the pieces, with the old calibers, have considerably greater range. The table on page 15 presents comparative range data for the old and new models of artillery.

This table characterizes the evolution of artillery since 1914. We see that artillery equipment was transformed during the war, having provided a 27 to 81 per cent increase in range compared with the prewar norm where all models are concerned.

In the first five years after the war, America rearmed all its artillery, while France invented models that left the successes

	1914 Artillery		*French Artillery in the Inventory*		*Modern Artillery American Artillery*		*New French Models*	
	Model	*Range (km)*	*Model*	*Range (km)*	*Model*	*Range (km)*	*Model*	*Range (km)*
Mountain Artillery	Russian Mountain Gun	5	M1906 6.5mm Mountain Gun	5	Mountain Gun	5	M1921 75 mm Mountain Gun	7.9
							Same, M1923	9
Light Gun	M1902 76mm Gun	8.7	M1897 75mm Field Gun	11.2	75mm Gun	13.7	M1925 75mm Gun	12.7
Light Howitzer	122mm Howitzer	7	—	—	105mm Howitzer	10.8	—	—
Heavy Guns	107mm Gun	11.2	M1917 155mm Gun	11.6	100mm Gun	18.5	155mm Gun (Corps)	15
					155mm Gun	23	Same (Army)	16.5
Heavy Howitzers	155mm Howitzer	8	M1917 155mm Howitzer	11.5	155mm Howitzer	15	—	—
					210mm Howitzer	17	—	—
Powerful Guns	—	—	M1903 240mm Gun	16.5	—	—	M1920 240mm Gun	55
			M1912 340mm Gun	22	—	—	340mm Gun Super Long Range Fire	150

achieved in the field of artillery technology by 1918 far behind. The range of post-war models of artillery pieces increased an additional 25 to 80 per cent.

But these achievements are not even considered the threshold. Problems facing artillery involving mechanization of the infantry and a further increase in defensive engineer resources (use of quick-set concrete in a field war) have not yet been solved completely. Modern artillery is called upon to provide not only increased range, but increased power of the projectile. So, an increase in field artillery calibers, especially of howitzer artillery, is unavoidable, as is an increase in the quality of the explosive charge (more powerful explosives). Stemming from this, the problem of mechanical traction in artillery, a new revolution in artillery technology, will be posed and solved once again.

We may use as our example those conditions, which, according to French and German gunners, the new artillery equipment must meet. The table on page 17 presents these conditions.

These conditions became programmatic in the years immediately after the World War. Where light calibers are concerned, these conditions were actually fulfilled; to a significant degree, they have also been achieved where heavy gun artillery is concerned. Although we have no knowledge of models of powerful howitzers (240mm) they too must be included in future corps artillery (instead of the 155mm howitzers within divisional artillery), and even if they do not yet exist, there are no data to show that they will not appear in the future.

The problem of transition to mechanical traction is more acute. Due to their fragility, dependence upon bridge strength, and difficulty in surmounting obstacles, the mechanical traction resources of today (automobile, tractor, self-propelled) are unsuitable for divisional and even corps artillery. Mechanical traction is acceptable only for reserve artillery. Extant mechanical traction models provide a march speed of 8–12 kilometers per hour and a march distance of 50–100 kilometers.

All these new pieces are at present at the experimental stage. The equipment presently in the inventory of European armies still remains at the 1918 level. There is so much of this equipment and reequipping is so costly that rapid reequipping is improbable not only during peacetime, but even in time of war. Artillery reequipment is considerably more difficult than infantry weapon reequipment since the former requires not only equipment manufacture, but production of new units of fire as well, which cost more by a

	French Views			German Views	
Missions	*Caliber (mm)*	*System Weight and Traction (kg)*	*Range (km)*	*Caliber*	*Range (km)*
1. Infantry Direct Accompaniment	65	Tracked	2.5–4	65	4
2. Infantry Direct Support and Defense	75mm Gun and 105mm Howitzer	2100 Horse	12–14 12	10cm Universal Gun	Flat High Angle 12
3. Destruction of Material Obstacles	155mm Howitzer	Horse and Vehicle	14	20- or 24cm Gun	18–20
	240mm Howitzer	Horse or Tracked	12–16		
	150mm Gun	Horse	20–25		
4. Long-Range Barrage and Harassing Fire	150mm Gun	Tracked	20–25	15–18cm Gun	30–35
	195mm Gun	Tracked	30		
5. Especially Powerful Calibers	400mm Howitzer	Railroad Mount	20		Howitzer 20
	240mm Gun		40		Gun 200
	270mm Gun		60		
	280mm Gun		200		

factor of 10 or even 20 than the pieces, depending on the model involved.[2] Therefore, even in time of war, when one must produce new equipment regardless in order to replenish natural losses, transition to new models will not be as easy as the transition to new small arms. For rich industrial countries, gradual replacement of old equipment by new is inevitable. Those countries less powerful economically will be forced to lag behind with old artillery for the next 5–10 years.

Significant changes are probable in the area of transition to mechanical traction for part of the artillery, battalion and reserve artillery first and foremost. This will fundamentally solve the problem of accompanying artillery and, to a considerable degree, increase reserve artillery operational mobility. Mechanical traction will make rapid concentration of great artillery resources possible at striking points and will facilitate the maneuver of artillery in the rear area of the front.

CHEMICAL WEAPONS

Chemical weapons promise the most surprises in a future war. In accordance with an extant international agreement, all states are obliged not to employ chemical weapons in a future war. Actually, there is not a single state that would not be working intensively on the problems of chemical warfare.

In peacetime, all armies have special services preparing and developing chemical warfare assets. Funds spent on research rise every year.[3]

Efforts are aimed not only at inventing new toxic agents, but on the purchase of supplies of already known and tested chemical weapons.

According to far from complete data, it can be assumed that an entire range of new toxic agents has been invented and the effectiveness of old toxic agents increased. New toxic smokes with high irritant properties have been discovered. Thus, 0.0003 milligrams of chlorocetophenone per liter of air suffice to seriously irritate the human eye. An entire group of new materials with analogous properties is known. As far as the old toxic agents are concerned, it should be noted that the effectiveness of mustard gas introduced into a molecule of bromine is increased and new compounds of carbon monoxide and arsenic hydride have been obtained. The absorbents presently in use in gas mask filters block these new compounds poorly.

The problem of smokes has been posed anew since the World War ended. New mixtures providing a larger cloud of thick impenetrable smoke have been obtained. Some smoke compounds not only possess a camouflaging capability, but also cause damage when they contact the skin, causing burns.

Significant changes have occurred in the methods of disseminating or dispersing toxic agents.

Spraying toxic agents from aircraft also deserves special attention. Tests in America demonstrate that spraying a poisonous liquid from an altitude of 600 meters provides good results and can cover (with one aircraft) an area of up to 14 hectares. Given average weather conditions, an aircraft expending 400 kilograms of smoke agent from the same altitude can create an impenetrable smoke screen 1.6 kilometers long and about 185 meters high.

The design of aerial bombs has changed to such an extent that terrain may be contaminated more uniformly.

The range of the Stokes mortar has been increased to 2–3 kilometers and that of the Livens chemical mortar to 1–1.5 kilometers.

The size of cylinders has decreased (from 28 to 9 kilograms) and, as a result, it has become possible to employ a gas cloud attack during maneuver warfare, too. The method of releasing the gas from the cylinders has been improved by electrically rupturing an entire battery of them.

Firing chemical projectiles now is a component part of the artillery field training of all armies.

Moreover, instruments for free dispersion of toxic agents during a withdrawal have been invented. These instrument systems may be portable or mobile, the latter on bicycles, motorcycles, and other mounts. Their employment results in significant areas of terrain being contaminated easily and rapidly by persistent toxic agents.

Chemical warfare in the future promises to undergo enormous development. Even today there is a completed system of means, which may be employed to disseminate (disperse) toxic agents widely. These means make it possible to carry out a chemical offensive not only directly against forces conducting combat, but also against deeper reserves, the rear area, and the country's residential centers. Aviation's range of actions defines the sphere of toxic agent employment in a future war. This normally will be 200–250 kilometers from the front, reaching 500–600 kilometers in some instances. The closer to the front, the greater the means for dispersion of toxic agents: artillery, special mortars and gas projectors, the gas cloud method, hand grenades, and free spraying. The scale of chemical warfare will depend on how many toxic agents a country can place at the disposal of its army. The World War demonstrated that capabilities in this area are enormous.

Efforts to improve equipment to defend against gas are underway at the same time. Filters to protect against toxic smokes and carbon monoxide have been invented and automatic breathing devices designed to supply enough oxygen from a cylinder to compensate for the stress under which an individual is working. Protective clothing remains unsatisfactory. Extant equipment continues to require improvement. It impedes individual activities too much. New compounds to decontaminate persistent toxic agents from the terrain have finally been invented, making possible easier and faster detoxification of presently-known toxic agents, mustard gas in particular. At present, defensive equipment lags behind offensive equipment. Extant filters are applicable only to the toxic agents known today. There are no guarantees against new secret chemical weapons. Moreover, the present state of affairs concerning protective clothing is completely unsatisfactory. The possibility cannot be excluded that, in future, there will be a requirement to be able to live and work not only in a gas mask, but in protective clothing as well. Meanwhile, not a single army has yet been supplied with chemical defense equipment of either the requisite quality or quantity.

TANKS

Tank construction entered a new developmental phase following the World War. No one today doubts the great tactical significance of tanks for a future war. The current increase of automatic weapons in the infantry, the tendency towards a further increase in these weapons and their qualitative improvement, broad distribution of artificial obstacles in the defense, and the fact that suppressive assets (artillery) lag behind defensive assets promote tanks as one of the mightiest offensive assets for a future war. In the future tanks can and must to a significant degree replace artillery during an infantry attack and breakthrough of the enemy defense zone. In the execution of missions of accompanying the infantry in combat, tanks have enormous advantages over the artillery. As the 1918 campaign on the Western Front demonstrated, artillery is unable to keep up with the infantry since artillery's movement on the field of battle is extremely difficult.

The tank problem occupies a significant place in the organizational development of all armies.

One may characterize the postwar period of development of tank construction as continous attempts to convert the tank from a tactical resource to a resource of great operational significance. Military technology was tasked to provide new, more mobile, faster tanks with a greater radius of actions to replace the former barely mobile, barely maneuverable, short-range (constrained radius of actions) tanks. This new tank must participate not only in a relatively fast-moving attack as it accompanies the infantry into combat, but in all phases of pursuit beyond the field of battle as well. The tank accomplishes these new missions as part of new vehicle-mounted (motorized) units. Moreover, designers were tasked to provide a tank powerful enough to be able to pave the way for smaller tanks without being afraid of artillery fire.

Military technology provided new models of tanks that accomplished these missions to a significant degree. New maneuverable tanks intended for infantry accompaniment travel at speeds of 25 to 40 kilometers per hour, carry an 8–12 hour fuel supply, and have a radius of action of 250–300 kilometers at a combat weight ranging from 6.5 to 12 tons.

A tankette (combat weight 2.1 tons) with sufficient speed (35–40 kilometers per hour on tracks and 50 kilometers per hour on wheels) has been designed for reconnaissance missions. And, finally, a powerful *breakthrough* tank with thick armor, but slow (5–8 kilometers per hour), and a constrained radius of actions, has also been designed. These new types of tanks have already entered the inventory of the British, French, and American armies, where they exist on an equal footing with old tanks from the World War.

The East European countries still have mainly old tanks in their inventories. But new high-speed tanks have already begun to appear in several of these states.

One may characterize this period in the development of tank affairs as a period of reconstruction and direct, as yet uncompleted, reequipping, when, at the same time, army inventories contain old, barely mobile and unmaneuverable tanks on an equal footing with fast, fully modern, tanks.

The properties that high-speed tanks possess dictate a new

tactic for them as well. They not only participate and accompany the infantry into combat, but they may also participate in other phases of an operation. Along with strategic cavalry, high-speed tanks may participate in reconnaissance, facilitating the cavalry's penetration into the enemy disposition and looking into the depth of this disposition. Along with this same cavalry, tanks may participate in the pursuit of the enemy off the field of battle, facilitating the cavalry's rapid surmounting the resistance of retreating covering units. Tanks may also accomplish reconnaissance and pursuit missions as part of special motorized units (part of the so-called mechanized cavalry).

There is no doubt that motorized units will develop widely in the future. The economic capabilities of each state define the scale of the motorization. In countries like Britain, America, and France, an entire series of separate independent motorized formations (motorized brigades), able to accomplish a significant portion of the missions previously assigned to the strategic cavalry, may be created in the near future. There will be fewer motorized units in poorer countries. The first stage of such formations is the creation of special motorized detachments within the division (corps) for the purposes of tactical reconnaissance. Subsequent stages are motorization of the signal units in the division, corps, and army, motorization of entire machine gun battalions, conversion of field artillery to mechanical traction, and so forth.

We are now witnessing the first experiments in motorization of the army. At present, it is still difficult to foresee the scale this will take in different states. In any event, this must be taken into consideration in all future calculations.

SIGNAL AND ENGINEER RESOURCES

Wire signal resources developed in the direction of improving transmission and reception equipment. New telegraph equipment, both operating with the Morse alphabet and with printers, is simpler in design and, at the same time, is more productive. Identical improvements are underway in the design of field telephone equipment.

But the main development in signal resources involved the radiotelephone. The conversion to shortwave stations necessitated the design of equipment just as portable as the field wire telephone. Thus, instead of being a strategic and operational signal resource, the radiotelephone has become a *tactical* signal resource. It is capable of serving not only the communications of the command element at corps and division level, but communications in the rifle regiment right down to battalion and company inclusive and in artillery down to its observation points.

Introduction of the radiotelephone into the army will make tactical communications more stable and independent of wire, which is often severed during combat. But, radio has retained its main shortcoming. The enemy can intercept radio transmissions, so use of a code or cipher is mandatory. Either complicates the use of the radiotelephone and, therefore, despite all its advantages, it still remains an auxiliary signal resource.

New light bridging equipment, rapid set (alumina) cements, improved field camouflage equipment, and several achievements in the area of destroying and restoring railroads are engineer resources worthy of attention.

New bridging equipment in the form of inflatable boats of varying systems and load capacity to the greatest degree successfully solved the problem of divisional assault river crossing assets. The inflatable boat for erecting column bridges has a load capacity of three to five tons while weighing about 120–140 kilograms. It can hold up to 20–25 people simultaneously. A ferry comprising two boats supports a gun with team and crew. A bridge built on these boats accommodates all equipment in a division and in a corps. The divisional set of this equipment along with its upper flooring is carried on 64 double wagons. Introduction of this boat with its upper bridging into the divisions makes them independent of heavy pontoons and facilitates actions on river barriers.

Use of rapid set cements makes it possible to have cement structures usable for military purposes within one to three days of their erection. Given secure supply lines from the rear area and proximity to railroads or major highways permitting wide use of vehicle transport, the capability to create elements of permanent fortifications during a field war and thereby raise the stability of a defense even more is not ruled out. The significance of heavy artillery calibers and an increase in the amount of howitzer artillery acquires special importance.

New field camouflage resources (nets of various types and designs, disruptive painting, and so on) make it possible completely to conceal separate batteries (machine gun and artillery), rifle groups, or larger objects from enemy ground-based and aerial observation.

The following resources intended for destruction and restoration of railroads are worthy of attention:

1. Devices for mechanical destruction of the rail bed, to cause destruction with great rapidity.
2. Mechanization of rail bed construction operations.
3. Use of light girders made of new grades of steel, which significantly accelerates the bridge restoration rate.
4. Invention and construction of special ferries to open rail communications across large rivers prior to restoration of permanent bridging. Such ferries will allow not only loaded cars, but locomotives, to cross the river.
5. Invention of special pneumatic stations to eliminate the enormous water towers and, to a significant degree, solve the problem of restoring the water supply on destroyed sections of railroad.
6. Diesel engines, which will pose the question of the exploitation of lead railroad sections in a completely new manner (they will eliminate the need to restore the water supply).

Moreover, an entire series of repair organizations has been developed and is in place. This will bring order to the task of restoring separate services on destroyed railroads (advance mobile repair trains, railway communications repair trains, water supply repair trains, repair subunits).

All this in combination facilitates present efforts both to destroy and restore railroads.

AVIATION

During the postwar years, aviation has been reequipped completely. In all indicators of the development of aviation technology, we see great changes. New engines exceeding those in the 1918 inventory by a factor of 2.5 have been designed and introduced. In this context, new types for all branches of aviation have been designed, starting with reconnaissance aircraft and ending with the night heavy bomber. Armament on aircraft equipped for aerial combat has been improved significantly. New types of bombs with greater power and better ballistic properties have been designed. Aircraft have received new equipment, better bomb sights and cameras, radios, and night flight instruments in particular, resulting in significantly upgraded aircraft tactical properties.

Thus, the sphere of combat aviation actions has expanded and its effect on ground-based targets has improved. Due to tactical improvements, aviation not only gained a better capability to accomplish its main mission during the World War (reconnaissance) but, thanks to its machine guns and bombs, has also become a mighty weapon participating directly in an operational engagement. Regarding its effect on enemy deep logistics units, aviation has gained all the advantages (projectile power, hit accuracy, morale effect) over very long range artillery.

The aforementioned aviation achievements naturally are not final. Aviation technology will grow rapidly and spasmodically. Higher records have already been achieved in individual aircraft in a whole series of categories.

The following records have been set according to extant 1928 data (naturally, not all records are listed here):

	1918 Data	*1927 Achievements*
Reconnaissance aircraft average speed (km/hr)	130	190
Fighter aircraft average speed (km/hr)	180	280–300
Average practical radius of actions (km):		
Reconnaissance aircraft	300	350–400
Bomber aircraft	300	450–600
Fighter aircraft	175	250–300
Light bomber payload (kg)	150	400
Heavy bomber payload (kg)	–	2000
Maximum weight of high explosive bombs	1000	2000
Average aviation machine gun rate of fire (rounds per minute)	1000	1600
Hit per cent from altitude of 1,500 meters	14–15	50–60
Hit per cent when firing machine gun at ground-based targets	approx 10	approx 75

Category	*Record*	*Aircraft Type*	*Engine HP*
1. One-way range	6300km	Wright-Bellana	220
2. Round trip range	4400km	Farman Goliath with Farman engine	450
3. Horizontal speed	448.17kph	Vernard-Ferbois with Hispano-Suiza engine	450–550

(continued)

Category	*Record*	*Aircraft Type*	*Engine HP*
4. Horizontal speed to a range of:			
more than 500 km	306.69	Nieuport Delage with Hispano engine	500
more than 1000 km	248.29	,,	,,
more than 5000 km	168.62	Breguet 19 with Hispano-Suiza engine	300
5. Duration with a 2000 kg payload	10h. 32	Rohrbach with three BMW engines	750
6. Range with same payload	1460km	,,	750
7. Ceiling with same payload	6262m	Caproni Ca. 73 with two Acco engines	1000

Naturally, these records are not characteristic for the combat aviation of today. The aforementioned figures were achieved by individual aircraft on which one particular aircraft property (horizontal speed, let us say) was developed lopsidedly to the detriment of other properties (payload, flight duration, and so forth). But we already have a sort of harmonic combination of speed and payload in the bomber records (the German Rohrbachs). One must anticipate that these records will become the normal tactical properties of future combat aircraft.

Possible Numerical Strength of Mobilized Armies

SMALL MOTORIZED UNITS OR MILLION-MAN ARMIES?

"War demands high-quality forces and in sufficient quantity."[4] But, for capitalist countries quality and quantity have become a contradiction to each other in the epoch of the proletarian revolution we are experiencing. One cannot meet the demands for quantity without universal compulsory military service and massive, virtually universal, mobilization of the entire able-bodied population. Even that portion of the able-bodied population that will not be taken to the front must be militarized since otherwise it will be impossible to satisfy the demand for a million-man army. On the other hand, massive universal mobilization will confront the bourgeoisie with the problem of the reliability of this armed force. The acute contradictions in the capitalist world and the class struggle stemming therefrom naturally will confront all bourgeois states with the problem of how to approach further organizational development of their armed forces.

In recent years we have been encountering in the press a flock of foreign military writers, who sharply attack "ghastly" multimillion-man armies and advocate creation of new armed forces small in number, but selected from among "reliable" professionals in military affairs. Quality must replace quantity in these new armies. To achieve this, small new armies must be supplied liberally with all modern weapons and be fully motorized for maximum mobility. The shock force of these armies manifests itself in a large number of high-speed tanks, motorized artillery, and combat aviation. In the main, the human just maintains these machines. Rifle units, liberally supplied with new automatic weapons, will be required only for occupation purposes.

According to the originators[5] of these proposals, such an army during the first period of a war will have the capability to employ large aviation raids to destroy proper functioning of vital centers of the enemy country, while mobile and well-supplied motorized ground forces units, by means of invasion deep into the enemy country, will smash and hurl the enemy army back, seize territory, and provide new airfields from which aviation can make deeper raids.

According to them, the method of creating armed forces employed until recently is absurd since the result is a "ghastly army", extraordinarily complex, clumsy, uncontrollable, stifling tactical creativity, and ravaging the country by taking people away from useful work. The modern army must be a mobile army of submachine guns and tanks. Defense of the idea of massive "ghastly" armies is conservatism.

It is barely possible to take seriously these individual assertions of some foreign and Soviet military writers. The idea that small, albeit motorized, forces can conquer modern states is naive. Such an army, having invaded deep into an enemy country, risks becoming isolated if it is not immediately supported by a stronger army. Modern states cannot be conquered by individual raids, even those conducted by a unique new cavalry. Aviation cannot operate every day and in every kind of weather. It cannot count on unpunished raids on the enemy rear area, if for no other reason than because the modern million-man ("ghastly") army has appropriate defenses (the same air fleet, antiaircraft artillery), which make it possible to counter this aviation, not only within its own territory, but outside its boundaries as well. A "ghastly" army also has the resources to battle both tanks and vehicle-mounted infantry. States with million-man armies have all capabilities required not only to drive out, but to isolate and destroy small motorized units that have invaded their territory. "The actions of a large state against Moscow or Warsaw require penetration 550–750 kilometers into the enemy country, occupation of 200,000–300,000 square kilometers of territory. This is a task for a capable army approaching nearly a million rather than a half-million men and requiring, even when crushing methods are used, at least 10–12 weeks, during which time appropriate replacements must be dispatched."[6]

We know that these ideas of Fuller, Zol'dan, and others are born from fear of the inevitable proletarian revolution, are caused by exceptional distrust of the masses, who have now become more class conscious than prior to and during the World War, rather than by the deep conviction of these writers that small motorized armies can in fact win a modern war.

Regrettably, capitalism, the capitalist system, has yet to reach that point in its development at which not individual writers, but statesmen, have been forced to abandon the idea of massive armies. On the contrary, we observe how the period of a temporary stabilization of capitalism we are now experiencing has given rise in the capitalist countries to an entire series of new measures directed towards insuring the capability for massive mobilization in the event of war. Universal military service still remains the only system for the organizational development of the armed forces of all states, the defense of which will be structured on the ground (France, Poland, Romania, and others). Periods of service (one and one-and-a-half years rather than the former three years) have been reduced everywhere to create the maximum number of trained personnel. Military industry has grown both qualitatively and quantitatively. Conversion of all industry in the event of war to military production is being prepared on a broad scale in all states. All capitalist states are presently maintaining the course towards mass production of weapons and accessories. It is natural that such enormous reserves are being prepared for other than small armies. The bourgeoisie still feels confident enough so that it hopes to employ the means in its possession (state apparatus, school, church, press, fascist organizations, social-chauvinistic parties, and so forth) to keep the masses in its own hands. And, it is taking an entire series of measures that would facilitate this effort in time of war. The French ("bonkurovskii") law on the defense of the nation, the British law on professional unions, exceptionally harsh laws against communist parties, are all directed towards creation of an outward appearance of national unity during war, preservation of a civil peace in the country, and freeing the government's hands against the revolutionary wing of the working class and its party during a war. Articles by individual military writers of Fuller's and Zol'dan's ilk characterize only the difficulties capitalism is now encountering in its relations with the masses and possible forms of organizational development of the armed forces in the event of a strong exacerbation of the class struggle. One must now consider that a future war, even for the capitalist countries, and provided it is not the result of some profound social upheavals or revolutionary explosions, will elicit from them the greatest military intensity these states are capable of handling. In the Soviet Union, where defense of the socialist fatherland is the affair and obligation of all the toiling masses, war will rouse the entire combat-capable population. Both we and the capitalist states will rush to the front not only all technical resources (machine guns, artillery, aviation, toxic agents) that a given country is able to bring to bear, purchase abroad, or obtain from allies, but millions of people en masse as well.

The best conditions for free maneuver, for extensive tactical and operational art, will be achieved not through a return to the small armies of the armchair warriors, but by the corresponding *increase in the mobility of modern million-man armies by improving the technology of transportation assets* (employment of vehicle transport, six-wheeled vehicles, wider development of railroads, and so forth). A country forced by political considerations, due to distrust of the masses, to return to small armies of professionals cannot count upon conducting a large war.

Therefore, our task is to study the maximum mobilization capabilities of the countries in which we are interested to determine the numerical strength of the armed forces they may be able to place at the front in a future war. We will examine the mobilization capabilities of these countries under the conditions of the present temporary stabilization of capitalism, assuming that the capitalist states will succeed in mobilizing "normally," that they will be able to employ completely all resources they possess for the goals of the war.

MOBILIZATION SEQUENCE

Theoretically, it would be advantageous for each state to achieve during peacetime that mobilization readiness that would make it possible at the beginning of a war to place its maximum possible armed forces immediately at the front. There would then be more chances to achieve superiority over the enemy at the very outset of a war. But there is no state economically capable of that degree of mobilization readiness. In peacetime, not all persons subject to military service even serve in the military in the majority of states. The number of peacetime cadres is such that they cannot train all those subject to military service. Supplies of weapons and equipment are limited. Military plants do not operate at full capacity and the bulk of a country's industrial enterprises take care of the civilian market. Given the modern system of defense organization, the moment of maximum military intensity is put off until the time of complete industrial mobilization. Of course, one cannot rule out the possibility that some states, poorly prepared for war, will be put out of action and will lay down their weapons before they are able to employ their maximum mobilization capabilities.

Two factors determine the degree of a state's threshold military intensity: first, the numerical strength of the population able to be called up for military service and, second, the condition of the country's economy, that is, a country's capabilities of producing weapons, equipment, ammunition, and other military items. The following determine the numerical strength of the army that can be placed at the front at the outset of a war:

1. The amount of peacetime materiel and ammunition reserves for mobilization.
2. Number of peacetime cadres.
3. Number of *trained* personnel (command and rank-and-file).

POSSIBLE NUMERICAL STRENGTH OF THE MOBILIZATION FIRST ECHELON IN DEVELOPED STATES

Understandably, we lack certain basic data determining the possible numerical strength of the mobilization first echelon. We have in mind information on equipment mobilization reserves maintained during peacetime in different countries. Extant information of that category indicates that the large capitalist countries retained enormous supplies of weapons, equipment, and ammunition after the World War.[7] The number of military plants in such countries as France, Britain, the United States, Italy, and Czechoslovakia is not less, but, in some countries, is more than in 1914. We know that such countries as Poland and even Romania during the postwar years built *their own* ordnance, cartridge, artillery, and even aviation plants, that, beginning immediately after the war, Poland and Romania and the Baltic states annually receive a certain amount of weapons and equipment from abroad. Although we are in no position to define the amount of accumulated mobilization supplies, having data on the numerical strength of peacetime cadres and trained personnel resources, we can establish the numerical strength of the mobilization first echelon. This is a fully solvable problem since armed forces organizationally are developed so that the requisite correspondence among cadres, trained reserves, and equipment mobilization reserves will already be achieved during peacetime. Even during the years of peaceful organizational development, the problem of what army numerical strength must be reached when mobilization is announced is predetermined and, accordingly:

1. Cadres will be maintained during peacetime.
2. A reserve of trained personnel will be trained and retrained.
3. Equipment mobilization reserves are accumulated year by year to insure both mobilization deployment of the army and its support until full mobilization of all industry.

Here, of course, we will consider those data of a *general* nature characterizing the mobilization equipment base in each given country.

The state of trained personnel reserves in various countries shows that no difficulties will be encountered in this area during a future mobilization. The contingent of trained personnel is 6.44 million in France, 2.8 million in Poland, and 2.2 million in Romania. Comparison of these data with the capability to mobilize peacetime cadres reveals that the latter cannot absorb this mass of people.

Cadres in all modern armies represent a *narrower* base for mobilization than those maintained immediately before the World War. Despite the fact that the organization of forces has become complicated compared with 1914 and modern weapons require more qualified and better trained personnel, the cadres we observe everywhere are weaker than those noted in 1913–14.

We grew accustomed to being amazed by the feverish energy, the harmony, with which the first operations were conducted at the outset of the World War, especially on the Western (Franco-German) Front. But very few realize that these operations could have been conducted with such intensity and with such art of maneuver, thanks to those significant cadres the Germans and French had and who insured the high qualities of the mobilized army.

The wartime German division numbered 16,500 men. The Germans considered that 12,000 cadres had to be maintained in peacetime in order to deploy such a division, that is, approximately 75 per cent of the wartime strength. True, only 42 per cent of all peacetime divisions were maintained that way. The remaining 58 per cent had just 10,000–11,000 each (about 66 per cent of the wartime strength), but the cadres of these divisions now remain unchanged numerically.

The wartime French division numbered 16,000 men. Until 1913, the French maintained a 7,500-man peacetime division or some 48 per cent of the wartime strength. But when war was in the air, these cadres seemed weak to the French. They introduced a law calling for a three-year term of service (the 7 August 1913 law), resulting in a one-third increase in peacetime cadres. This increase went not for newly-formed entities, but for an *increase in unit table of organization and equipment* (TO&E) in peacetime. After 1913, the composition of the company in border divisions was brought up to 200 men and the normal divisional composition to 10,000–11,000. The budgeted numerical strength of the French Army was increased to 863,000, while retaining the former number (47) of infantry divisions.

The Russian Army also had relatively powerful cadres. It had 21.5 per cent of its forces at three-quarters, 25.5 per cent at two-thirds, and the remaining 53 per cent at half the wartime TO&E.[8] Given a wartime division numerical strength of 18,000, this meant 13,500 and 12,000 for reinforced divisions and 9,000 for normal-strength divisions.

Given such powerful cadres, we observe in the table at the top of page 33 the picture of the mobilization deployment of first-line forces in these three largest armies.

It is evident from this table that the stronger the divisions in peace-time, the greater the per cent of first-line divisions formed during mobilization. The Germans, having 50 divisions with a rather strong cadre (8,000 and 12,000 men) during peacetime, were able to deploy 79 first-line divisions[9] (a 58 per cent increase). The French, having more powerful peacetime divisions, (12,000 and 10,000 men), given 47 peacetime divisions, deployed 79[10]

	Germany	*France*	*Russia*
Peacetime Army Numerical Strength:			
Total (Thousands)	761	863	1423
Infantry Divisions	50	47	78.5*
Mobilized First-Line Divisions			
Total (Thousands)	1887	1856	2500
Infantry Divisions	79	79	123.5
Per cent of Mobilization Strength Compared to Peacetime Strength:			
To Overall Strength	248	218	173
To Number of Peacetime Divisions	158	167	156

* Including rifle brigades.

first-line divisions as well (a 67 per cent increase). Russian divisions, weak with respect to cadre, provided only a 56 per cent increase in the number of divisions.[11]

At present, one notes an absurdly weak peacetime divisional composition in all states. At a time when a wartime divisional composition of 13,000–14,000 is planned (only the French plan to have a 14,000-man division), the numerical strength of peacetime divisions in the majority of states now does not exceed 5,000–5,500 (6,000-man normal and 8,000-man reinforced French border division), with this strength barely reaching 3000 in some states. The table below shows the picture that emerges if you compare peacetime and wartime divisional composition.

This is a consequence of the fact that, given an overall low peacetime budgeted army numerical strength, such an army will contain a very large number of divisions.

Country	*Divisional Composition Peacetime*	*Wartime*	*Ratio in per cent*	*Comments*
France	6000* / 8000	17,000	35 / 47	* Numerator shows normal divisional composition. Denominator shows reinforced division.
Poland	6300**	14,000	38	** Composition of all Polish divisions is identical. Border divisions have regiments reinforced at the expense of other regiments in the division.
Romania	3200 / 5000	14,000	23 / 36	
Estonia	2800	9000	31	
Latvia	3300	13,000	25	
Finland	4800	14,000	34	

Country	*Total Peacetime Army Strength (thousands)*	*Number of Peacetime Infantry Divisions*
France	603	32
Poland	293	30
Romania	158	23
Estonia	14	3
Latvia	22	4
Finland	33	3.5
Status before the World War:		
France	863	47
Germany	761	50
Russia	1423	78

The table above depicts the ratio between army numerical strength and the number of peacetime divisions in the largest countries and what our Western neighbors have.

If war broke out, given the existing state of affairs, we would have to assume that either the mobilization capabilities of today's armies were much lower than they were in 1914 or, given the identical factors for the organizational deployment of the number of divisions, the divisions in all armies had weaker cadres and, consequently, were weaker qualitatively. Given today's infantry division composition, one can scarcely count on the identical army organizational deployment factors that existed in 1914 or even lower ones. On the contrary, growing infantry mechanization and the increase in the modern division's technical resources (technical communications gear particularly) will require even larger cadres.

One must assume that the extant state of affairs *is not final. It is temporary* and is dictated by postwar economic conditions forcing one to use all available means to reduce military expenditures. The political situation and absence of a direct military danger for the time being are making it possible to maintain reduced peacetime cadres.

But it would be erroneous to think that mobilization for a future war will occur precisely based upon the extant reduced foundation. An entire series of postwar political conflicts has already shown that just a hint of the smell of military complications in the air suffices for the numerical strength of peacetime armies to increase. Reservists are called up and unit authorized composition is radically increased without any special stir.[12] The fact that a sufficient number of organizational formations, albeit relatively weak in composition, will already be maintained in peacetime makes it possible without any complications and stir whatsoever actually to increase the overall numerical strength of the army long before mobilization is announced. It is understood that such measures may be employed to increase only the *authorized composition of units*, not the *number of organizational formations*. An increase in the number of the latter (divisions) during peacetime involves forming new entities and increasing the annual contingent called up and is therefore not so easily accomplished.

That is why when calculating the possible numerical strength of future armies one must always consider that the future mobilization base can be *expanded* very rapidly and relatively easily to the dimensions of the 1914 mobilization. Thus, in any future mobilization, we at least must consider the army organizational deployment factor that existed in 1914.

The opinion exists that the number of wartime divisions may be doubled immediately compared with the number existing during peacetime. We consider such a view erroneous if for no other reason than a whole series of divisions disposed along a threatened border can hardly be burdened with the tasks of allocating secondary divisions, while the remaining divisions will be unable to allocate more than one additional division each. Not a single unit with modern cadres is capable of triple generation. Such (triple) deployment would seriously degrade force quality and would place their fighting efficiency in great doubt. Thus, the complete organizational deployment factor of an army during its mobilization will always be less than 100 per cent.

In 1914, the number of divisions increased by 58 per cent in the German Army, 67 per cent in the French Army, and 56 per cent in the Russian Army. A 60 per cent organizational deployment factor must be considered the maximum for the majority of modern armies. States such as Poland, Romania and the Baltic states but not Germany with a long *threatened* border cannot count on more than 60 per cent organizational deployment. On the other hand, France, having such a disarmed neighbor as Germany, can anticipate a much higher percentage of organizational deployment. It may reach 80 and even 100 per cent.

Given the aforementioned conditions, the number of wartime first-line divisions, which can be fielded by the states of interest to us, will be from 57 to 64 divisions in France, 48 in Poland, 36 in Romania, five in Estonia, six in Latvia, six in Finland, and five divisions in Lithuania. Deployment of this number of divisions, with all auxiliary institutions and hardware, requires a mobilized army of the following numerical strength: 2–2.5 million in France (the special features of French organization are taken into account), from 1.2 to 1.5 million in Poland, and up to 1 million in Romania.

Each Baltic state will have an army of 80,000–100,000 men.

FIRST-LINE AND SECOND-LINE FORCES

The aforementioned armies have an excess of trained personnel resources for deployment. Moreover, in all states, after the first mobilization echelon, there remains a very significant number of *trained* persons subject to military service (up to 4 million in France, 1.5 million in Poland, and up to 1.2 million in Romania), who cannot be called up due to a shortage of cadres and, in Poland and Romania because of a shortage of equipment as well. But this still does not signify that the aforementioned excess personnel will not be utilized. Even during the 1914 mobilization, we observed in all states a whole series of entities without cadres, comprising reserves exclusively. That same year, the Germans used 1.887 million of more than 4 million reserves for the mobilization of first-line corps. Including auxiliary institutions and reserve forces, the number of men mobilized passed the 3 million mark. But even after this, there remained a large number of trained personnel reserves, from which the Germans formed an additional 44 second-line (29 *Landwehr* and 14 *Ersatz-Reserve*) divisions. The numerical strength of the entire mobilized army reached 4.215 million[13], that is, not only was the entire trained contingent of reserves utilized, but up to 215,000 completely untrained men were called up for logistics institutions.

The French had fewer personnel reserves in 1914, 3.5 million trained and 329,000 untrained. Therefore, they were able to form just 13 second-line (territorial) divisions in addition to the 79 first-line divisions. As a result, they had to mobilize an army of 3.781 million men, that is, completely exhausting the relatively young age at the very outset of the war.[14]

Despite enormous personnel resources, the Russians had a very insignificant reserve of trained personnel (up to 3.5–4 million men) thanks to long terms of service. This reserve completely went for the replenishment and deployment of first-line forces and, therefore, the Russians did not succeed in creating any significant and reasonable second-line forces. These militia volunteer detachments which Tsarist Russia created in 1914 could not be compared quantitatively, qualitatively, or organizationally with the French territorial divisions, nor even with the German *Landwehr* and *Ersatz-Reserve* divisions.

Even in Germany, *Landwehr* divisions were inferior to first-line divisions not only in cadre manning, command element quality, and quality of the replenishment forces, but also in the quality and quantity of the weapons these divisions had.

This table shows the comparative strength of the 1914 German and French first- and second-line divisions.

	First-Line Divisions				*Second-Line Divisions*	
	Primary Cadre		*Reserve*			
Country	*Battalions*	*Guns*	*Battalions*	*Guns*	*Battalions*	*Guns*
Germany	12	72	12	36	6	6–12
France	12	36	12	36	4	6

Second-line divisions were weaker both in overall composition, and in the amount of artillery.[15] One battalion of German infantry had the following: six pieces in a primary division, three in a reserve division, and one or two in a *Landwehr* division. The same for France: instead of three pieces per battalion, as in first-line forces, a territorial division had a total of 1.5 pieces. At the outset of the war, the Landwehr and territorial divisions were divisions in name only. In essence, these were weak brigades of low-grade forces. Only during the war did they receive additional weapons, the requisite tempering, and satisfactory units were obtained from them. Both France and Germany, over a period of years, prepared feverishly for war, maintaining enormous armies under arms and, year after year, readying enormous weapons reserves at military plants. But, nonetheless, neither cadres nor a sufficient number of weapons was found for the second-line forces. That is why the question of second-line forces requires an individual approach to each country.

For modern Germany, even in the event of change in the existing military regime the Versailles Peace Treaty established, the center of gravity in its army will be in these same second-line divisions. Germany will be forced to mobilize an army out of "thin air," begin to weed out a large number of peace-time cadres, to a significant degree count in its mobilization upon illegal military alliances and organizations and on a command element left over from the World War, and to use experience from mobilization of the *Landwehr* in 1914. Second-line forces in Germany must comprise the basic mass of a mobilized army since first-line forces will absorb only an insignificant portion of those enormous amounts of personnel and materiel that even defeated Germany will be able to field in the event of war.

France will also have a large per cent of second-line forces. At present, it maintains an army smaller numerically than in 1914. The disarmament of Germany permits this. The first-line forces that can be deployed from the 600,000-man peacetime French Army will take second place to the 1914 mobilized army where numerical strength is concerned (even given a higher organizational deployment factor, France will field only 57–64 infantry divisions rather than 79). After that, France will still have so many assets, both personnel and materiel, that she will be able to deploy a very powerful second-line army, up to 20–25 new divisions at least.

A different picture is observed in such countries as Poland, Romania, and the Baltic states. Mobilization of first-line forces alone will require them to manifest a materiel effort of which they are hardly capable. Let us recall that even Tsarist Russia, possessing a relatively large military industry, having counted on purchases of armaments abroad to a degree no less than that now seen in Poland and Romania and with its economy on the upswing, went to war nevertheless with first-line corps short of artillery and with a great shortage of machine guns. Meanwhile, Poland and Romania must to a significant degree acquire even basic infantry weapons abroad, not to mention artillery equipment and other hardware.

Nonetheless, modern Poland and all the Baltic states (the same is true of Germany) now have certain conditions favorable for second-line formations, conditions not present in 1914. We have in mind so-called "concealed armed forces," these being fascist organizations. They number 30,000–50,000 in small and up to 150,000–200,000 in average-size states, with this figure topping 2.5 million in several large states.

These forces will be fully satisfactory cadres for newly-formed entities and, if the appropriate quantity of weapons and equipment is found, the capability to form new divisions fairly quickly will also manifest itself.

Of course, these second-line entities may be employed successfully only for secondary missions. Nonetheless, they will free the entire field army from internal security missions and observation of neutral borders and, here and there (in secondary sectors), will even accomplish direct combat missions well.

It is very difficult to foresee the numerical strength of these second-line entities since it will depend upon weapons and equipment mobilization reserves, information about which we lack.

Personnel resources suffice everywhere for deployment of a second army of the identical numerical strength of the first-line forces. However, we consider such a numerical strength for second-line forces impossible even for France since, at the very outset of a war, it would have to take from the country immediately more than 5 million workers directly engaged in this or that productive labor. This would disrupt fundamentally the country's economy. Personnel must be mobilized for the army sequentially so the national economy will have an opportunity gradually to replace more qualified workers leaving for the army with less qualified and less capable workers. Other states are confronted with the same problem to a certain degree. Only Germany, for which these second-line entities will also in essence represent its mobilization army, will be able to have second-line forces exceeding by several times the numerical strength of the first-line divisions. This is dictated by the special conditions in which she finds herself.

Considering all these data, we think that the number of second-line divisions in the aforementioned countries will be up to 25–30 in France, 15–20 in Poland, five in Romania, three in Finland, and up to one in Latvia.

Besides this, one must consider the cavalry in each of these countries (with respect to the number of peacetime divisions): five divisions in France, three in Germany, four divisions and five separate brigades in Poland, and two divisions in Romania. Thus, the overall numerical strength of armed forces that might be mobilized at the outset of a war is depicted in the following way:

	First-Line Forces			*Second-Line Forces*			
Country	*Inf Div*	*Cav Div*	*Numerical Strength Including Service Institutions and Reserves (thous.)*	*Inf Div*	*Strength (thous.)*	*Inf Div*	*Strength (thous.)*
France	57–64	5	2000–2500	25–30	700	82–94	3200
Poland	48	5.5*	1500	15–20	300	63–68	1800
Romania	36	2	1000	5	100	41	1100
Finland	6	$\frac{1}{3}$	100	3	60	9	160
Estonia	5	$\frac{1}{3}$	75	–	—	5	75
Latvia	6	$\frac{1}{3}$	100	1	20	7	120

* Considering separate cavalry brigades as well.

Right now, only the *number of organizational formations*, that is, the divisions maintained during peacetime (this does not include Germany), supports peacetime deployment of such armies from the cadres standpoint. The numerical strength of a peacetime army is insufficient for deployment even of first-line forces. But, we assume that, just prior to a war, the numerical strength of armies overall and division composition in particular will increase by the simple call-up of reservists or by other measures. Thus, it is fully possible to make the aforementioned calculations for first-line forces. The problem of the numerical strength of second-line forces is more complex since the calculation we use is based upon certain prerequisites of a theoretical nature, the validity of which may be contentious. But, in any case, the calculations made depict the *maximum* mobilization capabilities of the mobilization first echelon. Even modern France will not exceed this figure.

Certain states (for example, France) probably will not encounter any difficulties where logistical support for mobilization of armies of the aforementioned numerical strength is concerned. Other states *do not have* such equipment and are forced to procure it (and in all certainty are doing so) in times of peaceful respite.

SUCCESSIVE MOBILIZATION ECHELONS

We pointed out that the moment of threshold intensity during a modern mobilization is reached during a war itself, by the time the entire economy of the country succeeds in transitioning to direct service of the goals of the war. This circumstance provides economically powerful states the capability not only to supply the active army dispatched to the front, but also to create new units (infantry divisions) and hardware during the war. Moreover, partial or complete reequipping of the army is even possible during a war.

In this regard, the experience of Germany and France during the World War is indicative.

Germany entered the war with 123 infantry divisions. It set about mobilizing the second echelon virtually the day after the wave of the first mobilization crested. Over a two-month period (16 August–10 October 1914), 13 new infantry divisions were formed. Fifty infantry divisions were formed right on their heels during the period 13 November 1914–20 January 1915. Forty-eight were formed in 1916, an additional 10 in late 1916–early

1917. Fourteen new infantry divisions were formed in the spring of 1917 and, finally, the last eight infantry divisions were formed in the summer of 1917.[16] All told, 275 infantry divisions were mobilized during the war, that is, their number increased by a factor of more than two.[17] As of 15 August 1914, there were 92 infantry divisions in the French Army. This number had reached 109 by 1 January 1916 and was 118 on 1 January 1917.[18]

France's constrained personnel reserves did not permit her to develop the scale of newly-formed entities that had been reached in Germany.

Supplying men to a modern army requires very large reserves.

The French Army, having 2.6 million men in the active army, lost 528,000 killed and captured and 580,000 wounded and sick during the first six months of the war (4 August 1914–31 January 1915), that is, a total of 1.108 million, comprising 43 per cent for six months of war or 86 per cent of the initial numerical strength of the active army in one year of war fighting.

The Russian Army, having 2.5 million men in the active army at the beginning of the war, lost 3,403,013 men over the period of one year, which comprises 130 per cent of the initial numerical strength of the army in the field. These losses include approximately 1.5 million captured or missing in action.

Losses in a future war will be even more significant with the expansion of the sphere of enemy actions (aviation, long-range artillery), with wider employment of toxic agents, and also the possibility of the appearance of new weapons. Thus, after a year of war, there will be a requirement for at least 100 per cent of the overall numerical strength of the army mobilized at the outset of a war in order to replenish personnel reserves. Given such an expenditure of personnel, only France, the USSR, and Poland (in part) will find more or less significant reserves for newly-formed entities.

The following figures express the number of individuals qualified for military service by country: 9.8 million in France, 5.86 million in Poland, 2.5 million in Romania, 525,000 in Finland, 165,000 in Estonia, and 270,000 in Latvia.

The table on page 42 will express the picture of the balance of personnel resources for a year of fighting.

If you disregard France and Poland, the personnel reserves of other states are so small that some newly-formed entities may be established only at the very outset (the first months) of a war.

But the question of newly-formed entities depends not only on

	Number Qualified For Military Service (thousands)	*Requirement For 1 Year of Combat Including Mobilized Army (thousands)*	*Number Not Used During the First Year of a War (thousands)*
France	9800	6400	3400
Poland	5860	3600	2260
Romania	2500	2400	100
Finland	525	320	205
Estonia	165	150	15
Latvia	270	240	30

personnel reserves, but (and this is decisive) on logistics capabilities as well. Given identical personnel reserves, but a different *rate* of accumulation of weapons, equipment, and ammunition, the capabilities of newly-formed entities will vary greatly for different countries.

If the Eastern European countries do not succeed in creating more or less significant newly-formed entities at the outset of a war, their creation during a war will be extremely doubtful since a significant portion of the personnel reserves will go for replenishment of natural losses in the active army and the rest may be lost completely if they are in territory that the enemy might occupy.

During the World War France managed to increase the number of her divisions from 92 to 118 only in a period of $2\frac{1}{2}$ years. Now, given the state of her industry and the reserves she possesses, she can reach the same number of divisions during the first year of a war and perhaps even faster than that.

For Poland (and the remaining Eastern European countries as well), the problem of newly-formed entities during a war in the near years boils down to the rate of receipt of material support from abroad since the most general calculations show that, even to supply the army mobilized at the very outset of a war, she will be called upon to import approximately 75 per cent of all requirements from abroad.[19] Therefore, given conditions most favorable to her, Poland can only count on an insignificant increase in the number of her divisions during a war, even though personnel reserves would allow her potentially to bring their number up to 70–75.

Thus, France and perhaps Poland may be able to achieve a significant increase in their armies during a war. The maximum number of divisions that one can anticipate during the first year of a war will be 118–120 for France and 70–75 for Poland.

The numerical strength of the armies in the other aforementioned states will remain at the mobilization first echelon level or may even be reduced.

NUMERICAL STRENGTH OF AVIATION

A modern army is unthinkable without aviation. All states are working on both a qualitative improvement in aviation equipment and, in parallel, on its quantitative growth.

This table depicts the number of ground forces and naval aircraft in the inventory (peacetime).

Country	*1923*	*1927*
France	1350	1640
Britain	385	700
Italy	250	800
United States	420	700
Poland	120	260

But these numbers very poorly characterize possible aviation activity in a future war. Germany in 1914 began the war with a total of 232 aircraft. In 1918 at the end of the war, she had 5,000 *active* aircraft on all fronts. Over the course of the war, she built 47,637 aircraft.[20] France entered the war with 162 aircraft of various types and ended it with 4,408 in combat units alone,[21] of which 3,430 were operational, having built some 52,000 aircraft during the war.[22] One can say without exaggeration that the air fleet, both where equipment and personnel training are concerned, was created *during the war itself*, so miserly were the aircraft and the personnel reserves available to all countries that went to war.

The base for aviation deployment for a future war differs completely. Air fleets comprising up to 700–800 and even 1,500 aircraft are being established in peacetime. Personnel are trained in line units and special schools at an increasing rate from year to year. An enormous number of new (not to mention old) aircraft are stored as a mobilization reserve directly in line units and at military depots. It suffices to point out that the French have in reserve at least 1,500–2,000 new aircraft, the British more than 1,000, and the Poles up to 500 (purchased from the French). These reserves alone permit not only replenishment of natural equipment losses during the first months of a war, but formation of an entire series of new aviation units as well. It would be extravagant in peacetime to maintain in the inventory all the aircraft that a country has available and no state is in a position to do so.

And, in addition, the state of the modern aviation industry cannot be compared to the situation during the World War.

The aviation industry of five countries – France, Germany, Britain, Italy, and the USA – in 1914 comprised 8–10 aircraft plants and eight engine plants with a work force totalling 3,000. According to 1925 data, there were 75 aircraft plants and 34 engine plants with a work force totalling 100,000 in these same countries.

The table below depicts the annual peacetime production of the aviation plants.

Country	*No. of Aircraft*	*No. of Engines*
France	2500	3500
Britain	1800	1200
Italy	1200	500
Germany	600	800
Poland	300	100

With wartime transition to two or three work shifts and a certain amount of additional retooling, the production capabilities in different countries increase by a factor of 2–3. According to approximate data, the annual aviation plant production of the aforementioned countries will reach 30,000 aircraft and 26,000 engines in wartime.

The most careful calculations show that the number of aircraft could double during the first six months of a war and quadruple by the end of the first year of a war.

Based on these considerations, the table on page 45 expresses the numerical strength in the first year of a war of the air fleets of the countries of interest to us.

France will approximately achieve its 1918 level during the first six months and will surpass this level by a factor of 1.5–2 by the end of the first year of a war. The remaining countries will create air fleets unlike those they had during the World War. Even in the eastern theaters, one must anticipate the appearance of 800–1,000 aircraft on each side at the front at the end of the first six months of a war, reaching more than 1,500 aircraft at the end of the war.

Countries	No. of Aircraft At Outset of the War	At End of First 6 Months	At End of 1 Year
France	1640	3200–3500	6500–7000
Britain	700	1500	2800–3000
Italy	800	1500	3000
United States	700	1500	3000
Poland	260	600	1000–1200

Note: Of course, these figure apply to the near years. The entire picture will change over time. Poland may achieve these figures only given abundant supply of equipment from abroad. Its aviation growth during a war cannot be especially significant without such support.

One must keep in mind here that such countries as Poland, Romania and others, owing to Article 16 of the Regulations of the League of Nations and the treaties existing among these countries and France, may and surely will be supported by the air fleets of their allies.

PROBLEMS OF FORCE QUALITY

Million-man armies are not only an enormous force operating on the defense, but also an enormous incrustation on the body politic, an enormous burden on the neck. Million-man armies are that bulky and cumbersome object, which, given well-known conditions, can turn into its antithesis. From a weapon of defense of a given state structure, this object can be converted into its grave-digger.

Creation of million-man armies denotes unavoidable armament of the enormous mass of the people. Virtually the entire able-bodied male population, to a man, must be called up into the army for a prolonged war. If in the nineteenth century, the epoch of the flowering of the bourgeoisie, this presented no special danger for the people, at the present time, the epoch of the strong development of class contradictions and class struggle, such universal arming of the populace can be tolerated without caution only in those states in which the ruling classes have faith in the masses, and in which the masses are interested in maintaining the state structure. The Soviet state, the Soviet system of state power, has every reason to rely upon the broad toiling masses, but the capitalist world must consider the “unreliability” of these masses and undertake mass mobilization with certain circumspection, certain constraints, and additional measures.

The problem of the "unreliability" of million-man armies for the capitalist countries exists with such acuity that, in recent years, capitalist Europe's military scientific thought has been working feverishly on a solution of the problem of a "reliable" army. Early in this chapter, we expressed the opinion of certain military theoreticians regarding this "ideal" army, which must comprise reliable professionals dedicated to capitalism and armed with all types of modern weapons. Instead of the masses, high technology, maximum mobility, maximum firepower. Everything that has been improved, everything modern technology had created – the best automatic weapon, light and powerful artillery pieces – must be mounted on a vehicle, tank, and aircraft and transferred to the hands of a small, but dedicated army.

At the beginning of this chapter, we provided an assessment of these views on the modern army and pointed out the completely utopian nature of the aspirations of those individuals desiring to employ small armies to defend modern states possessing enormous resources for goals of the war.

The bourgeoisie understands not only the danger of mass mobilizations, but also the fact that, at the same time, primacy in war will go to the side employing high technology and able to field the *larger* army at the front. Therefore, in all capitalist countries, we *essentially* see a further strengthening of the foundations of universal military service: the transition to shorter (one-year) terms of service, training of personnel reserves on a massive scale for the purposes of war, *weapons production on a massive scale*, preparation for war of an industrial base capable of serving the maximum conceivable army for a given country. The capitalist world continues to hope that it can employ the power and pressure of the state apparatus, skillfully conducted agitation and propaganda, and creation of those additional (fascist) organizations, which, along with the remaining attributes of the capitalist system, must preserve civil peace in the country, and maintain the obedience of mobilized armies, in order to solve the problem of the "reliability" of its forces. The bourgeoisie still has not and cannot repudiate the masses. On the contrary, it introduces those laws that envision mobilization of the entire population, to a man, in wartime. The bourgeoisie still senses that it retains sufficient power, so it decides to create million-man armies in case of war. All peacetime preparations are also directed towards this end.

But all this of course does not mean the bourgeoisie has or will succeed in eliminating the prerequisites defining the unreliability of the armed masses for capitalist countries. Class, national, and other contradictions undermining the capitalist system will not only remain, but *inevitably will increase* in wartime, reach the threshold of exacerbation, and certainly lead to unavoidable social upheaval in more than one country.

The impact of those contradictions (class and national) that exist in every capitalist country, but, during peacetime, cannot be reflected in the army to a noticeable degree (isolated location of barracks, reliable cadres, severe military discipline), will begin to penetrate into the army on a wide scale when mobilization begins and will create more fertile soil for revolutionary feelings than during peacetime.

The war of million-man armies is linked with unavoidable new mobilizations, and hardships in the country, and unavoidable depression of the entire economy. Earlier, we enumerated that one year of war requires mobilization for such countries as Poland of up to 3.5 million and, for France, up to 6 million people. This will comprise an enormous percentage of the able-bodied population of these countries.

War does not require only people. An enormous quantity of ammunition and new equipment is required. The ammunition and equipment requirements of million-man armies are so great[23] that their satisfaction demands that the entire metallurgical industry of even the most powerful capitalist countries fully mobilize and shift to "defense" work.

Transition of virtually the country's entire economy to production of military goods signifies an unavoidable reduction in the supply of the peaceful needs of the population and a complete depression in industry. The work of branches of industry of no significance to defense will have to cease very quickly and those of significance to defense be developed intensively.

War will levy enormous requirements not only on industry, but on agriculture as well. While ammunition is required in large quantities only during a period of intense combat, food and forage must be supplied daily and regularly, regardless of whether combat is in progress at that time or there is a lull.

The 1916 Russian Army required up to 300,000 tons of flour and groats, some 100,000 tons of meat or about 810,000 head of livestock, and about 16,000 tons of fats monthly. Delivery of this cargo required up to 2500 trains per month. The figures representing the food requirements for future large European armies will be at least as large.

A future war, if it drags on, will unavoidably lead to an even greater disorganization of the entire economy than the 1914–1918 war caused and this despite the preparation for war in all respects taking on broader dimensions and being underway in a more planned manner than prior to the World War.

Two to three million able-bodied members of the populace will be removed from industry and the economy at the very outset of a war. During the first year of a war, 4–7 million people in each of the warring states will be called upon for military purposes. Industry and agriculture to a significant degree will be devoid of a work force. Masses of people, who are simply consumers and who produce nothing, will be fed only at the cost of reducing the needs of the population remaining within the country. All of industry must convert to work for the goals of the war to satisfy the army's ammunition and equipment requirements and, consequently, consumption within the country must drop radically. All of this involves unavoidable privation for the civilian population, with an unavoidable depression in the entire national economy.

The World War with its consequences led to great social upheavals (revolution in Russia, Germany, Hungary, major and minor mutinies in the French and British armies), while future wars, which will be more ruinous in nature, will unavoidably create even greater prerequisites for major revolutionary explosions. The slogan of conversion of the imperialist war into a civil war will find more fertile soil in the future than was the case in the World War. Against the backdrop of these general difficulties, those contradictions existing in each given country will inevitably receive broad dissemination and more acute manifestation inside the country.

For our neighbors, these internal contradictions are mainly concealed in agrarian and national problems.

Approximately 65 per cent of the Polish population is occupied in agriculture. Poor and semi-poor peasant farms comprising about two-thirds (64.7 per cent) of all peasant farms occupy a total of 14.8 per cent of all land at a time when 2.7 per cent of the kulak farms occupy 9.8 per cent of all the land, with 0.5 per cent of the landowner farms occupying 44.8 per cent of the land. The share of the land in the eastern regions occupied by large landholders reaches 54.1 per cent. Thus, the wartime Polish Army, more than two-thirds of which must comprise peasants, will unavoidably reflect the dissatisfaction that exists among the peasantry even in peacetime due to this land distribution. The Polish government will not eliminate the preconditions for this dissatisfaction for it would then have to cease being a bourgeois government.

National contradictions also exacerbate these class contradictions. In spite of the fact that the Polish nationals in the country comprise about 62 per cent of the total population, Belorussians, Ukrainians, and Jews make up approximately 50–80 per cent in the eastern regions.[24] This denotes that, overall, oppressed national minorities will comprise a quarter to one-third of the strength of a mobilized Polish Army, while forces stationed in the eastern regions, even considering extraterritorial manning and mobilization, will comprise 40–50 per cent. Given the national policy the Polish government is pursuing regarding Belorussians, Ukrainians, and Jews, these national contradictions will naturally find their widest reflection in the Polish Army, too.

Peasant and national contradictions will make it very difficult to maintain the army's proper political stability and morale.

If a series of peacetime measures (significant cadres, extraterritorial manning, concentrated propaganda, and the like) can still provide to the proper degree the appropriate mobilization first echelon force quality for the outset of a war, then, during a war, when cadres will be diluted and the hardships and travails of war increase, it will be very difficult to maintain this requisite level of quality.

The picture will be virtually analogous within the Romanian Army as well.

This country, where 82.4 per cent of the population are peasants, has 83 per cent peasant farms possessing an insignificant share of the land. All remaining land is in the hands of landlords and kulak farms. Moreover, Hungarians, Moldavians, and Ukrainians, who gravitate towards the neighboring states (Hungary, Ukraine) where the bulk of their nationality resides, comprise 35.4 per cent of the population.

Of course, we will have our difficulties, too. We know on the basis of the experience of our history that all difficulties the country experiences will inevitably lead to exacerbation of both the urban and the rural class struggle. Surviving capitalist elements will raise their heads and begin to manifest themselves actively. This class struggle naturally will be exacerbated during a war, which will require great intensity on our part and inevitable privation for the population remaining in the rear area.

But the principal difference between us and the capitalist countries will be that our broad mass of toiling population will be the linchpin of the state and only separate, relatively insignificant, capitalist strata will be in opposition and we must suppress them. The opposite is true in the capitalist countries. An insignificant part of the hierarchichal strata of society must keep the dissatisfied millions in the population obedient.

Broad prospects unfold during wartime for political propaganda and agitation, both ours and our foe.

But force quality problems are problems not only of the political stability and morale in the army, but of the degree of combat training and cohesiveness of the forces as well.

An increase in the weapons in the inventory of the modern army and new ways to conduct combat providing small organic subunits and individual soldiers greater independence now also require better trained forces. An insufficiently trained army that is not cohesive is doomed, because it will lose its weapons and be captured in droves.

The general prerequisites for creating *highly-qualified* soldiers at the present time are less favorable than they were prior to the World War. Despite the incontrovertible general technical and cultural growth of the populace, mastery of contemporary military affairs given the great variety of weapons and equipment that modern armies possess still requires more time and greater effort than before. Besides that, everywhere we are faced with a reduction in terms of service (two- and one-year terms now, instead of the three- and four-years terms prior to the World War) and, at the same time, there is the radical reduction in peacetime cadres. The composition of peacetime companies, battalions, and regiments has been reduced significantly compared with 1914. The share of the reserves fed into organic units is increased considerably due to the large wartime organic unit organizational deployment factor. Despite the readiness training sessions for which they are called up periodically, the combat training of these reservists cannot be considered fully sufficient for the conduct of modern combat. Short terms of service and the complex conditions under which combat is conducted make it impossible to release a fully-trained soldier to the reserve. Reservists, who stay in the reserves for a long time, suffer a significant loss of professional skills. That is why many organic units will have to be knocked together (to a significant degree) and receive appropriate tempering during the war itself.

During the first months of a war, forces will be better prepared for those forms of combat not requiring complex shifts or maneuvers. These forces will be stronger in the defense than in an offensive. In offensive combat, the assault tactic will be more widespread than the fire tactic in these forces. As far as their combat qualities are concerned, during the first months of a war, these forces will be more reminiscent of the 1916–17 divisions diluted by a great number of hastily-trained reserves than of the forces that entered the war in 1914.

However, the peacetime breather, if it continues very much longer, may still change many things and bring modern training up to the level of training of the 1914 German Army. The tempo of the efforts involving combat training we are seeing in all armies provides a basis for thinking that such changes may still occur.

Established Force Organization

CORRELATION BETWEEN DIVISION AND CORPS DEFENSIVE AND OFFENSIVE RESOURCES

Not only the quality of armaments, their properties, but also their numbers, the degree to which different organic subunits are saturated with a particular weapon, that is, the problem of force organization, is of tactical significance.

The so-called "mechanization" of armies must be considered the distinguishing trait of postwar force organization.

The reasons why mechanization in different armies has occurred unevenly are purely economic. All armies can be divided into two groups where degree of mechanization is concerned. The Western European armies form the first group. The French Army is a clear representative of this group. The East European armies form the second group. The Polish and our Red Army must be considered typical of these armies.

The major difference between the first and second group is that, given an almost identical degree of infantry mechanization, the amount of divisional artillery in the second group has remained at the 1914 level.

The force organization the Western European armies (including the French Army) adopted is in essence a sort of rectification regarding artillery of how these armies were organized in 1918, at the end of the World War.

Infantry organization essentially remained unchanged. The 1918 French battalion had 36 light and 12–16 heavy machine guns and two infantry pieces. The contemporary organization of the French battalion envisions 36 light and 16 heavy machine guns and two infantry pieces. The 1918 German battalion had 24–32 light and 12 heavy machine guns (trench pieces, six mortars, were in the regiment). The present battalion composition has 18 light and 12 heavy machine guns. If you disregard the decrease in the number of light machine guns in the modern German battalion, which is a consequence of the change in the platoon organization due to the small *Reichswehr* the Treaty of Versailles established, one must consider the organization of the infantry battalions in both armies identical to that of 1918.

In organizing their infantry, the Eastern European armies copied the infantry organization of the Western European armies. The Polish and Romanian armies adopted the French organization, having included 36 light and 12 heavy machine guns and two infantry pieces in the infantry battalion (the Romanians have only eight heavy machine guns in the battalion due to a shortage). Given this battalion organization, the following is the number of infantry automatic weapons and infantry pieces found in a rifle division:

Division	*Light Machine Gun*	*Heavy Machine Gun*	*Infantry Piece*
French	324	144	18
German	162	108	–*
Polish	324**	108	18
Romanian	324	72	18

* The Germans have a mortar team in the regiment.
** This drops to 162 when light machine guns replace hand-held machine guns.

French infantry, with the greatest number of both light and heavy automatic weapons, is the most liberally supplied with automatic weapons. The Polish and Romanian armies, given the same number of light automatic weapons, takes second place to French infantry in the number of heavy machine guns (in the division, the Poles have 75 per cent and the Romanians only 50 per cent of the heavy machine guns found in the French division). The German division has 50 per cent less light machine guns and 25 per cent less heavy machine guns than the French division.

Organization of infantry in all modern armies radically differs from the prewar organization. The 1914 battalion had exclusively rifles in its inventory and the only two heavy machine guns it could call upon were in the regimental machine gun team. As far as automatic weapons in the infantry division are concerned, there was a total of 24–32 heavy machine guns and not a single light machine gun. Modern infantry in all armies must be considered really mechanized. Fluctuations in the number of automatic weapons in the divisions of various armies do not change the crux of the matter.

Organization of the artillery is something entirely different.

The Western European countries studied the World War experience and included powerful artillery within the division. It is impossible to surmount the resistance of mechanized infantry without a large amount of artillery. Using the World War experience, we can observe the major changes mechanization of the infantry has introduced into artillery organization.

	1914	*1916*	*1918*
France:			
Light machine guns	—	24	36
Heavy machine guns	2	8	12
Germany:			
Light machine guns	—	12	24–32
Heavy machine guns	2	8	12
Russia:			
Light machine guns	—	—	—
Heavy machine guns	2	8	8–12

The number of machine guns in a battalion rose, as the table on the previous page shows.

Thus, by the end of the war, the number of heavy machine guns in the infantry increased by a factor of four–six. Moreover, up to 24–32 light machine guns appeared in the French and German battalions. The fire power of a battalion rose by a factor of 2.5 at a time when its strength decreased from 1,000 to 650 men. In order to provide the forces' operational capabilities, all armies had to:

1. Increase the artillery numerically.
2. Increase the share of howitzer artillery at the expense of gun artillery.
3. Increase the numerical strength of the heavy artillery, introducing it even into the infantry division.

The German Army entered the war having 8,404 pieces, of

which 2,076 (about 34 per cent) were heavy. At the end of the war, it had 18,019, of which 6,819 (about 38 per cent) were heavy.[25] At the beginning of the war, the French Army had 4,648 pieces, of which only 688 (about 15 per cent) were heavy. It ended the war with 12,220, of which 5,740 (about 47 per cent) were heavy.[26] Correspondingly, the Russian Army had 7,088 pieces, of which 240 (about 3 per cent) were heavy. It ended the war with 12,299, of which 1,430 (about 12 per cent) were heavy.[27]

This numerical increase in artillery alone made it possible in offensive operations to concentrate the enormous masses of artillery required to break through a front of mechanized infantry.

The artillery support norms per kilometer of front during the World War rose in the following manner:

	Year	*Number of Pieces (Light and Heavy) Per Kilometer of Front**
Field Maneuvering Period (French Army)	1914	20
Champagne (French Army)	1915	50–55
Somme (French Army)	1916	70
Flanders (French Army)	1917	150
Riga (German Army)	1917	140
Picardy (German Army)	1918	128
Maneuvering Period	1918	80

* Err, *Artilleriya proschedshego, nastoyaschego i budushchego.*

It is evident from this table that the artillery support norms per kilometer of front underwent an interesting evolution during the World War. Beginning in 1914, they continuously rose, reaching the maximum figure of 150 pieces per kilometer of front at the end of 1917. But, already by then, these norms begin to drop, initially to 128 pieces in the German Picardy offensive and then even to 80 pieces in the 1918 maneuvering period.

One must not look at the evolution of these norms in isolation. They must be examined first from the standpoint of the evolution of tactical views on artillery employment and, second, from the viewpoint of the development and employment of tanks in offensive operations.

Primacy of the French artillery doctrine characterizes the period of positional warfare until 1917: solution to the problem of a successful offensive against an enemy dug in and braided with wire had to be sought exclusively in a mass of iron and steel.

Therefore, an enormous amount of artillery and an even greater number of projectiles are required, as are several days in which to issue them. According to the French, artillery had not only to catch the enemy in a slit trench, but also achieve his complete destruction. Only after that did the infantry move in and occupy the area.

The wartime experience did not justify this method of action. Prolonged artillery preparation provided the defense time to bring the requisite reserves to the combat area and to localize the offensive.

In 1918, the Germans changed their tactics. They combined a concentration of efforts, including those of the massed artillery, with surprise and succeeded in achieving great results with a relatively smaller amount of artillery (128 pieces versus the 150 enemy pieces per kilometer of front).

In the latter half of 1918, when the Allies concentrated an enormous number of tanks at the front, the artillery support norm fell even more, dropping to 80 pieces per kilometer of front, as indicated.

Nonetheless, by the end of the World War, in its maneuvering period, these norms were greater by a factor of four than in the 1914 maneuvering period, not counting the tanks, which replaced the missing artillery to a significant degree. It would be correct to assert that the norms for *suppressive assets* (considering tanks and artillery together) by the end of the World War rose by a factor of six–eight compared with 1914.

The armies of all countries had to resort to the creation of reserve artillery, that is, artillery not in the divisions and corps, in order to gain the capability to maneuver artillery assets so widely.

The table on page 56 characterizes the amount of reserve artillery in France and Germany at the end of the World War and its relation to the overall artillery numerical strength of these countries.

Thus, the artillery outside the divisions and corps would have sufficed (not counting high-powered and antiaircraft artillery) for the formation in the French Army of 20 three-division corps (figuring 168 pieces per corps) and, in Germany, 51 three-division corps (figuring 150 pieces per corps).

The problem of the ratio between gun and howitzer artillery was also linked closely with the accumulation of reserve artillery. Before the war, there was an average of one howitzer for every two guns. By the end of the war, there were four howitzers for

Category	*France*	*Germany*
Light Field Artillery:		
Number of Pieces	1332	3200
Per cent of Total	24	31
Heavy Field Artillery:		
Number of Pieces	2040*	4480
Per cent of Total	50	58
High-Powered Heavy Artillery:		
Number of Pieces	750	200
Per cent of Total	100	100
Anti-aircraft Artillery:		
Number of Pieces	900	2558
Per cent of Total	100	100

* Less trench and dismounted artillery

every five guns and the tendency was towards a ratio of 1:1, both in light and heavy artillery.

These conditions alone, to wit, bringing artillery support norms down to 120 pieces (if partially replaced by tanks, down to 80) per kilometer of front, a virtual doubling (for the French tripling, for the Russians quadrupling) of heavy artillery, and a strong upsurge of howitzer artillery, made it possible to supply divisions with the corresponding offensive capabilities. As a rule, given lesser artillery support norms and weak heavy and howitzer artillery, attacks foundered (Russian Army attacks).

Both the French and the Germans strove to put this experience to use in the postwar organization of their divisions and corps. True, the Germans are not permitted to have the artillery they would want. But the "theoretical" division, which they call the "modern division"[28] and with which they operate in their tactical drills, indicates their conclusions from the experience of the World War when organizing forces.

Given infantry's modern saturation with machine guns and using French data, the norm for artillery support to the attack is as follows: one field piece every 25 meters of front and one heavy field piece every 50 meters of front, which provides 40 light and 20 heavy pieces per kilometer of front, that is, a total of 60 pieces per kilometer of front.

With respect to its infantry assets (nine battalions), the modern division can conduct a successful attack on a 1.5- to 2-kilometer front (figuring 500 meters per battalion and three–four battalions in the division first echelon). Based on these calculations, a division must have 90–120 pieces, 30–40 of which are heavy, just for infantry support missions alone.

Moreover, according to these same French views and given the aforementioned weapon saturation in combined-arms formations, countering the enemy artillery requires one counterbattery group piece per 50 meters of front, that is, 20 pieces per kilometer of front or 30–40 pieces in the division sector.[29]

The French and German organizations to a significant degree stem from the aforementioned norms. Since inclusion of so much artillery in the infantry division would increase the length of the divisional column so much that it would be impossible to commit all the forces of the division over a period of a day (given that the division moves in one column), both the Germans and the French assigned divisional artillery only infantry direct support missions, while the missions of the counterbattery group were transferred to the corps artillery (French corps artillery has 48 heavy pieces, the German 35, 15 of which are howitzers and the rest guns). As a result, the Germans structured their divisional artillery (the "theoretical" division) with 72 pieces, of which 24 are light guns, 24 light howitzers, and 24 heavy howitzers, that is, howitzers comprise two-thirds of all artillery and half of these are heavy. The French adopted divisional artillery comprising 72 pieces (some data indicate 60), of which 36 are light guns and 36 (24 in the second variant) heavy howitzers, that is, only half is howitzer artillery, but all of that comprises heavy howitzers.

One must consider this loading of the division with artillery more or less sufficient, given that the counterbattery group's missions have been levied on the corps artillery. The division can be provided with conditions appropriate for an offensive through corresponding contraction of the division front or attachment of reinforcing artillery.

The French clearly still consider this divisional artillery to be deficient and, therefore, even in peacetime, maintain powerful cadres for deployment of the "main artillery reserve". During peacetime, the latter comprises 12 light gun and howitzer regiments, two mountain artillery regiments, nine heavy artillery divisions, of which seven are tractor and two are caterpillar traction, and two railroad heavy artillery regiments (not counting trench and antiaircraft artillery), which comprises up to 25–30 per cent of all the peacetime artillery in the French Army. During the first six months of a war, it is understood that the French will succeed in forming the same amount of strategic artillery they had in 1918.

The Treaty of Versailles does not permit the Germans to have peacetime cadres for strategic artillery but, according to press accounts, they operate such artillery in their drills.

	Divisional Artillery				*Corps Artillery*				
Army	*Light Gun*	*Light How.*	*Heavy How.*	*Total*	*Light Gun*	*Light How.*	*Heavy Gun*	*Heavy How.*	*Total*
Polish	24	12	—	36	—	—	12	12	24
Romanian	36	16	—	52	—	—	12	12	24
French	36	—	36	72	—	—	48	—	48
German	24	24	24	72	—	12	8	15	35
For Comparison: Theoretical Norms	—	—	—	90–120	—	—	—	—	60–80

Thus, in the richest army (the French) artillery requirements have been considered to a sufficient extent (although, for purely historical reasons, the amount of howitzer artillery in the army is slight) that it provides its divisions appropriate offensive capabilities through the degree to which the division is loaded with pieces (72) and through maintenance of powerful strategic artillery.

This is not the picture we see in Eastern European armies.

First, not a single one of these armies turned out to be in a position to include heavy artillery in the divisional artillery complement. Second, not one of them was able to maintain the correct ratio between gun and howitzer artillery. Third, divisional artillery (this also applies to corps artillery) is relatively weak numerically.

The table above illustrates the composition of the divisional and corps artillery of these armies.

This table demonstrates that the divisional artillery of all Eastern European armies is 55–80 per cent smaller than the norm developed based on wartime experience and 35–50 per cent less than the artillery in the French and German divisions; that the ratio between gun and howitzer artillery is 2:1 and even 3:1 at a time when wartime experience requires at least a ratio of 1:1 or better yet 1:2 (as the Germans adopted); that heavy artillery is not only lacking in the division, but that there is very little of it overall; that corps artillery is so weak that it is unable to accomplish even counterbattery missions; that reinforcement of a division with heavy artillery can only be looked upon as a random possibility.

Moreover, there is absolutely no strategic artillery in the Eastern European armies. In essentially all the Eastern European armies, there is not a single battalion of light and heavy field artillery outside of organic artillery. There are only a few pieces (one–two battalions) of more powerful calibers (210mm), but this artillery cannot serve as reinforcing artillery (which a significant portion of the strategic artillery must be). And there is so little of this that it can accomplish only some episodic missions in wartime.

Thus, a known contradiction, which can be termed *unilateral mechanization*, has formed the very foundation of the army organization of the Eastern European armies. The infantry fire weapons in all these armies approximately tripled compared with 1914, but the artillery assets not only do not exceed the artillery load of the 1914 Russian Army division, but, in several countries, are even below this norm.

This gap between the artillery requirements and artillery capabilities of the Eastern European armies may be intensified even more during wartime since it will be more difficult for the economically weak countries to create additional artillery than to upgrade infantry automatic weapons qualitatively and quantitatively.[30] Issue of a total of one or two automatic weapons to each rifle platoon may upgrade infantry firepower slightly at a time when increasing the artillery support norm to the requisite degree now requires virtually the same number of weapons that these states have in their present inventory, the only difference being that virtually all this additional artillery must comprise light and heavy howitzers.

The assumption is that such artillery saturation is not required on the Eastern Front since the density of the fronts there will be significantly less and it is difficult to employ such artillery due to purely local conditions (roads, supply, maneuver). Actually, the significantly lower density of the front to a certain degree eases the crisis of artillery saturation in the armies of the Eastern countries, but, as will be indicated below, the gap between the "ideal" norm and reality still remains so great that, given the exsting situation, it is difficult to organize major operations that pursue a decisive goal.

MODERN CAVALRY

Mechanization has also affected cavalry to a significant degree. Even during the World War, cavalry fire weapons were increased in the French and German armies. Armored cars were introduced into the inventory, the number of machine guns almost doubled, artillery was reinforced, and bicycle units were attached. In 1917–18, the cavalry in the West was employed as a powerful mobile

	French Cavalry 1914	*Modern Cavalry* French Cav. Div.	American Cav. Div.	Polish Cav. Div.
Light machine guns	—	315	102	96
Heavy machine guns	6	98*	92	72
Field guns	8	24	24	24
Armored vehicles	—	36**	24	19
Tanks	—	—	24	—
Bicycles	—	270	—	—
Aircraft	—	—	13	—

* Of this number, 30 antiaircraft, 12 in the bicyclists' group, and eight in the artillery.
** One machine gun and one gun on each armored vehicle.

fire reserve. It is quite natural that, given the density of the fronts that existed in the West during the World War and infantry fire weapon saturation in the French and German armies, the cavalry could not even dream about combat in cavalry formation. It was forced to move on horseback, but fight in dismounted formation.

The cavalry in all armies increased their fire weapons even more after the World War. They received light machine guns and included them in the squadron TO&E, increased the number of heavy machine guns, and were reinforced by artillery, armored vehicles (by tanks in American cavalry), bicycle units, and even aviation.

The table above demonstrates the firepower of the modern cavalry division as compared with 1914.

The cavalry converted entirely from cold steel to fire weapons. This naturally caused a change in views on the combat employment of cavalry, too. Strong development of automatic weapons made it impossible for cavalry formations to conduct combat in mounted formation. The time is long past when a cavalry attack decided the fate of an engagement. Modern combat is unhurried and is conducted exclusively with rifles, machine guns, artillery, tanks, and armored vehicles. The cavalry can participate in this combat only with its fire weapons. It has the horse only so that it can rapidly reach those points from which commitment of a large fire reserve promises the greatest results. Rapid achievement of favorable points for an offensive, surprise commitment of fire weapons to the action, rapid disappearance after success is achieved, and, finally, appearance anew for new participation in combat are characteristic peculiarities of cavalry combat.

Cavalry attacks can only occur during combat with enemy

cavalry or during the pursuit of a disorganized enemy. And even then a combination of an attack and actions in dismounted formation is unavoidable.

AVIATION ORGANIZATION

Significant changes have also taken place in the past in the ratio of the various branches of aviation. At the beginning of the World War, aviation was exclusively a reconnaissance resource. Fighter and bomber aviation did not exist. These branches of combat aviation only began to be formed in late 1914. At the end of the war, France had an inventory of 3,430 aircraft, of which 1,600 (48 per cent) were reconnaissance, 1,220 (36 per cent) fighter, and 610 (16 per cent) bomber aircraft.

At present, the share of bomber aircraft (day and night) in peacetime French land-based aviation has risen to 21–22 per cent at the expense of fighter aviation. Reconnaissance aircraft comprise 33 per cent, fighters 23 per cent, and bombers 44 per cent of the British land-based air fleet. Reconnaissance aircraft still comprise the bulk of the aviation in the air fleets of other countries and this is understandable. A small air fleet will always be constructed initially mainly as reconnaissance aviation, which accomplishes bombing missions in parallel. Combat aviation begins to manifest itself only with a further growth in aviation, when requirements to conduct reconnaissance in support of the ground forces are met sufficiently. Thus, the nucleus of Poland's bomber aviation has begun to stand on its own two feet in the past two years. We see exactly the same thing in the Red air fleet.

In the future, one must anticipate that bombers will gradually comprise one-fourth to one-third of all aviation. The main trend in aviation growth during wartime will be an increase in the number of bombers and, to some extent, fighters.

At present the organizational forms of an air fleet have also stabilized. The aviation detachment of 8–10 aircraft is the basic tactical entity. Detachments are combined into squadrons, the latter into aviation regiments and aviation brigades. Moreover, two air divisions have been formed in France.

All armies consider that the modern infantry division must now have its own organic aviation. But even French aviation still lacks the number of organizational entities that would allow introduction of aviation into the TO&E of all infantry divisions. As a rule, army corps everywhere have their own organic aviation comprising one aviation detachment (8–10 aircraft).

According to the French view, every army must have one reconnaissance aviation and one fighter aviation group (a group comprises three to four aviation detachments). An army group (what we call a *front* administration) should have one reconnaissance aviation group and two observation squadrons. All remaining aviation, including bomber aviation, forms a general aviation reserve, which the higher command element employs *en masse* in a particular sector, depending upon the situation.

COMBAT ARMS CORRELATION

The German Army entered the war in 1914 with a composition of 62 per cent infantry, 17 per cent artillery, about 5 per cent cavalry, 7 per cent engineer troops, and 0.3 per cent aviation. Other auxiliary units made up the rest. In 1918, infantry's share in the army composition fell to 49 per cent, that of cavalry dropped to 1.6, while the artillery, air forces, and engineer troops composition rose to 20.6, 2.3, and 115* per cent, respectively. The composition of the British, French, and partially the Russian armies had a similar evolution.

Appearance of a light automatic weapon and an increase in the number of heavy machine guns made it possible in static warfare to make do with less infantry and simultaneously required an increase in artillery, since an offensive became impossible otherwise. The rising firepower of armies constrained the employment of cavalry. On the other hand, more engineer troops were required, the necessity for which in an enormous theater of military actions greatly increased during a prolonged war. Not only did the scale of fortification work increase, and the communications network expand, but there was a requirement for them continually to monitor paved roads, dirt roads, and railroads, maintain enormous vehicle transportation, and so forth.

Aviation was rebuilt during the war. Its growth is completely understandable.

Organization of postwar armies remained intact at the level of the 1918 requirements and the Western European powers retained that degree of infantry mechanization achieved in 1918. In so

* (Translator's Note: As it appears in the original text)

doing, they greatly predetermined the ratio among infantry, artillery, and cavalry. Infantry's share in peacetime cadres will fluctuate from 42 to 45 per cent. The amount of cavalry was reduced greatly.[31] On the other hand, stronger cadres for artillery, aviation, and engineer troops are retained.

Calculations show that the combat arms correlation in future mobilized armies will be approximately the following:

Combat Arms	*Western European Armies (French Type) Per cent of Total*	*Eastern European Armies (Polish Type) Per cent of Total*
Infantry	33	46
Artillery	24	14–16
Cavalry	2	3.8
Air Forces	2.5	1.1
Engineer Troops	9	5
Auxiliary Troops	29.5	28–30

Thus, infantry and artillery will comprise the basic mass of future mobilized armies. The figure given for aviation is not representative, because not so much the personnel, but the number of aircraft in an air fleet is of significance. And the figure for the beginning of the war is 1,640 for France and 300 for Poland.

Infantry and artillery will mainly conduct a future war. Tanks (augmenting and partially replacing artillery) will act in direct concert.

In line with its numerical strength, cavalry will perform auxiliary missions, replacing infantry where its mobility is insufficient (conducting operational reconnaissance, in actions on the enemy flanks and in his rear).

Aviation in Eastern European armies will also play an auxiliary role due to its present numerical strength. Therefore, even its independent actions (raids to the deep rear area) must be linked with respect to time and axes with the actions of the ground forces at the front.

Tank and engineer troops are relatively poorly represented in all armies. The composition of each is limited to separate companies and battalions, rarely regiments.[32]

THE MODERN ARMY'S TRANSPORT RESOURCES

The increase in machine guns in the infantry and partial increase in other weapons led to a radical increase in the complement of horses within the division. The 20,000-man World War division had 3,920 horses and 910 wagons. The modern division, even with reduced artillery, given 12,000–15,000 men, has about 7,000–8,000 horses and 2,000–2,500 wagons. An infantry division of the French type has 8,000 horses, 2,000 wagons and about 400 vehicles.

Naturally, logistics within the corps also increased. The old army corps had a total of 6,500 wagons for 15,000 horses. The modern rifle corps has 10,000 wagons for 25,000 horses. Approximately 550–600 double wagons are required to haul one day's food and forage issue for the authorized personnel of a corps with reduced artillery, with 1,500–2,000 double wagons needed to haul one unit of fire. This transport requirement will increase by a factor of 1.5–2 in corps organized on the Western European model.

To base an army, organized on the French model, upon horse transport is impossible in practice. Logistics are so enormous that, being stretched out behind the divisions, they will not fit on the roads, not to mention the fact that army mobility and maneuverability are greatly reduced. Thus, corps and partially division logistics in the Western European armies have been motorized.

In France, corps artillery parks completely and divisional parks partially have been converted to mechanical traction. All strategic artillery has parks based on mechanical traction. Logistics for strategic cavalry have been mechanized. The entire army link in the supply chain has been converted to mechanical traction. The identical picture is also seen in the British Army as well, where not only army and corps logistics have been converted completely to mechanical traction, but the division level in the supply chain has been partially converted as well.

In the Eastern European armies, the organic level in the supply chain (division, corps) still remains based completely on horses. Even the army level in the supply chain in these armies has been mechanized only partially at present. This circumstance increases the number of horses in the eastern countries' wartime armies and makes them less mobile and maneuverable.

Transport assets required to support the modern offensive operation are enormous. An army comprising five rifle corps reinforced with 15–20 regiments of additional artillery requires the concentration of from 16,000 to 22,000 double wagons for each day's march (20–25 kilometers) of the army link in the supply chain. If a shock army has a restricted front, this amount of transport cannot be accommodated on the roads allocated to this army and, for that reason, supply for such an army must be virtually completely converted to vehicle transportation. A vehicle is three times more economical than horse transport. One hundred to 150 motor transport detachments, each comprising 20 three-ton vehicles, can support an army requirement to a distance of 40–50 kilometers (that is, twice as far). The problem of mechanization of logistics at the army link in the supply chain and of strategic artillery completely and the corps link in the supply chain partially is a matter of daily concern in the armies of the East European countries.

* * *

Thus, armies of the future, armies that will initiate and conduct the next war, are million-man armies, massive armies. The mobilization first echelon will take to war masses of people, 2 to 2.5 million in the large states (like France) and 1 to 1.8 million in medium states (such as Poland and Romania). Only small states like thc Baltic states will have an army of 80,000–120,000 men.

Where the small states are concerned, the mobilization first echelon will all but exhaust their personnel and materiel resources. Remaining states will still retain capabilities to reinforce the army in the field. It is difficult at this point to predict the scope of this reinforcement, but it will not be very great during the first year of a war, especially for such states as Poland and Romania, which have limited capabilities to accumulate military equipment and accessories.

Million-man mobilized armies will more completely and more acutely reflect the state of mind existing in a country than will the small peacetime cadres in the capitalist armies artificially isolated from the country. Class, national, and even religious contradictions present in the capitalist countries will inevitably find fertile soil for development in the mobilized armies of these countries. In this regard, the Red Army will find itself in conditions *differing in principle* from those in which the armies of the capitalist states find themselves.

The general level of training, the cohesiveness of organic units, and their mobility and maneuverability will drop to a great degree due to the infusion of a large number of reservists into the wartime army. These shortcomings may be corrected only by increasing peacetime cadres and making reservist refresher training more intense.

The special distinguishing feature of modern armies is the so-called mechanization. Armies are divided into two groups in this respect. The first comprises the Western European armies, armies in which the combat arms are mechanized uniformly (we have in mind the ratio between defensive and offensive assets). The second is made up of the Eastern European armies, with a unilateral mechanization implemented sufficiently fully only in the infantry and partially in the cavalry. There are two major defects in the second group of armies: first, incomparably weak suppressive assets, weak artillery, an insignificant number of tanks, weak combat aviation composition and, second, a peasant rear that does not correspond to the requirements of even just a mechanized infantry.

New hardware (tanks, chemical weapons, aviation) is represented in sufficient quantity only in the Western European armies. Tanks and chemical weapons remain very weak in the East. They may be employed only spasmodically due to their numbers. Qualitatively, aviation essentially is at the same level (with a certain lag in the East) in all armies, but it remains weak quantitatively in the Eastern European armies. The nucleus of combat (bomber and ground attack) aviation is still very weak in the aviation of the Eastern armies.

Much may still change prior to a war and is changing year after year. Based on the trend in the development of armed forces discernible in the measures of all states, in the next few years one can anticipate for the Western European armies further qualitative improvement in the latest hardware, namely in the type of tanks, materiel, and aviation, introduction of new chemical weapons, antiaircraft artillery, and radio communications gear into the inventory, and introduction of an off-road vehicle into the army.

One cannot anticipate *massive* qualitative changes regarding rifle and artillery weapons in the next few years. A qualitative change in these types of weapons is possible during a war, this occurring earlier in the infantry than in the artillery for production and economic reasons. Even during the first year of a war, the infantry may transition to a general or a partial armament with automatic weapons and may receive self-propelled and lightly-armored infantry artillery. The artillery itself (divisional and corps) will still retain its present equipment for a long time.

Major changes in the Eastern European armies are also inevitable prior to a war. Basic efforts here will certainly be directed towards a certain levelling between defense and offensive resources, that is, towards an increase in the amount of artillery and the number of tanks, improvement in their quality, and increase in chemical weapons. A rise in tank and even artillery construction may be observed even in the Polish Army. During the past year, regimental artillery entered the inventory, the number of tanks rose significantly, and orders have been placed for much new equipment.

A growth in aviation has been noted literally every year and, in this regard, the present state cannot be accepted when making calculations, even for the near future. Qualitative and quantitative changes are possible here even prior to a war.

In all probability, the contradictions between a mechanized front and peasant rear will be ameliorated to a significant degree. For reasons of a purely economic nature, the vehicle and the tractor are forcing their way into both the urban and rural economy decisively in all states (ours included) and are forcing the peasant horse out. Vehicle and tractor construction are developing rapidly, even in the Eastern European countries. The base that will undoubtedly make a gradual transition to motorized rear possible is beginning to be formed here as well. Prerequisites for the transition (wholly or partially) of the army level in the supply chain to automotive traction, both in Poland and in the USSR, already exist now. During a war itself, when the interests of the front will take precedence over everything, vehicles will be taken off farms, some will be purchased abroad (the latter approach is obviously denied to us), and the needs of the army will be satisfied.

We must always take into account the major assistance our neighbors can obtain from abroad during a war. Back during the World War, the first Russian Army armored detachments were maintained by French crews, and were obtained intact via a convoluted route (via Murmansk). The Tsarist Army even had aviation units of like origin. All the special-purpose artillery Russia had created by 1917 was imported from abroad.

There is no doubt that both Poland and Romania will have such assistance on a broader scale. One must consider not only normal logistical supply (which Tsarist Russia put to use via Murmansk and Vladivostok, and which Wrangel used via Sevastopol), but the appearance on our front of complete organic units, aviation and tank primarily. Much of the Western European technology may appear on our front directly at the outset of a war, even more during the war. During the war, the Russian Army doubled its machine gun units, depending to a significant degree on Colt machine guns obtained from America.

It is very difficult to forecast the scope of our enemies' reinforcement. Such predictions must always be adjusted.

PART TWO

Operations of Modern Armies

Premises

DENSITY OF THE OPERATIONAL DEPLOYMENT IN THE EASTERN EUROPEAN THEATER OF MILITARY ACTIONS

Our Western Theater of Military Actions has a length of about 3,000 km (from the Arctic Ocean to the Black Sea). Some 1,500 kilometers involve the border with Finland, about 380 with Estonia and Latvia, and 800 kilometers with Poland, of which 400 are north and 400 south of the Pripyat'. The Romanian sector of the border encompasses 320 kilometers.

As indicated earlier, a mobilized Polish Army will number approximately 68 infantry and 5.5 cavalry divisions in the mobilization first echelon. Even given that Poland will conduct war only in the east, of these forces at least five rifle divisions will remain on the western border and, consequently, up to 63 infantry and 5.5 cavalry divisions will be deployed in the east, which averages out to 12–13 kilometers per infantry division (cavalry is not included in count).

This figure (12–13 kilometers) is of more statistical than practical value. It is more important for us to establish the *thresholds* of the fluctuations in the density of the front, paying attention to the main and secondary theaters of military actions and possible fluctuations of the front to one or another side of the state border. The aforementioned fluctuations are of great significance, because the Polish sector of the front, if you take its depth from the state border to the line of the Vistula and San rivers, diminishes as one moves from east to west. It extends 800 kilometers at the Dnepr, but drops to 500 kilometers on the Vistula–San line. Even given uniform force distribution along the entire front, there will be only eight kilometers per infantry division on the Vistula and San instead of the 12–13 kilometers on the Dnepr. If one adjusts for the main and the secondary theater, the density of the front in the main theater will naturally be higher.

It is immaterial to us where the Poles deploy main forces, north or south of the Pripyat', since the dimensions of both sectors are almost identical: 400 kilometers each on the Dnepr and on the line of the state border, and 250 each on the Vistula and the San.

Defense on a 400-kilometer front (considering the special features of a defense in the Poles'ye as well) in one of the theaters requires:

a) up to 50 infantry divisions given normal divisional sectors (eight kilometers per infantry division);
b) up to 33 infantry divisions given wide divisional sectors (12 kilometers per infantry division) and
c) up to 20 infantry divisions given extended divisional sectors (20 kilometers per infantry division).

Of the 63 infantry divisions the Polish Army can allocate for actions on its Eastern Front, no more than 20 can be allocated for defensive missions in a secondary theater and, consequently, for one of the theaters, operations at the very onset of a war will immediately boil down to an extended defense. Given identical forces, the density of the defense here will increase more and more by virtue of movement from east to west and may reach 12 kilometers per infantry division, that is, a transition from an extended defense to a more stable defense with "wide" divisional sectors, is possible.

Up to 43 infantry divisions, a large portion of which is cavalry, will remain in the main theater. This will mean an average per infantry division of 9–10 kilometers on the Dnepr and 5–6 kilometers on the San and Vistula. Of course, these figures define the possible *operational* density of the front. *Tactical* density, even in the main theater, will differ. The front will be more dense than the aforementioned figure in assault sectors of the front and more extended in secondary sectors.

The degree of density of the front in the Romanian Theater will differ little from the aforementioned figures. If one considers that the Romanians will be able to allocate to the eastern border 35 of the 41 infantry divisions it mobilizes, this averages 10–11 kilometers per infantry division, figures approximately identical to the corresponding ones in the main theater of the Polish sector of the front. The tactical density here will also differ, of course.

An entirely different picture must be anticipated in the Baltic

Theater, Where there will be no more than 8–10 infantry divisions on 380 kilometers of front, that is, 35–40 kilometers per division. Even presence of numerous lakes and swamps in this theater does not change the overall situation since, with the exception of the Lubana Lowlands, they cannot constrain the maneuver of the forces. These conditions only permit so-called "detachment" warfare. A solid front in this theater is out of the question.

The density of the front for the southern axis (the isthmus between the Gulf of Finland and Lake Ladoga) in the Finnish Theater can be taken to approximate the density of the front in the main Polish theater, that for the northern axis (between the Arctic Ocean and Lake Ladoga) being less than the density of the front in the Latvian and Estonian theaters.

The density of the front indicated for the Poles and Romanians formally (regarding the number of kilometers per infantry division) is virtually identical to the density of the front in Galicia in 1914. At that time, on the same front (400 kilometers), the Russians initially deployed 32 infantry and 16 cavalry divisions, the Austrians 28 infantry and 11 cavalry divisions. During the Galicia battle, the number of divisions increased to 41 for the Russians and 33 for the Austrians. This means 12–13 kilometers per infantry division when deployment began and 10 kilometers during operations.

But, in essence, the density of future fronts in principle will differ greatly from such a period of the World War on the Russian Front.

In 1914, the Russian and Austrian infantry division had a total of 24–32 heavy machine guns and 36–48 field pieces for every 10 kilometers of front. In a future war, there will be the same number of pieces, but *162* light and *108* heavy machine guns per the same 10 kilometers of front, providing the following results per kilometer of front:

1914	0 light	2.4–3.2 heavy machine guns
Present	16.2 light	10.8 heavy machine guns

or a density of machine gun *fire* greater by a factor of approximately 6–8 than in 1914.

These data characterizing the density of *fire* of future fronts pose an entire series of serious problems, both in the realm of tactics and in the realm of operational art.

AVIATION DENSITY

There will also be differences between 1914 and the present time where aviation density is concerned. True, not one of the aviations of our neighbors, with their present aircraft inventories, can be assigned major operational missions.

At present, the most powerful aviation in the Eastern European countries has a total inventory of 260–300 aircraft, comprising 130–150 reconnaissance aircraft, 90 fighters, 30–50 bombers, and the rest seaplanes. An army comprising 60–70 infantry divisions needs as a minimum organic aviation comprising 120–160 aircraft (figuring six–eight aircraft per corps) and army reconnaissance aviation comprising 90–120 aircraft (figuring one squadron per army, two per army on main axes) to meet its *normal* timely aviation reconnaissance requirements.

Thus, the aviation reconnaissance requirement alone demands resources about equal to the present aircraft inventory in the Eastern European armies with the strongest aviation assets. Since reconnaissance aviation presently cannot meet both organic and army reconnaissance requirements, the problem immediately boils down to depriving corps of aviation assets and transferring the entire aviation reconnaissance mission to army level. All the same, each army will gain only one or two 19–aircraft reconnaissance squadrons. This degree of reconnaissance aviation saturation must be considered very weak since it can service only the most important requirements of the army command element. Corps and divisions will be served spasmodically and randomly. Given such conditions, artillery fire adjustment missions are essentially dropped completely.

The number of fighters that the strongest aviation in the East possesses suffices only for simultaneous coverage of a space of 35–40 kilometers[1] along the front *or* three important targets in the rear area, that is, they do not suffice even to cover the front of one shock army.

Three bomber detachments would be capable of accomplishing only spasmodic missions against individual targets.

Aviation in the Eastern European armies as comprised in peacetime still cannot play the role of an operational factor, despite the very modern equipment it possesses. This aviation could only have operational significance if it comprised 800–1,000 aircraft. Then, after allocating up to 300 aircraft to meet the reconnaissance requirements of the forces and of the army command element, aviation would still have approximately 500–700 combat aviation aircraft (fighters, ground-attack aircraft, bombers), which, being massed in specific sectors, could produce the required effect.

Creation of such aviation is the business of the next two to three years. Since war does not wait for tomorrow, appearance of that many aircraft on our Western border is not only not ruled out, but is probable. Special attention must be paid to this since several squadrons, predominently combat aviation, which the Western European states may allocate, must be added to the amount of aviation our neighbors have. In any event, it would be rash to count only on the peacetime aviation inventory when planning the actions of our forces. The situation can change more rapidly in this area than in any other. Thus, looking ahead somewhat, one must count upon the enemy having more powerful aviation.

DIVISION AND CORPS DEFENSIVE AND OFFENSIVE CAPABILITIES

Based on wartime experience, density of fire is considered sufficient if fire weapons in a given sector can provide five rounds per minute per meter of front. Observing echelonment requirements, the modern battalion can move up to one-third of its fire weapons forward for fire ahead of the main line of resistance, which provides approximately 5,000 rounds per minute (the fire-power of a Polish battalion is 14,000 and that of our and a French battalion 16,000 rounds). Thus, a battalion can occupy a frontage of one kilometer (5,000/5 = 1,000 meters) for a firm defense, with the depth of its disposition when maintaining the same density of fire within the line of resistance (five rounds per meter) reaching one kilometer. Usually, such a density of fire is considered necessary only in the most important sectors. One of the main missions of the defense is to free forces for an offensive on decisive axes. Thus, in the defense, one often has to resort to a relatively large dilution of combat formations to release forces for offensive missions. One has to stretch battalions along a frontage and depth of 1.5–2 kilometers. The latter figure (two kilometers) should be considered the threshold since, even using this norm, the resultant density of fire is less by a factor of two than what is required.

Stemming from these calculations, one should figure that a rifle division *with its own infantry* resources can occupy for the defense normally from four to eight kilometers, having four to five battalions in the first (holding) echelon and the remainder in the second and third (shock) echelons. The depth of the division's defense zone given such disposition (which we will conditionally call "normal") will reach five–six kilometers. If the division is disposed in "wide" sectors, the defensive front may reach 8–12 kilometers (at least six battalions in the holding group, three or less battalions in the shock group). The depth of the division's disposition in this case drops to three–four kilometers. The density of fire ahead of the forward line can be brought to 3,000–5,000 rounds per kilometer of front if approximately a half to one-third of the battalion fire weapons are moved forward. Finally, the division front in an extended defense may reach 12–20 kilometers. Battalions are distributed the same as in the second case, the only difference being that unoccupied gaps each stretching 1–1.5 kilometers are left between battalions. It is natural that, given such a disposition, the density of fire cannot exceed 2,500–3,000 rounds per kilometer of front, even when up to two-thirds of a battalion's fire weapons are moved forward. The density of fire ahead of the forward line remains just as significant, but it will be reduced dramatically in depth. In an extended defense, the front will be broken through simultaneously when the resistance (depth) of the holding group is overcome. A shock group in an extended defense will exert no influence on the course of combat actions.[2]

But occupying the aforementioned front firmly enough from the density of infantry fire point of view, a division lacks the capability to support it from the *artillery* standpoint.

A battery (four 76mm pieces) with its fire can reliably support a 200-meter front.[3] Based on these calculations, a division with its own artillery can reliably provide this support: 1,800 meters given 36 pieces (Polish), 2,400 meters given 48 pieces (Red Army), and 3,600 meters given 72 pieces (French).

Our artillery regulations consider[4] that a division can support creation of a continuous destruction zone with full employment of the might of effective artillery fire on a front not exceeding three kilometers (2.5 kilometers would be more correct). Thus, artillery can cover only individual sectors on the front of a divisional disposition despite the fact they are smaller by a factor of three (a factor of four for a Polish division) than those of the normal infantry front of a division in the defense.

If the divisional frontage exceeds 8–12 kilometers, the force of the defense lies *mainly in the infantry resources, in machine gun fire*. Artillery in the defense will serve *as a supplement* to infantry fire. When a division is disposed on a normal front (up to four–eight kilometers), being completely or partially centralized (given favorable terrain conditions), the artillery can provide sufficiently deadly fire in a sector with an overall expanse of up to 2,500 meters (up to 3,600 meters for the French), having created a *continuous destruction* zone in this sector. In this event, within the constraints of this figure shifting its fire from one sector to another, it can *successively* inflict perceptible losses on the enemy.

If a division is disposed on a front exceeding eight kilometers, the capability to centralize artillery command and control is essentially ruled out. In this case, artillery is distributed among the regiments. The density of its fire drops to such an extent that its role will boil down to creation of a curtain of fire in small sectors separated from one another.

Therefore, an attacker must primarily consider the enemy infantry fire system.

Banking mainly upon organic and attached artillery (or tanks), a division and a corps can surmount the enemy defense zone system. The role of infantry resources for this purpose is relatively small. They are helpless against machine guns the defense has dug in or has skillfully adapted to the terrain. Therefore, offensive combat requires not only a sufficient number of forces overall, but artillery (or artillery plus tanks) primarily as well. Offensive actions demand a great amount of artillery.

Based upon wartime experience on their front the French think that, during a war of maneuver against an enemy that has not fully reinforced himself, the average artillery supply norm per kilometer of front attacked must equal 12 75-mm batteries (48 pieces), six heavy artillery batteries for destruction (28 [sic] pieces), and six long-range artillery batteries for counterbattery fires (24 pieces).[5] The total is 96 pieces per kilometer of front, of which 76 are direct support artillery.

Our artillery regulations consider "that approximately seven batteries, *if only in the area* of the main blow, are required to suppress enemy infantry and its fire weapons in a one-kilometer sector of the defense zone. At least two batteries per enemy battery are required to counter enemy artillery successfully." Even in static warfare, 20–35–50 pieces[6] per kilometer of front are considered sufficient, depending upon the strength of enemy reinforcements. Some 10–15 batteries, including counterbattery, are normally required per kilometer of enemy front.

The Polish Field Service Regulations establish three artillery attack support norms: reinforced ("in large numbers") – one artillery battalion (12 pieces) per battalion advancing in the first line; average – one artillery battalion per two battalions; reduced – one artillery battalion per three or more first-line battalions. According to the regulations, "allotment in great quantity is based on experience. A battalion supported by a battalion of artillery may attack and penetrate 2000 meters deep into the enemy position *without significant losses*, despite enemy infantry resistance." Given the narrowest sectors assigned to a battalion in a war of maneuver (50 meters)[7], according to the Polish regulations, the attack support norm per kilometer of front is 24 pieces, being 36[8] not counting counterbattery artillery in static warfare (300–400 meters per battalion).

Thus, we have completely *different* norms for identical conditions of maneuver warfare. The difference becomes so great that it cannot be explained by making a trite reference to the fact that the conditions of the Western Theater, density of the front primarily, differ so greatly from those in the Eastern European Theater. Naturally, one must make an adjustment due to the varying density of future fronts in the West and in the East, but the figures contained in both ours and the Polish regulations are understated as well regarding the density of fronts we must anticipate as an average during decisive clashes even on the Eastern Front.

Let us make a calculation.

During an offensive against one infantry division defending on four to eight kilometers, one must always anticipate approximately the forces of one infantry battalion per kilometer of front.

The attacker must simultaneously accomplish the following missions:

1. Suppression of infantry fire weapons;
2. Destruction of artificial obstacles;
3. Maintenance of fire against enemy batteries (considering that their suppression has been achieved prior to fire being shifted to the enemy infantry).

In accordance with established artillery fire norms, the following are required to accomplish these missions:

Missions	*Targets*	*Number of Shells Per Target*	*Total Number of Shells*
1. Suppression of enemy infantry fire	About 12 heavy machine gun nests	100 bombs	1200
	24 light machine gun sections*	75 bombs	1800
	24 rifle sections**	50 bombs	1200
2. Destruction of natural obstacles, considering one path per first-line platoon 12 meters wide each, considering 2 linear meters per 50 grenades	16 paths	300 bombs	4800
3. Maintenance of fire against suppressed enemy batteries (considering that 2–3 enemy batteries may be operating on a division front)	—	1–2 batteries	—
Total shells			9000

* Considering the requirement to be suppression of two-thirds of all machine guns and rifle sections. Infantry resources are assumed to have the task to suppress the remaining one-third of the machine guns and rifle sections.

** The fact that this is not an exaggerated calculation can be seen from the combat example in our artillery regulations (Attachment 9), according to which 7,959 shells (of various calibers) are to be expended in a division attack against an enemy lacking artificial obstacles. Besides, the same source states that this expenditure "is far from the maximum."

If the dimensions of the paths are halved (to six meters each), the number of shells will drop to 6,600 (approximately 2,400 shells will be required for the paths). Thus, preparation of an offensive on a one-kilometer front will require from 6,600 to 9,000 shells. Given that up to four–five hours[9] generally are devoted to artillery preparation, not counting the time required to counter enemy artillery, we get the following calculation for the required amount of artillery. The threshold number of shells that can be fired in a period of four to five hours is: 150–180 shells for the 76mm gun and 100–120 shells for the 122mm howitzer. Given attack artillery comprising 50 per cent 76mm guns and 50 per cent 122mm howitzers, 125 shells on the average can be fired per gun during a four-hour period, this rising to 150 shells per piece over a five-hour period. Consequently, firing that number of shells over a period of four–five hours requires on the average from 45 (more precisely 44) to 60 pieces, of which half are light guns and half light howitzers. Inclusion of heavy calibers in the attack artillery composition hardly changes the overall picture. The power of the shells will increase, while the rate of fire will decrease (a 152mm howitzer can fire no more than 80–90 shells in five hours). Moreover, up to eight pieces will be required to maintain fire against suppressed enemy batteries. Given that the engagement with the enemy artillery will be fought simultaneously with the suppression of enemy infantry assets, the amount of counterbattery artillery will have to be increased up to five to eight 3-gun batteries (15–24 pieces). *Thus, these artillery support norms must be considered sufficient for the East European Theater:* for each kilometer of front, 45–60 pieces (15–20 3-gun batteries) for infantry support alone and 75–84 pieces in those instances when the engagement with the enemy artillery proceeds simultaneously with suppression of enemy infantry assets. On average, the following can be used to figure the support for the *main* attack (per kilometer of front): (1) for infantry support alone – about 50 pieces; (2) for infantry support and maintenance of fire against suppressed enemy batteries – some 60 pieces; (3) for infantry support and a simultaneous engagement with enemy artillery – up to 75 pieces.

Tanks may replace part of the artillery. One must have 20–30 tanks per kilometer of front in operations designed to a slight depth. Usually, one tank is required in the first echelon of attacking units per 100 meters of front, which will provide 10 tanks per kilometer of front. Maintenance of uninterrupted first-echelon actions requires having the same number of tanks in the second echelon and in the reserve, a total of 20 tanks per kilometer of front. One must envisage a high percentage of losses during an offensive against a well-defended enemy. In this case, the number of tanks per kilometer of front must be increased to 30. This norm must be doubled in longer operations since tanks can operate continuously for two days only, after which about two days of rest are required so that mechanisms can be cleaned.

The aforementioned figures undoubtedly more accurately reflect the artillery requirement than those contained in both ours and the Polish regulations.

According to our and the Polish regulation norms (21–24 pieces per kilometer of front), it is possible to advance only against an enemy who has hurriedly fortified himself, lacks barbed wire entanglements, and occupies more than 12 kilometers per infantry division. Given a more dense defensive front, even if he does not have barbed wire entanglements, the artillery support norm must be increased to 27–33 pieces or an average of 30 pieces per kilometer of front.

If the enemy has more solid defensive fortifications and artificial obstacles and the front is more dense, an offensive supported by such artillery resources will be unable to lead to a complete breakthrough of the enemy zone. It will be accompanied by extraordinary infantry losses (despite what the Polish regulations assert) or an artillery preparation that takes too long. In either case, it is difficult to count on rapid success and the appropriate rate of development of combat actions. In the first instance, the infantry will be called upon to spend a long time employing its own resources to surmount the enemy resistance and, in the second, it will encounter better-organized enemy counterattacks, which the enemy will have sufficient time to organize.

Ours and the Polish regulation artillery support norms stem from an *incorrect* prerequisite that the density on the Eastern Front will not exceed 12 kilometers. Our calculations demonstrate that one can count on such a density in a secondary theater only. The density of the front (operational) in a main theater of military actions will fluctuate from five to 10 kilometers. Decisive operations will ensue if the density of front is greater by a factor of two or three than that envisioned by regulation artillery norms. Therefore, reality will overtake these norms.

More artillery assets will be required for decisive actions. Given the norms the regulations envisage, partial successes are possible only against extended enemy sectors and this only prior to the approach of enemy reserves. An offensive will unavoidably be stopped, it will founder, when the reserves appear on the field of encounter.

The aforementioned norms envision very strong, morally steadfast, and well-trained troops on both sides. Given a less-stable enemy, these norms may be decreased to some degree. On the other hand, they must be increased correspondingly if the enemy is powerful and steadfast and friendly forces are poorly trained.

It would be erroneous to think that the aforementioned required suppressive asset norms denigrate the role of the infantry and shift the conduct of an engagement and an operation exclusively or mainly to the artillery and other hardware, that, thus, the *quality* of the personnel in the infantry is being underestimated. The moral–political steadfastness of the soldiers, the unswerving will to fight, the devotion to the ideal for which the war is being fought – all this remains the primary condition for success in battle and victory in war. Abundant hardware, if it is entrusted to the hands of politically unreliable or poorly-trained and unprepared troops, will be of no use to them. In the best (for the government concerned) case, it will be surrendered to the enemy and, in the worst case, will even be turned against their own ruling classes.

But, it certainly does not follow from this that troops with high moral–political qualities can and must be sent into battle without sufficient weapons and improperly trained to employ what they do have. In this case, the troops would suffer incredibly heavy losses and would rapidly lose those high qualities, without which it is senseless to wage war. They would lose confidence in the possibility of victory.

A million-man army must be built on the foundation of a person with average gifts and average qualities. The large modern army cannot count on a 100 per cent complement of heroes. Thus, one must look upon the above norms as mandatory average conditions under which forces with high moral qualities can fight a prolonged major war.

The human, and the infantry in particular, has the decisive word. As usual, the infantry must transfer to its shoulders the most difficult, the bloodiest, stage of battle – the direct clash with the enemy, the attack, and surmounting the entire depth of the enemy disposition. Abundant infantry fire weapons must be retained for the conduct of this close combat, for overcoming the resistance of surviving enemy nests, individual pockets of his disposition, which always survive and live to the final moment. And, even in this struggle, in this clash at close ranges, it is impossible to avoid direct assistance from the artillery, given the present-day system of defense of advancing infantry. The infantry needs the accompaniment of the artillery not only with fire, but also with wheels.

Infantry lacking the requisite artillery support tasked to attack a modern defense abundantly supplied with automatic weapons and echeloned in depth will very rapidly be dispersed and put out of the game. The infantry must be supplied with favorable conditions for combat, must be preserved, must not forced to take superfluous losses, and must not be forced to make fruitless and unsuccessful attacks. Otherwise, it loses its trained cadres, it must be brought up to strength hastily with untrained and unprepared bearded men or beardless kids. Such infantry rapidly loses it combat verve.

Creation of high-quality infantry is no easy task, even for us, who have great and reliable human material. It is possible to lose this infantry very soon if you employ it injuriously, without taking the changing conditions of combat into account.

If you start from the artillery support norms in offensive combat that we calculated, the authorized amount of artillery in an infantry division should be considered sufficient to support an attack on a front:

Nature of the Offensive and the Defense	*Attack on a Front in Divisions Supported by Artillery (in meters)* West European Armies	East European Armies	*Note*
1. In an advance against a defense with normal or wide divisional sectors (8–12 kilometers per infantry division)	800–1100	500–800	Corps artillery tasked with all counterbattery missions
2. In an advance against an extended defense (20 kilometers per infantry division) under meeting engagement conditions	2500	1500–2000	

Meanwhile, even in offensive combat, infantry resources within a division suffice for accomplishment of broader missions than these artillery capabilities envisage. A 400–500 meter front is considered the minimum front for a battalion in offensive combat. Narrower zones for an advance will call for an extraordinary accumulation of personnel and the greater superfluous losses that accrue thereto.

Complete breakthrough of the enemy defense zone will require penetration normally 8–12 kilometers into his disposition since, during combat, some enemy batteries and infantry will unavoidably withdraw to new positions and, naturally, the initial depth of his defense zone will expand. The attacker will always have to organize his battalions in at least three echelons to surmount such a depth of the enemy disposition. But even given a division with its infantry assets organized in three echelons, it will fully suffice for an offensive on a 1.5–2 kilometer front (three to four battalions in the first echelon, the rest in the second and third echelons). In those cases when the attacker is facing a weak defense, it is sufficient to organize divisions in two echelons and assign each battalion broader offensive frontage (up to 800–1,000 meters). Then, a division's infantry assets will suffice for an advance on a front of three–four kilometers.

Thus, the following ratio between the artillery and infantry capabilities of the modern division results:

Nature of the Offensive and the Defense	*Infantry Sufficient for Advance on Front*	*Front Supported By Artillery in Divisions* West Euro. Armies	East Euro. Armies (*in meters*)
1. In an advance against a defense with normal divisional sectors (8–12 kilometers per infantry division)	1500–2000	800–1100	500–800
2. In an advance against an extended defense (20 kilometers per infantry division) and under meeting engagement conditions	2000–3500	2500	1500–2000

Within corps boundaries, given that missions to counter the enemy artillery will be assigned totally to corps artillery (apparently temporary assignment of infantry support groups to counter the enemy artillery will still become necessary), the attack frontage of a three-division corps where its artillery resources are concerned cannot exceed: in the first instance, two–three kilometers given infantry capabilities of 4.5–6 kilometers and, in the second instance, 4.5–6 kilometers given infantry capabilities of 6–10 kilometers.

The accepted regulation norm is from 4 to 10 kilometers per corps.[10]

ADDITIONAL SUPPRESSIVE ASSETS FOR A DIVISION AND A CORPS IN OFFENSIVE COMBAT

Thus, we see that the artillery capabilities in offensive combat are less by a factor of approximately two than infantry capabilities, both in the division and in the corps.

The shortage of artillery in divisions during offensive missions is recognized in all armies.

The French consider that, in maneuver warfare, a four-division corps attacking an enemy not fully fortified must normally commit the artillery of its second-line divisions immediately. But the army commander then must also reinforce the corps with one or two regiments of 75mm guns transported on vehicles, two regiments of short-range heavy artillery, and two regiments of long-range heavy artillery,[11] that is, with five to six regiments of additional artillery. All of this, along with organic artillery, comprises approximately 550 pieces (figuring 72 pieces in a division), which provides up to 135–138 pieces in the sectors of the main attack (corps front of about four kilometers) and, given auxiliary actions (corps front eight kilometers), 68 pieces per kilometer of front.

We too, in our tactical exercises, in order to reinforce organic artillery, very often are forced to commit additional High Command Reserve Artillery (ARGK) or to mass artillery in the sector of the main blow at the expense of the third division in the corps. But reinforcement of divisional artillery from the High Command Reserve Artillery for us is an intermittent phenomenon.

Meanwhile, conditions for the offensive turn out to be such that a corps with its own artillery assets cannot carry out a decisive attack envisaging deep penetration into the enemy disposition. A corps left to its own devices in such an offensive artificially will have to reduce the attack frontage, refuse to employ all its infantry, or throw into battle about half of the infantry without sufficient artillery support, thus condemning them to extra losses without any hope of success. Such an offensive must unavoidably founder, misfire. Corps, which by the nature of their missions have to surmount *any* enemy resistance, and carry out assault missions, without fail must be reinforced by additional artillery or tanks.

A tactical requirement – to balance corps artillery and infantry capabilities, to create conditions whereby a corps would be capable of employing its infantry resources fully so that the frontage of its actions and its capabilities to maneuver will not be reduced – defines the amount of artillery a shock corps requires.

We have defined both the infantry capabilities of a corps and the artillery support norms per kilometer of front under various conditions of offensive combat.

Stemming from these data, a shock corps must have the following amount of artillery: about 300 pieces for an offensive against a densely-occupied defensive zone prepared promptly and figuring the corps attack frontage to average five kilometers and the minimum artillery support norm to be 60 pieces per kilometer of front. The support norm must be raised to 75 pieces per kilometer of front given stronger fortified structures or conditions in which a fast rate of advance is required. Then a corps will require up to 375 pieces. Since a corps has only 171 pieces, it will require a minimum of 130 and a maximum of 200 pieces for reinforcement, that is, a minimum of four and a maximum of six–seven artillery regiments. A corps will also require up to 300 pieces or about 130 pieces (the same four artillery regiments) of additional artillery during an advance against an extended defense and in a meeting engagement with weak enemy forces, considering an attack frontage of 10 kilometers and an average artillery support norm of 30 pieces per kilometer of front (we calculated that norm to range from 27 to 33 pieces). Thus, one may consider that a shock corps *normally* requires four artillery regiments of additional artillery.

This artillery will provide a capability to employ corps infantry assets fully both in a meeting engagement and during an offensive against an enemy that hurriedly has gone over to the defensive. In an offensive against a more stable defense, the amount of additional artillery will have to be raised to six or seven artillery regiments.

Tanks in part may replace additional artillery. As indicated above, one must start from a norm of 40–60 tanks per kilometer of front in calculations for a major and prolonged operation, that is, given our tank unit organization, two tank battalions may replace one regiment of additional artillery.

CHEMICAL WEAPON TACTICAL EMPLOYMENT NORMS

Employment of chemical weapons provides a great effect in combat. Toxic agents, even in a weak non-lethal concentration, force an enemy to don gas masks, hamper the actions of soldiers, force them into shelters, and ease the conditions under which an attacker operates. Employed in great quantity and in sufficient concentration, they inflict great damage on an enemy lacking chemical defenses and significantly restrict enemy actions even if he has such defenses.

A peculiarity of the tactical employment of toxic agents is the large amount that must be expended to accomplish various tactical missions.

A chemical cloud attack requires the greatest expenditure of toxic agents. Some 30–35 tons of gas per kilometer of front under attack (with this quantity having to be released over a period of one hour) are required to achieve the requisite concentration of toxic agents. The dependence on weather conditions for this method of releasing gases is commonly known. Based upon these calculations, an attack on a 10-kilometer front requires 300–350 tons of toxic agents, the entire load having to be brought directly to the forward lines of the troop disposition.

This task is so difficult that it is achievable only under static warfare conditions. New lighter gas cylinders make it possible to employ a chemical cloud attack under maneuver warfare conditions as well if the front has been stabilized. However, the drawbacks to this type of employment make all armies consider this method obsolete and disadvantageous.

A relative saving in toxic agents expenditure is achieved when they are released employing artillery shells, by chemical projectors, sprayed from aircraft, and freely dispersed. It is easiest of all to use these methods to place toxic agents where desired and they provide the desired result.

If one begins with the norms established in the artillery for the firing of chemical shells, the amount of ammunition shown in the table on page 86 must be expended to accomplish various tactical missions.

The data in this table demonstrate that a very large quantity of artillery is required when chemical shells are fired to accomplish more or less important tactical missions. Nonetheless, several of these missions are also fully achievable given those artillery support norms we have established above. Thus, the success of a surprise chemical attack employing shells containing volatile toxic agents against individual important sectors in the enemy disposition is fully possible given these norms as well. Using short attacks by fire for 15 minutes prior to an attack itself during the period of preparation for the attack, an attacker will be capable of engulfing the enemy disposition on a one-kilometer front in a thick cloud of volatile gas (this requires up to 44 76mm guns or 40 107mm guns or 33 152mm howitzers). This quantity of artillery can undoubtedly be allocated if up to 60 pieces are available per kilometer of front.

Considerably fewer capabilities accrue when firing shells with persistent toxic agents, mustard gas in particular. A very large expenditure of ammunition and, consequently, a large quantity of artillery, is required to achieve a specific concentration of toxic agents when firing on large areas. Even though the firing of this type of chemical shells can be continued over a longer period than

TABLE OF EXPENDITURE OF ARTILLERY AMMUNITION REQUIRED FOR ACCOMPLISHMENT OF VARIOUS TACTICAL MISSIONS WHEN FIRING CHEMICAL SHELLS

Missions	*Caliber*	*Shelling Duration*	*Rate of Fire* *of One Gun*	*Requirement* *Shells*	*Guns*	*Batteries (3-Gun)*
1. Sudden chemical attack on an enemy battery using non-persistent toxic agents to put it out of action (front less than 10 meters)	76mm 107mm 152mm	3 minutes 3 minutes 3 minutes	6 rounds 4 rounds 2 rounds (per minute)	200–240 120–150 50–60	12–15 11–12 8–10	4–5 4 3
2. To maintain a contaminated atmosphere for 1 hour on the indicated target	76mm 107mm 152mm	1 hour 1 hour 1 hour	60 rounds 40 rounds 24 rounds (per hour)	200 120 50	3–4 3 2	One battery essentially must be assigned
3. Sudden chemical attack on the forward edge of a center of resistance (Polish infantry type – frontage 1 kilometer)	76mm 107mm 152mm	15 minutes 15 minutes 15 minutes	3 rounds 2 rounds 1 round (per minute)	2000 1200 500	44 40 33	15 13 11
4. To maintain a contaminated atmosphere on an enemy center of resistance for 1 hour	76mm 107mm 152mm	1 hour 1 hour 1 hour	60 rounds 40 rounds 24 rounds (per hour)	2000 1200 500	33 30 24	11 10 7
5. To contaminate with mustard gas one enemy battery or one company level point of resistance	76mm 107mm 152mm	Up to 4 hours Up to 4 hours Up to 4 hours	150 rounds 100 rounds 72 rounds (in 4 hours)	500 300 200	3 3 3	Approximately against one battery
6. To contaminate one Polish infantry center of resistance (frontage and depth of 1 kilometer)	76mm 107mm 152mm	Up to 5 hours Up to 4 hours Up to 4 hours	180 rounds 120 rounds 90 rounds (in 5 hours)	50,000 20,000 5,000	276 165 55	92 55 18

is the case when firing shells with volatile toxic agents, all the same, it is possible prior to an offensive in maneuver warfare to shell only individual important targets in the enemy disposition and mainly those that friendly troops will not attack directly. Given today's artillery rate of fire and today's quantity of artillery in the Eastern European armies, it will be difficult with the aid of artillery alone to contaminate significant areas in the enemy disposition with mustard gas. Even such targets of attack as an individual center of Polish infantry resistance require an extra-ordinary expenditure of ammunition. Today's artillery will be capable only of missions in which shells containing persistent toxic agents are employed to neutralize individual important targets (short-range batteries, flanking structures, important approaches, and so forth). Broader possibilities in this direction are opened for Western European armies, which possess more artillery.

It is possible to employ gas projectors with much greater success to create the requisite concentration of gases. Chemical mortar rounds are several times more economical than artillery shells (by a factor of three–five). It is possible to create a high-concentration toxic cloud more rapidly when they are used. But their employment involves great inconvenience. First, they have a short range and, second, their employment requires a great dcal of preparatory work to set them up prior to firing. Normally, up to two to three nights are devoted to this, which means their employment in field warfare is virtually excluded.

More advantageous dissemination of toxic agents is achieved with the aid of the air fleet. For this purpose, aviation either employs special chemical bombs, which will contain a higher percentage of toxic agent than artillery shells[12] or free dispersal (spraying or dumping) from aircraft is practiced.

Aerial bombs are filled with toxic agents prior to use. Individual internal vessels (made of sheet iron, porcelain) containing various toxic agents exist for each type of bomb. They make it possible to fill the bombs right in the aviation unit prior to take-off, employing the agent the nature of the target requires at a given moment.

The action of aerial chemical bombs is still barely discussed in the literature. Tests run in various armies are held in the highest secrecy. Such calculations are found in our literature.[13] A mustard gas bomb weighting one pood (16.38 kilograms) can contaminate 1,000 square meters of land surface (that is the same area 50 75mm shells can cover). A bomber group comprising six aircraft, each carrying 160 kilograms of bombs, contaminates 60,000 square meters of land surface. A 60-man team requires one hour to decontaminate this area. A squadron capable of dispatching three six-aircraft groups twice a day can put a railroad station out of action for 12 hours a day (figuring six hours for decontamination and six hours for preparatory operations: assembly of the team, supply of materials, and so forth).[14] These calculations envisage aircraft carrying only 160 kilograms of bombs. If you take into account the day bombers of today carrying 400–500 kilograms each, the effect of the chemical action should be considered greater by a factor of 3–3.5. Night bombers carrying up to 1,000–1,400 kilograms of bombs will provide an even greater operating effect.

Presence of two to three bomber squadrons in a given operational sector makes it possible to maintain individual rail junctions and important industrial and political targets under the threat of chemical attack continuously for 7–10 days. Large rail junctions within 200–250 kilometers of the front can be made the subject of systematic chemical attack from the air and their operation can be seriously impeded or disturbed for a specific period of time (up to 7–10 days).

More distant targets will be subjected only to sporadic raids. Troop concentrations, if reconnaissance aviation detects them beforehand, may be subjected to the identical action from the air and aviation has special chemical fragmentation bombs or instruments permitting direct application of liquid toxic agents.

For free dispersal, an aircraft (conventional day bomber) can lift up to 250–300 liters of liquid toxic agents, which, when dispersed from an altitude of 600 meters, suffice to cover an area of 15–17 hectares. Repeat spraying of the liquid from follow-on aircraft achieves the appropriate toxic agent concentration. This method may be employed to contaminate a sufficiently large area in residential centers in the enemy rear area or individual approaches to the organic rear area on the battlefield. Live targets are sprayed with one pass by the aircraft.

Thus, the possibilities of chemical attacks have at present expanded more than was the case during the World War period.

Even under maneuver conditions, one can anticipate cases when entire sectors of the front will be covered by a thick cloud of volatile gases of sufficient concentration for a period of several minutes for the purpose of forcing everyone to don gas masks and mortally to contaminate those lacking them. Such a cloud may be maintained without any special difficulties for the prolonged time of regular shelling. At the same time, artillery and aviation may be employed to inundate individual, especially important, points (flanking machine gun nests and gun positions, observation points and command posts, the area of several important batteries or the disposition of large reserves, approaches to positions) quite rapidly with mustard gas.

Important rail junctions, industrial centers within 200–250 kilometers of the front, locations of bases and warehouses, and crossing sites that cannot be bypassed by transport carrying rations to the front may be subjected to *systematic* air attack with bombs containing persistent or volatile toxic agents. More distant points (up to 600 kilometers) will be the subject of sporadic chemical attacks.

Given a more or less stabilized front, when there will be two–three nights to prepare for an attack, a heavy gas attack is always possible using chemical projectors, especially if a given area facilitates supply of requisite materials due to transportation conditions.

In *static* warfare, the scope of such attacks will grow since it may take longer to supply the shells. Firing from chemical projectors, and sometimes a gas cloud attack, will be more widespread. Individual sectors of the front, as well as the rear of the enemy dispositions, may be kept under mustard gas for weeks at a time. It may be possible to make some routes directly inaccessible to the enemy.

As a rule, there will then be the requirement to live and work in gas mask and protective clothing.

Naturally, the scope of the employment of chemicals will depend entirely on the degree to which a country can supply these articles of extermination to the army. Experience from the World War demonstrated that countries with a developed chemical industry can achieve enormous results, even if the entire effort to supply these weapons to the army is improvised during the war.

The Germans fired the first chemical shells in late October 1914. They did not provide satisfactory results. On 27 March 1915, the Germans fired bombs causing lachrymation in the Ypres sector and, on 23 April of that year, they released the first gas cloud (chlorine) in the same sector. Five months later, in September, the French responded by releasing their own gas. By the fall of 1918, the number of chemical shells had already exceeded one-fourth of the entire number of artillery shells. In some operations, half the shells both sides fired were chemical shells.

Peacetime preparations for a chemical attack are underway on a large scale in all states. In future, one can anticipate a faster rate of chemical warfare expansion than during the World War. One can get an idea of the scope of future chemical warfare just by the attention being paid in all countries to the problems of chemical *defense*.

Requirements levied on the new gas mask (and they have been met to a significant degree) include the capability to accomplish various combat functions (firing, operating a telephone, command, and so forth) *normally* for a lengthy period of time. The gas mask must not constrain the soldier, it must become his normal equipment during combat.

Not only the entire active army, but the entire population of the country, especially in large industrial centers, must be equipped with such a gas mask.

But a gas mask by itself does not suffice. Normally, each soldier must also have clothing that protects against blistering toxic agents. Various forms of such clothing have been invented in different countries.

Various types of gasproof shelters are being popularized widely everywhere and they are being introduced not only into military construction, but into general civilian construction as well.

Preparation is underway on such a scale that the normal work of the army and the largest center is insured even under the conditions of a prolonged stay in a contaminated atmosphere.

The Operation

SHOCK ARMY

The "shock" army of the German right-flank type that advanced in 1914 through Belgium to the Marne or the right-flank Red armies during our 1920 offensive to the Wisla, that is, an army intended for action in the sectors of the main blow, must be organized so that *it will be capable with its own forces of conducting a series of successive operations from start to finish. It must have the resources that will allow it to surmount any enemy resistance, both at the outset and during operations.* Rifle units, additional suppressive assets, aviation, auxiliary troops, all must be designed for and adapted to those missions facing them. The composition of the army must be so designed to insure tactical success during a clash with the enemy in a situation anticipated during a given operation.

One must envision an unavoidable change in the situation during combat actions for operations designed to go to great depth and pursuing decisive goals: unavoidable reinforcement of the enemy, an increase in the density of his front, appearance of an entire series of positions reinforced hurriedly and beforehand on routes of advance. From the very outset, a shock army must have all those resources that will permit it, without loss of time, to organize an uninterrupted blow in any situation possible during planned operations. In operations with a decisive goal, one usually must envisage a clash with the main mass, with the main forces, of the enemy. These enemy forces may either appear in front of the advancing forces at the very outset of the operation or appear on the front during the operation as result of a major regrouping made via railroads, a march, or with the aid of vehicle transportation.

Rifle units must be included in the army composition in such strength that the army can form a sufficiently *dense offensive* grouping when combat is joined.

Stemming from the maximum capabilities of a rifle division and rifle corps, the attack frontage of the latter in a meeting operation and during an offensive against an insufficiently strong enemy defense should be considered to be no more than 10 kilometers, this dropping to 4.5–6 kilometers in an offensive against a sufficiently dense defense prepared beforehand. The *maximum* infantry capabilities of a division and corps disappear given these norms.

The first echelon alone of a shock army must comprise three to four rifle corps if the width of the attacked frontage has to be increased to 25–30 kilometers in order to achieve an operational breakthrough of the enemy disposition.

In modern combat, especially in frontal engagements, infantry suffers heavy losses and requires frequent replacement for rest. Moreover, the front takes on a broken shape during an operational engagement, frontage increases, and density is diluted. New forces must be committed to retain the requisite density of the front. This requires that the second and third echelons comprise up to half or one-third the number of first-echelon divisions.

Thus, the overall composition of the rifle units in a shock army will rise to 12–18 rifle divisions. Unavoidably, one must have several four-division corps (first-echelon corps desirably) to insure normal command and control of such a number of units.

Then, one must consider the additional suppressive assets required.

According to our calculations, a three-division corps carrying out shock missions under the conditions of a meeting operation normally requires four regiments of additional artillery, with this number having to be increased to six or seven regiments in an offensive against a deliberate dense defense. Thus, normally, each first-echelon corps must be reinforced by four artillery regiments of additional artillery. Moreoever, a certain number of additional suppressive assets also must remain at the disposal of the army to allow it to increase the additional artillery of all or of the most important corps to six or seven artillery regiments when attacking a deliberately reinforced position. It is advisable to have this second portion of additional assets in the form of tank units. It is possible to use one tank battalion per artillery regiment as the replacement norm since tank units are required only for breakthroughs (rather than as a replacement for additional artillery during the entire duration of the operation).

Thus, a shock army comprising four–five rifle corps will require up to four–five artillery divisions (16–20 artillery regiments) of additional artillery and up to 8–12 tank battalions.

Such an army requires a whole series of auxiliary troops for its support. In view of the fact that the final decision as to the force grouping in an operational engagement on an army scale must be made again within two days' march of the enemy, there must be reconnaissance assets at the disposal of the attacker sufficient for timely receipt of the requisite information about the enemy. The amount of army reconnaissance aviation must insure regular daily reconnaissance at least three times a day, considering night flights as well. One must consider that each shock army requires at least two reconnaissance squadrons.

One cannot bank upon aviation reconnaissance alone. First, it depends greatly on weather conditions and, second, the fact that a flight takes off does not signify that it will see what needs to be seen. In 1918, British and French aviation even missed the large concentration of troops the Germans put together on the Western Front prior to their March offensive, despite the fact that there were flights regularly almost every day.[15] And, finally, even if it will detect the enemy somewhere, it is unable to provide more detailed information as to subordination of particular units, distribution of forces, and so on. Besides aviation, the army commander must provide himself with reliable ground-based reconnaissance.

The army zone of movement will equal about 50–100 kilometers. An army requires one, better two, cavalry divisions reinforced by aviation, high-speed tanks, and bicycle units to provide reconnaissance on such a front.

Along with organic antiaircraft assets, air defense of the mass of forces a shock army will possess will require at least an additional four to five fighter squqdrons.[16] Moreover, special antiaircraft assets will be required to defend the most important points in the rear area (railheads, airfields, bridges, and the like). One must consider one to two antiaircraft battalions as the minimum per defended point.

Actions in an area abounding in river obstacles will require inclusion of pontoon units in the army composition, figuring a minimum of one heavy bridge per shock corps.

A significant number of signal troops will be required to provide the communications for such an enormous mass of forces.

In a majority of cases, bomber aviation (light and heavy) may reinforce a shock army. Since this branch of aviation is employed as a rule *en masse*, its composition will be significant. All or a major part of the combat aviation a given army possesses may turn up here. In any event, it will comprise at least two or three aviation brigades so it can make systematic attacks either against enemy forces or his close-in logistics.

Finally, a shock army probably will be reinforced by chemical weapons. Chemical shells for artillery are not part of its permanent property. They belong to the High Command and are supplied to armies accomplishing shock missions. Chemical companies with gas cylinders and gas projectors finally are distributed if the front is stabilized. As a rule, bomber aviation will have an unlimited number of aerial bombs. Individual squadrons will be adapted for free release of toxic agents.

The aforementioned figures, of course, are not absolute; they may not be suitable, of course, for *all* cases. The nature of the army's mission, the quality of friendly and enemy forces, terrain conditions, and other situational data will always introduce some adjustments into these figures. One thing is clear, however. The composition of an army formation cannot be defined on the basis of the "inspiration," the "caprice," of a particular commander. This effort, especially the part that concerns definition of suppressive assets requires calculation and may be computed. We would like here to demonstrate only the kind of figures an operator must deal with when making calculations concerning a prolonged major operation.

Countries lacking sufficient suppressive assets and other hardware will be constrained to the greatest degree when forming those armies that will have to accomplish assault missions. Lack of additional suppressive assets will force them to reduce the overall suppressive asset support norm per kilometer of front, will force them to supply these suppressive assets only to the most important corps within the composition of the shock armies, or resort to artificial concentration of artillery assets to the detriment of secondary sector corps and divisions. Additional artillery or aviation will be employed more intensively in armies that have tanks, but are deficient in suppressive assets. Their forces will be accelerated. These units will be worn down more rapidly than when they are employed normally.

Given all of the above, advancing infantry will find itself in conditions rather difficult for the conduct of the battle. It must attack a defense that is not completely disorganized and suppressed, it will have to employ its fire weapons more intensively to suppress the defending enemy. High-quality and trained infantry can be successful under these conditions as well, especially during actions against an enemy that has not yet dug in or that does not fight very efficiently. But losses naturally will be greater than in armies that have sufficient suppressive assets. The percentage of unsuccessful attacks and of those that founder will also be high. Operations undertaken without sufficient suppressive assets will be bloodier and more wasteful from the personnel standpoint.

APPROACH MARCH TO AN OPERATIONAL ENGAGEMENT

Although those large marches that an army made before its operational deployment no longer occur (these movements mainly take place via railroads), an army must still make major improvements of the entire mass of its forces during the course of an operation. Regardless of how close the selected operational deployment area is to the enemy, several transitions always have to be made, especially at the outset of a war, from this area to the clash with the main enemy forces under meeting operation conditions. During an offensive against a defending enemy, operational deployment may occur in direct proximity to the enemy defensive position. Therefore, the requirement for such marches for the initial operation vanishes. On the other hand, the entire operational deployment for subsequent operations must occur in march formation and the entire mass of forces must do this simultaneously to preserve the continuity of the blow. There is a high degree of difficulty associated with such large movements today, given the complex organization of forces and the increasing threat from the air.

Movement is complicated by the circumstance that, even under conditions whereby armies have significant attached additional artillery and tank assets, selection of movement frontage when organizing the approach march to an operational engagement will still depend upon very many conditions. One must move on as wide a front as possible for convenience and rapid movement, for convenience of positions for rest, for more rational and fuller employment of local resources, and to retain freedom of maneuver. The broader the movement frontage, the smaller the march formation columns, the faster the march maneuver progresses, the easier it is to hide forces from aerial observation, the fewer the inconveniences in positions for rest, the more food and especially forage that can be delivered, and, consequently, fewer supplies and logistics. Broad movement frontage provides greater opportunities for envelopment and turning the enemy flanks. But a desire for very broad frontages may lead to complete loss of the offensive power of the forces, the pursuit of conveniences in movement and positions for rest may lead to an operational cordon unable to accomplish any offensive missions at all. When organizing the march formation of large masses of forces, one must find that movement frontage *threshold* from which it will be possible rapidly and easily to transition to *frontage* dimensions that the offensive capabilities of a given group of forces allow without loss of time, without extraneous regroupings.

We have calculated that up to three–four rifle corps with 16–20 artillery regiments of additional artillery and 8–12 tank battalions are required for a breakthrough on a 25–30 kilometer front. This density is required during an offensive against an enemy, who has deliberately gone over to the defense. The approach of such a mass of forces to the area of the operation presents no special difficulties if the front is stabilized. It can be accomplished piecemeal over a period of several days, by echelon. It is more difficult to organize the approach march of such a mass of forces to an operational engagement in the event of a meeting clash or during the period between successively developing operations, when simultaneous movement by the entire army front is required.

In a meeting operation, as well as when proceeding to the area of a new operational deployment, not only the march frontage, but the initial frontage of the operational engagement may be significantly wider than the frontage in which the main mass of both infantry and artillery with tanks will later deploy for the main attack. In order to provide the shock army greater freedom of action, it is advisble to have in its composition not three or four corps (based upon the amount of additional suppressive assets), but five corps. Then, depending upon the circumstances, the army will be able to assign auxiliary missions to one or two corps and task the rest, with the entire mass of artillery and tanks, to carry out the main attack.

So, let us use as our example an army comprising five rifle corps, with the aforementioned additional artillery and tanks. Such an army in a meeting operation can provide a sufficiently dense offensive infantry grouping deployed on a front of no more than 50 kilometers (an average of 10 kilometers per corps). Already one or two days' march from the enemy, the army on the march must have a movement frontage that does not especially exceed this figure. One must consider a front of about 75 kilometers possible, still two days' march from the enemy. Over the two-day period, given simple movement forward, it is always possible to reduce the army frontage to the required norm (50 kilometers) simply by narrowing the corps boundaries. Far from the enemy, three to four or more days' march away, the army movement frontage may be even wider and reach 90–100 kilometers. The latter figure should be considered a threshold, even when a significant distance from the enemy. Movement on such a front (90–100 kilometers) provides the army maximum possible conveniences for the march and positions for rest and, at the same time, provides the army commander the capability to organize maneuver within this zone in order to obtain an advantageous distribution by the moment the operational engagement begins. The basic mass of additional artillery and tanks must be placed directly at the army commander's disposal to facilitate his freedom of action when making the final decision about the distribution of forces for combat. Presence in the second echelon of a certain number of divisions capable of being maneuvered depending on the situation is extremely important for the same purpose.

There is no requirement to create a large accumulation of forces on one road three or four days' march from the enemy. Therefore, all suitable roads in the army offensive zone must be used for movement during this period.

No special difficulties are encountered when *structuring the march formation* of an army moving on a 100-kilometer front, even given the conditions of our Western Theater of Military Actions. If you take a large-scale map, you can find one road every five–seven kilometers of front in any area north or south of the Pripyat' and east or west of the border (especially in the area west of the Neman River–Rovno–Kamenets-Podol'sk line), that is, a minimum of one individual road may be assigned to each division on a 100-kilometer front. True, a significant portion of these will be country roads and bridges will require repair. But there is no other choice in the East European Theater of Military Actions and one must count on more difficult movement conditions. It is possible that some corps moving under especially unfavorable conditions will be forced to use only two roads, even when a significant distance from the enemy, necessitating two divisions on one road.

All additional artillery, since it is horse-drawn, must move simultaneously with the divisons. It is disposed between corps, four to five artillery regiments per corps, only for movement until the army commander makes his final decision as to the distribution of forces.

One regiment of additional artillery moves with each of the three divisions when a corps moves via three roads, while the fourth regiment moves as a separate echelon via the best road.

Tanks move as independent echelons. They are moved by rail to railheads and, from there, move by bounds behind the forces on trucks or under their own power (high-speed tanks) over a period of two–three days. Pontoon and engineer units normally within the composition of divisions and corps, but subordinate to corps commanders, move as independent echelons. Corps logistics are distributed uniformly for the move via all corps roads.

The depth of each column when a corps moves via three roads reaches 50 kilometers, figuring from the head of the security forces.[17] Near the enemy, when the corps will have to transition to movement via two roads, the organization of the two divisions remains unchanged. The third division, less the additional artillery, moves as a special echelon behind corps logistics via both roads. The additional artillery moving with this division transitions to one of the divisional columns and moves ahead of divisional logistics along with the other artillery regiments.

The depth of a march formation organized in this manner reaches 65–70 kilometers if the movement frontage remains unchanged. It is natural that, given such a depth of forces located on one road, movement of all of these forces simultaneously (day or night) is out of the question. Different echelons will have to move at a different time of day. Units closest to the enemy (lead divisions with the additional artillery moving with and behind them) primarily move at night. Divisional and corps logistics move during the first half of the day. Second-echelon divisions move simultaneously with the lead divisions, either during the second half of the day or at night. Thus, a march formation depth of 50–70 kilometers does not signify that organic columns of the aforementioned length simultaneously will be on the movement routes. These 50–70 kilometers characterize only the echelonment depth of the entire corps. Columns moving simultaneously will have much less depth.

Corps echelonment to a depth of 50–70 kilometers must be considered normal since organic logistics have also been figured for precisely that depth (2.5 days' march). Despite this, it will be difficult to conceal the movement of such a mass of forces from aerial observation. In any event, it is possible using organizational measures (movement at different times of day, full use of night time) to conceal the scope of such a movement from aerial reconnaissance. Nonetheless, deep columns of forces undoubtedly will serve as an object of actions by enemy bomber aviation (if available to the enemy). Therefore, special attention must be paid to air defense of columns moving during the day and of troop rest areas. Corps antiaircraft artillery assets suffice for simultaneous cover of an area with a frontage and a depth of 10 kilometers. If organic antiaircraft machine guns and field guns on special mounts are tasked to defend troop rest areas (following a night march), antiaircraft artillery assets will turn out to suffice only for cover of the point at which the flanks of adjacent divisional and *corps links in the supply chain* meet (the area of greatest accumulation of wagons in day-time). Additional antiaircraft artillery assets must cover the movement of second-echelon divisions and logistics, as well as that of army logistics. The amount of these antiaircraft assets must be determined separately each time depending upon the nature of the area of actions and how active is enemy aviation. An additional antiaircraft artillery battalion will usually be required for each of the most important and exposed movement routes.

Semi-mobile antiaircraft artillery must cover the area of railheads and distribution stations. In view of the duration of an operation and even if there are up to four squadrons per army, fighter aviation can be tasked only for specific periods of time to cover limited areas through which will pass a certain column or group of columns not supported by other assets.

During the period of direct deployment, which most of the time will occur during the day, fighter aviation will have to employ all its forces to cover this army maneuver.

The way columns on the march are organized will vary greatly.

An army advancing with both flanks covered by neighbors will usually have column heads on the same line. This will allow the army to join with the enemy along the entire front more rapidly, employing superior forces, to achieve an outcome mainly by means of the power of a frontal onslaught. Maneuver is possible essentially exclusively within the boundaries of individual corps and divisions directly during the joining and conduct of the operational engagement. It is advisable that an army advancing on a flank organize columns echeloned to the rear (six–eight kilometers per corps). This organization will provide maximum cover for one's exposed flank and permit subsequent envelopment of the flank of enemy units that have been engaged on the front.

Presence of several second-echelon corps outside the advancing army's exterior flank is mandatory for deeper and more decisive turning of the flank of the enemy operational disposition.

The magnitude of a day's march for the entire army is approximately 15–20 kilometers, being 25–30 kilometers for individual columns.

It may be that such an army march formation structure is too unwieldy and, thereby, barely mobile and unmaneuverable.

We recall that, in 1914, three right-flank German armies comprising 16 army corps (32 infantry and 5 cavalry divisions) deployed on a 65-kilometer front (Vise-La Roche), having four kilometers per corps (two kilometers per infantry division). The two subsequent armies (2d and 5th) comprising 10 army corps (20 infantry divisions) had a 75-kilometer deployment front (Trier-Didenhofen), that is approximately 7.5 kilometers per corps (about four kilometers per infantry division). Following an assault crossing of the Meuse River, the 1st and 2d Armies comprising 12 corps (24 infantry and three cavalry divisions) had an offensive (movement) frontage of 60 kilometers (Hasselt-Leuven), that is, five kilometers per corps or 2.5 kilometers per infantry division.

Right up until the border operational engagement, three corps (III, IV, VII – reserve corps) moved in the second echelon. And under these conditions the movement frontage of each first-echelon corps did not exceed seven kilometers.

During the frontier operational engagement, each first-echelon division had an average of no more than four–five kilometers. During the pursuit, the movement frontage of the 1st Army (five army and one cavalry corps) did not exceed 40–50 kilometers. The 2d Army, comprising four army and one cavalry corps, moved on a front of 30–35 kilometers, while the frontage of the 3rd Army three corps) did not exceed 20–25 kilometers, being 18 kilometers on 27 August.

When deployment began, there were 20,000 men and 59 pieces per kilometer of front in the 1st Army, with 8,000 men and 30–40 pieces each in the 2d and 3rd Armies.

And this mass of forces, which moved seemingly with such extraordinary density, demonstrated the maximum conceivable mobility and agility. The rate of advance of these armies averaged 16 kilometers per day, with entire armies moving 20–25 kilometers some days. During the Battle of the Marne, the 1st German Army made a brilliant regrouping, with the pullback of all corps of the army and their deployment towards the flank, having to the rear of the initial front such a water barrier as the Marne. Meanwhile, the right-flank IX and III Army Corps covered a distance of 70–80 kilometers in two days (7 and 8 September). After disengagement, the entire transfer took place in divisional columns (a corps via two roads).

During the German offensive of March 1918, the 17th Army comprising seven corps (28 infantry divisions) had a deployment frontage of 35 kilometers (five kilometers per corps). The 2d Army comprising five corps (21 infantry divisions) had an offensive frontage of 38 kilometers. The artillery support norm on the average reached 82 pieces, in certain sectors 100 pieces, per kilometer of front, and this given the aviation both sides had available in 1918.

One clearly must recognize that only such massing of forces and artillery provided the capability to achieve tactical success. Only presence of a powerful force grouping with a high saturation of artillery on the right flank of the strategic front of the German armies allowed them sequentially to push back the Belgian Army, roll up the 5th French and British Armies in a frontier operational engagement, and overrun all French and British attempts to halt this German offensive all the way to Paris itself. This same dense grouping allowed Kluck to attack decisively and push units of the 6th French Army back following the 7–8 September regrouping.

But on the other hand, throughout the entire World War, we see how operations undertaken with an insufficiently dense front were suppressed or rapidly foundered. The experience of the old Russian Army is especially revealing in this regard. Before the World War, the reigning view in the Russian Army was that the best form of approach march to an operatonal engagement is organization of divisions by brigade (brigade columns of two regiments each). And experience showed that, during a clash with a more or less dense enemy front, the Russian Army always yielded, unable to achieve a swift outcome. Very often, its thin front, similar to an operational cordon, turned out to be broken through.

Two right-flank Russian armies (4th and 5th) comprising 10 corps advanced on a wide front (200–220 kilometers) with a density of one infantry division per 10–12 kilometers and, lacking a strike fist, conducted two weeks of futile combat with the Austrians, who had advanced essentially with the identical density of front, and, as a result, were broken through and pushed back to Lublin. The only thing that saved the situation on the Southwestern *Front* was the approach of new forces by rail and the formation of a new 9th Army on the right flank.

Brusilov's offensive had initial success because the Austrians did not expect it at all and because a certain concentration of forces at the points of attack was artificially achieved in the initial blow.

The 8th Army had a total of 12 infantry divisions and occupied a front of approximately 180 kilometers. It chose a 20-kilometer sector for the blow and concentrated seven infantry divisions and some 430 artillery pieces there, that is, three kilometers per infantry division and about 20 pieces per kilometer of front). Small sectors of about two–six kilometers each in which the appropriate concentration of forces was achieved at the expense of all army units were selected for an attack in the sectors of the three remaining armies. The initial blow was successful because it occurred on a relatively weak Austrian front, but the offensive very rapidly played out since the offensive grouping dissolved immediately following the first blow. The total depth of advance of the 8th Russian Army, which made the first blow, was 50 kilometers. This distance was covered from 23 May to 14 June, a period of 21 days, with half this distance covered during the first four days of the offensive. On succeeding days, the army made more futile attacks than advances. Careful study of this Russian Army experience demonstrates that, unless you have a sufficiently dense force grouping, it is impossible to complete operations in depth that pursue a decisive goal.

The aforementioned data concerning the requisite density of front and procedure for the approach march to an operational engagement by large masses of forces are fully substantiated and stem from the peculiarities of modern armaments and modern armies.

Armies not wishing to understand these simple truths, or unprepared for actions in such massive groupings, cannot count upon great victories in a future war. Their fate is to repeat the sad experience of the old Russian Army. It is impossible employing a sparse front and spread fingers to surmount the resistance of a defense saturated with machine guns and echeloned to great depth. An offensive operation undertaken with an insufficiently dense front will bog down, it will founder, as soon as new enemy forces confront the advancing troops.

INITIATION AND CONDUCT OF AN OPERATIONAL ENGAGEMENT

The commander must make his decision as to the final force grouping for commitment to an operational engagement long before column advance guards close with the enemy. In essence, this decision must be predetermined as early as two days' march from the enemy. Now the commander must decide on which wing (or in the center) corps must be committed in a more massive manner, in more compressed time intervals, and, from this time, using appropriate regulation of the corps starting time for the march, he must configure the army march formation appropriately: he must decide whether his corps are to move in a line of columns, with their heads at the same level, or if he should echelon the march formation to one flank or the other or in the shape of a wedge. From this moment on, he must finally target his corps appropriately if he desires to attack from the front or to envelop the enemy flanks. He will be in no position to make any major changes later.

It is quite evident that the aforementioned decisions to a great degree predetermine the army's initiation procedure and distribution of forces in the operatonal engagement. Therefore, the commander must concern himself with timely organization of reconnaissance to avoid preconceived decisions. Reconnaissance must be sent as far forward as required to guarantee collection of information about the enemy by the time the army is within two days' march of him. Modern aviation's radius of action naturally insures timely receipt of information on large accumulations of enemy forces. But only ground-based reconnaissance will be capable of providing more precise data on what enemy forces have occupied what local points along the army route of advance. Army cavalry must be sent forward promptly three–four days' march from the enemy to obtain such data.[18]

Our task does not include an examination of how the cavalry and aviation conduct reconnaissance. We will confine ourselves here only to pointing out that not only cavalry, but aviation as well, surmounting enemy resistance, battling his security units on land and in the air, are tasked to obtain the necessary information. Therefore, fighter aviation should support reconnaissance aviation promptly to insure the latter observes those areas the enemy will carefully cover. It will often be advisable to dispatch two-place fighters to reconnoiter such areas.

Cavalry reconnaissance will be even more difficult. It will be able to obtain more or less detailed information only after it has not only overrun the enemy cavalry, but the infantry units protecting it. Therefore, seriously-organized reconnaissance in force must be conducted. Tasking individual cavalry troops to conduct reconnaissance does not promise results of an operational nature. Cavalry must employ regiments supported by powerful artillery (heavy artillery as well) and armored units to conduct reconnaissance. High-speed tanks, with the aid of which the cavalry will be able to surmount the resistance of covering enemy infantry units, will strongly assist the cavalry. If tanks are lacking, it is mandatory that heavy artillery and vehicle-mounted infantry reinforce the cavalry.

The army commander's decision to initiate an operational engagement, will envisage the final distribution of forces (sector of the main and secondary blows), number of divisions assigned to the first ecelon, grouping of second-echelon divisions distribution of additional artillery by corps, and the decision about the tank battalion supply area (if this has not yet been made).

One must insure that sufficient forces, both infantry and artillery, are immediately committed. One division will be required for every two–three kilometers of front in the sector of the main blow. A sector of up to 8–10 kilometers may be assigned for division auxiliary actions. This is the case even if the main attack frontage will be only 25 kilometers and eight rifle divisions will be required for this. Another two–three divisions will be required for auxiliary actions on a front of 20–25 kilometers, that is, from 10 to 11 infantry divisions must be committed immediately. The remaining four to five infantry divisions must receive directions as to which area to go to and to whom they are to be subordinate. Shock corps usually have to retain their third and fourth divisions. The third divisions from those corps accomplishing auxiliary missions will be removed and transferred to the area of the main attack. A minimum of 30 pieces per kilometer of front must be committed in the sector of the main blow on the first day of combat, so it is mandatory that one regiment of additional artillery be attached to each first-echelon division in that sector. Divisions acting in an auxiliary sector retain just their own artillery. The main thing is that some of them will be reinforced from corps artillery. All remaining additional artillery is assembled at the area of decisive actions. The army commander may intervene further during an operation by allocating his remaining additional artillery, tanks, chemical assets, and second-echelon divisions and directing the efforts of combat aviation appropriately.

On the second and third day of an operational engagement, the enemy will go over to the defense in many sectors and fortified structures will appear. One should not anticipate especially strong fortifications during a operational meeting engagement, but, all the same, simply the erection of conventional machine gun nests will strengthen the defense to such an extent that it will necessitate commitment of new artillery. One must be prepared without delay on the front of a shock corps to increase artillery fire density successively to 45–60 pieces per kilometer of front, to bring up tanks at the first signs of stabilization of the front in the combat area, and to distribute them among the appropriate corps.

Tank employment is linked with terrain. Therefore, they must be directed to the area of those corps acting in terrain favorable for armor. Corps reinforced by tanks transfer a portion of the follow-on additional artillery to neighbors deprived of tank support. As will be indicated, the operation will last at least 5–10 days. Based on their properties, tanks can operate continuously no more than two days, after which they require a two-day rest for inspection of their engines and drive trains. Thus, if tanks are required not just for the breakthrough, but for participation in the entire operation, distribution of tank battalions and the procedure for moving them to the front must insure replacement of first-echelon tank battalions every two days.

As far as artillery is concerned, the commander still has up to 8–10 artillery regiments. If distributed properly, he will always be able to raise artillery fire density in the sector of the main blow to the levels indicated above (45–60 pieces per kilometer of front). Even greater fire density can be created on the front of individual corps (and moreover of divisions) by distributing additional artillery appropriately.

Directions relative to chemical weapon employment must also be given at the time the commander is making his decision. Chemical shells in motor transport companies are sent to the area of those corps where their employment is considered most advisable. Chemical companies are moved closer to the front, prepared at any moment to join the battle line.

Chemical shells can provide an effect only when employed *en masse*. Thus, their distribution must provide the capability for a powerful effect on the enemy in individual decisive sectors. Several thousand chemical shells are required for each powerful chemical attack, even in the sector of one infantry division. Therefore, it is advisable to supply a complete unit of fire of these shells to individual artillery regiments in the requisite sectors. This ammunition must be delivered from railheads directly to the area of artillery parks. This presents no difficulties if vehicle transportation is available. Shells can be delivered to batteries within a day.

Commitment of chemical companies (gas cylinders, gas projectors) will require more time and will be possible only on more stabilized fronts.

Even prior to the beginning of deployment, aviation must be prepared to operate from new airfields no more than 25 kilometers (organic aviation) and 30–35 kilometers (army aviation) from the front line.

We have already discussed the nature of reconnaissance during the period combat is joined. The interests of the forces that have joined combat require more details and systematic reconnaissance over the field of battle. Therefore, all organic aviation will operate over an area no more than 15–25 kilometers in depth from the combat front from the time the operational engagement is joined until it ends. If the enemy has motorized units and strategic cavalry, organic aviation (special additional corps detachments or individual reconnaissance detachments attached to corps from reconnaissance squadrons) perform *mandatory* systematic flights to a depth of 50–80 kilometers in a given sector (depth of a day's march for strategic cavalry and motorized units).

Systematic observation of all routes by which deep strategic reserves can arrive must be established early after the operational engagement begins. These include railroads with their junctions and possible railheads, major highways, and areas where agents or other sources have previously established the presence of reserves. If the attention of troop commanders is focused entirely on enemy forces directly on the field of battle, the command element at the army and *front* level must direct its main attention to the enemy rear area to detect promptly areas of supply of new enemy forces. This reconnaissance requires systematic flights to the *maximum* range of strategic reconnaissance aircraft.

When combat is joined, fighter aviation directs the center of its efforts to support the deployment of the shock grouping, its artillery in particular. Unconditional air supremacy over appropriate areas must be a requirement during periods when the shock grouping will be transferred. Fighter aviation efforts must be differentiated on subsequent days. Aviation will not be in a position to have continual air supremacy for a long time on a wide front. Therefore, it receives missions to cover particular points or organic formations forced during combat actions to move in large columns during the day (deployment of additional artillery, movement of corps executing turning movements, tank transfer and deployment, individual points in the rear of the forces, friendly airfields, and so forth).

In the early days of an operation, bomber aviation directs its main efforts against forces detected directly on the front and their close-in logistics. The mission of combat aviation is to prepare for and assist the destruction of this first target of the actions of the friendly shock grouping. Therefore, enemy organic columns, especially artillery units, initially will serve as the targets of its attack, with reserves and organic logistics the targets on subsequent days. At the moment arrival of new troops (major strategic reserves in vehicles or via rail) in the area of the operation is detected, combat aviation will shift the center of its efforts against these forces: against enemy detraining stations, assembly areas, and columns moving both by rail and via dirt roads.

As has been indicated, an operation will last approximately 5–10 days. If weather conditions do not interfere, intensive work by aviation will be required *on a daily basis* during this entire period. Thus, even if all branches of aviation are provided in sufficient numbers, their personnel will be required to do more intensive work than envisioned by normal sortie rates.

An operation does not develop equally along the entire front. Success is achieved at various times, first in one, then in another, sector. For this one reason alone, the front line takes on a broken form. Moreover, each organic unit in combat will strive to move far enough to the side to envelop or to turn the enemy flank. All this unavoidably leads during combat to elongation of the front and a reduction in its initial density, to dilution of the shock grouping.

During their movement from the Meuse to the Franco-Belgian border, two right-flank German armies had a front of only 60 kilometers. The density of this front was extraordinary – 2.5 kilometers per infantry division. The front of both these armies during the frontier operational engagement reached 100 kilometers, with the density in the first army of five–six and that in the second of 4.5 kilometers per infantry division. Its dimensions dropped to 70–80 kilometers only after the operational engagement ended, when the armies' front equalized.

Through commitment of his second-echelon divisions and partial regrouping during the operation itself, the army commander must retain the requisite force saturation in that sector where he seeks resolution of the operation.

DURATION AND DEPTH OF AN OPERATION

Success in a modern operation is achieved slowly, only as a result of enormous efforts, repeated attacks. An operation (especially a meeting operation) reaches its culminating point of development only a long time after its initiation. In actuality, forces from both sides are echeloned to a depth reaching 70–75 kilometers. Just the commitment of these forces alone will require at least two–three days.

A rifle division reinforced by one regiment of additional artillery and moving via one road requires from 4 to 6 hours to deploy, depending upon the degree of training of the forces.[19] Deployment will last 2.5–3 hours, even where a division is able to split into two columns ahead of time.

Deployment of main forces will end only at the end of the first half of the day if combat is joined after a march covering 10–12 kilometers (2.5–3 hours march). No results will be achieved during the second half of the day even in a case where the enemy that appeared in front of a given division is weaker. Only a breakout on an exposed enemy flank with a large mass of artillery can promise quick success and, after two–three hours, a new front comprising forces from the second and subsequent echelons and reserves brought up from the depth forms ahead of the advancing forces.

A final outcome then can be achieved only when all enemy forces have been exhausted, all his reserves committed. In a meeting clash, this is marked by the time required for commitment of the divisions of the second and, if it exists, the third echelon. If combat is joined with superior enemy forces moving in a shock grouping identical to that of the advancing forces, the commitment of the second-echelon divisions alone will require up to two–three days.[20] Deeper reserves will arrive on the field of battle later. All in all, given a clash with superior enemy forces under the most favorable conditions (sufficient superiority in forces overall and in suppressive assets in particular, their uninterrupted commitment, highly-trained forces), an outcome cannot be achieved in less than four–five days. If the forces are poorly trained and are not distinguished by special mobility and agility, these time frames can be increased by a factor of 1.5 to 2, even given a sufficient superiority in forces. It goes without saying that outcome periods *can be extended even more*, given any shortage of forces, artillery especially. Given an overall shortage of forces, there may not be any outcome: the operation will founder.

Experience from the World War has already demonstrated the greatly increased duration of an operation. Despite an enormous superiority in forces and advantageous operational position, the Germans in 1914 spent a full five days (from 21 through 25 August) surmounting the resistance of the 5th French and the weak British armies in a frontier operational engagement. During the 1914 Galicia Operation, combat among the 4th and 5th Russian armies and the left-flank Austrian armies continued without interruption from 23 through 30 August (seven days) and only on 31 August did the 5th Russian Army begin to withdraw towards Lublin. Virtually a 2:1 superiority in forces on the right flank of the Germans (in a frontier operational engagement) allowed them to achieve an outcome significantly more rapidly than did the Austrians, who in 1914 in the Lublin sector had forces essentially equal to those of the advancing 4th and 5th Russian armies. Combat between the 13th Red Army's shock group near Orel and the advancing Whites in October 1919 lasted an entire month since neither side had a noticeable superiority of forces. But in 1919, the Western *Front*'s shock grouping, enjoying great superiority over the Poles, over a period of two–three days disrupted the left flank of the Polish armies and forced the entire Polish Northeastern Front to withdraw. Such a duration of operations is inherent not only in meeting clashes, when a great deal of time is spent on deployment of columns, but in operations as a whole since the significant depth of modern fronts so stipulates.

The defensive disposition of a formation such as an army will reach a minimum of 20–35 kilometers. In actuality, the depth of the defensive zone of a division will reach four–six kilometers, corps reserves are disposed about 8–10 kilometers from the front line, while the distance of army reserves from the lead units will reach from 25 to 30 kilometers. If the defense has a large quantity of vehicle transport adapted for mass movement of forces, part of the army reserves may be moved back to 80–100 kilometers. We are not talking about deeper reserves, which can be considered strategic rather than operational (most of the latter reach the field of battle via rail).

Achievement of an outcome in a modern operation means to surmount the entire depth of the enemy tactical disposition and, immediately thereafter, to push back those units, which, during that time, will be brought by a means of a march, in vehicles, and via rail to the area where combat had been joined.

All in all, combat will extend to a depth of 25–35 kilometers.[21] It will take five–six days to surmount just the depth of the operational disposition of forces directly at the front. As wartime experience showed, the daily advance of forces in contact in a frontal offensive on average does not exceed five–six kilometers.[22] Only especially favorable conditions (weak enemy resistance, advantageous operational situation – breakout to the enemy flank or rear area, enemy demoralization) can provide a faster pace. We recall that, in 1914, the daily advance while in contact with the German armies fighting a sufficiently powerful enemy reached five–six kilometers and only those armies facing insignificant enemy forces advanced 8–10 kilometers on the average. In 1915, Mackensen's offensive on the Russian Front (Gorlice) on days in contact achieved no more than two–four kilometers. During the March 1918 German offensive in the largest operational engagement of the World War (in number of forces committed), the average daily advance did not exceed 3.5–5 kilometers. The tendency towards further development of automatic weapons, the difficulty of maneuver with artillery on the battlefield, and so on will erect major obstacles to increasing this norm in the future as well.

Only commitment of a larger number of tanks will elicit an increase in the daily norm for the advance of infantry in a day. Even at that, it will hardly exceed 10 kilometers per day since, in the final analysis, tanks also will not cancel the infantry's requirement to fight with its own assets in the depth of the enemy defensive zone.

At the same time combat is joined, the defender adopts a whole series of measures to reinforce the forces under attack. As indicated above, immediate reserves initially will flow there. Deeper reserves and even forces taken from other fronts (or sectors of the front) will also flow there if the site of the unfolding events is in a sector important from the standpoint of the conduct of the war (or of operations).

Duration of an operation greatly depends on the number and rate of accumulation of new forces by the defense. If reserves begin to arrive immediately and in sufficient quantity, an operation may then enter a new phase and last a very long time, as was the approximate case in the March 1918 German offensive. The Allies entered that operation with an enormous quantity of free reserves. Of the 175 infantry divisions they had at that time, 61 (more than 30 per cent) were in the reserves in the immediate and deep rear area. In their rear area, along with an enormous amount of vehicle transportation, the Allies had a powerful rail network that made it possible on a daily basis to bring up to 290[23] trains to the area where combat was in progress. This made it possible to bring reserves up to the breakthrough area at a high rate. Combat began on 21 March and, after six days (by 27 March), 10 infantry divisions, five cavalry, and one dismounted cavalry division *in toto*, as well as the lead units of six new infantry divisions, arrived in the area of the 3rd and 5th British Armies. The number of forces transferred to the breakthrough area by the end of the operation (5 April), 40 infantry and six cavalry divisions and 20 artillery regiments, was enormous. Simultaneously, 15 corps staffs, two army staffs, and one *front* (army group) staff were transferred for the command and control of this new mass of forces. The operation lasted an incredibly long time (more than 10 days) and required that both sides commit an enormous mass of forces. However, it did not lead to a shift of the defensive frontage and came abruptly to an end.

Combat actions take a completely different turn when the defense lacks a large number of free reserves or when the defense is incapable of supplying forces swiftly to the area of the operation (constrained transportation assets), as occurred with the Allies following the 1914 frontier operational engagement or with the Poles after our Western *Front*'s 1920 offensive.

In 1914 during the German offensive through Belgium, the French lateral movement of troops occurred much more slowly than in 1918. From the onset of the operation and until the end of the frontier operational engagement, only two corps were transferred by rail and some other units marched to the left flank of the French armies. The total reinforcement of the French 5th and 4th Armies until the end of the frontier operational engagement did not exceed three corps and three cavalry divisons. Due to their small numbers, these new forces were unable to impact the course of the operation. They neither achieved a turning point nor prolonged the operation to any extent. The frontier operational engagement ended on 26 August at the moment the depth of the disposition of the forces that had been in the area of the operation from the very beginning was surmounted.

The Poles supplied reserves at an even slower rate in 1920. They did not have completely free forces and had to employ a rail network that had already been disrupted during the World War. Therefore, the Western Front's July operation boiled down to surmounting the resistance only of those units located directly at the front.

All prerequisites are present for an increase in the duration of operations in the future. The increase already underway in the number of machine guns in all modern armies and the tendency towards further automation of infantry weapons to a significant degree are increasing the infantry's ability to resist and are making the defense more stable and prolonged. The shortage of artillery, to which we have more than once referred, will always impact unfavorably on the support of an artillery attack. Any shortage of suppressive assets, any reduction in the norm for artillery support for attacking forces, will prolong the period in which the infantry will be able to overcome the resistance of the defense. The process of penetrating the enemy defensive disposition will also be complicated in future to a major degree because the problem of pieces accompanying infantry during an attack has yet to be satisfactorily resolved. The 1918 German offensive was prolonged to a significant degree due to the crisis surrounding these assets. Horse-drawn organic artillery was unable to follow the infantry at the same rate and remain close enough to provide the infantry timely and sufficient support. In the early days of combat, the shortage of horses was so great that the artillery lost the required tactical mobility and fell behind the infantry. The advancing infantry, left alone and not supported by sufficient artillery, suffered enormous losses, was quickly worn down, and unable to cope with the defense's machine guns.

All the Eastern European armies now have a very insignificant number of tanks. The operational significance of the extant number is nil. Thus, the existing shortage of suppressive assets continues to increase. Finally, the state of rail transportation has also changed radically compared with 1920. The status of transportation in 1920, both for us and for the Poles, ruled out the possibility of any kind of large operational shifts. Divisions shifted by rail to a breakthrough area during an operation can be counted on the fingers of one hand. The present status of rail transportation makes it possible to supply at least two to three divisions per day from the rear area to the front, a distance of 100–120 kilometers. It is possible in the space of one week to shift from a quarter to one-third of Poland's armed forces to an area of decisive actions.

All this in aggregate (reinforcement of defensive assets, shortage of suppressive assets, the crisis of assets accompanying the infantry during an attack, improved conditions for maneuver by rail) promises to make future operations longer and more difficult. Given the present number of tanks and equipment (infantry artillery) that the Eastern European armies now have, the nature of these operations will be more like the slowly developing actions of 1918 than the 1914 German actions replete with pressure and maneuverability or the Red Army actions of 1920. Given today's ratio between defensive assets and suppressive assets overall and infantry accompaniment into combat in particular, the number of unsuccessful attacks that cause offensives to misfire, the futile attacks accompanied by heavy losses, will be even greater than in the old Tsarist army during the World War. *Only as a result of increased suppressive assets, commitment of a greater number of tanks, and widespread force motorization can the rate of development of an operation be elevated to the 1914 level.*

ATTACK FRONTAGE

Given today's elongation of the fronts of million-man armies and stability of the defense, it is impossible to break open these fronts by means of breakthroughs in a narrow sector.

A blow in a narrow sector, even though made to the entire depth of an operational front, engages a very insignificant portion of the enemy forces. Both the forces located on the entire remaining enormous front and numerous reserves in the immediate or deep rear area remain unengaged. These forces succeed not only in forming a new front around the attacker's penetrating forces, but also in organizing a counterblow against them.

The entire experience of the static period of the World War, the March 1918 German offensive in Picardy in particular, will serve as a clear example of the futility of such breakthroughs. In this operational engagement, the Germans chose an 80-kilometer sector for a breakthrough on an overall front 730 kilometers long. There were only 29 infantry divisions in the attack sector out of the 175 infantry divisions the Allies had at that time. Of the remaining forces, 85 infantry divisions occupied the remaining front, while 61 infantry divisions were in reserve. The German offensive, undertaken with a great superiority in forces, was successful and wedged 55–60 kilometers into the enemy disposition. But, despite this, it could not lead to a shift even of the sectors adjacent to the breakthrough area. The Allies turned out to have so many free forces that that they were able to localize this breakthrough by supplying up to 40 infantry divisions, three cavalry divisions, and 20 artillery regiments to the breakthrough area. Subsequent German offensives in May and July 1918 suffered an identical fate.

Achievement of large breakthroughs to a great degree has become complicated now, at a time when the role of the railroads in warfare has increased significantly, when a capability exists to shift up to 10–15 divisions with a large amount of artillery and special machine guns to a weak sector of the front over a period of three–five days. A breakthrough can count upon success only in the event that it involves a significant portion of the enemy forces occupying a given front and when the direction of the blow is selected so that the penetrating forces will break out to an advantageous operational position relative to the remaining enemy front, if the attacker's shock grouping will break out on routes from which it is possible to develop the blow against the flank and rear area of the enemy front not involved directly in the offensive.

The first blow must engage at least half, minimum one-third, of the enemy forces occupying a given front to deprive the enemy of the capability of making a wide maneuver with reserves. To do so, the attack frontage must be so wide that liquidation of the resultant breakthrough will require forces equal to another third or the other half of his forces. It is natural that such a maneuver, such a regrouping, of defensive forces will require much time. Thus, it cannot be done without a large rearward bound of the entire front.

The attack frontage in the frontier operational engagement reached 120 kilometers (of the 340 kilometers of the overall Anglo-French Front) and encompassed three (out of five) French armies and the entire British Army. The width of the main attack in our 1920 offensive was 140 kilometers (of the 500 kilometers of the entire front north of the Pripyat') and engaged half of the Polish forces defending north of the Poles'ye (8 of 16 infantry divisions).

The 1918 Allied offensive was wreathed with success to a significant degree thanks to the fact that it encompassed virtually the entire German Army front.

In the future, one cannot count upon one army being capable of achieving success, let us say, in the Galicia or Belorussian sector of the Soviet–Polish border.

One shock army can attack decisively only on a sector of 25–30 kilometers. In relation to a 400–kilometer front, this literally is a pin prick. Such an operation can have only limited, local, goals.

Decisive success on the aforementioned frontages requires an attack on a sector of at least 150–200 kilometers, which requires deployment of forces numbering 50 or more divisions in the first echelon alone.

A blow on a front of 150–200 kilometers, if undertaken in a theater where the main enemy forces are deployed, will immediately engage at least 15–20 of his infantry divisions (figuring at least 40–45 divisions in a main theater).

A significant portion of these forces will be disorganized if selection of the sector of the first blow is correct. Organization of any kind of significant counterblow against several of an attacker's shock armies not facing serious resistance requires a shift to the area of the operation of at least another 15–20 infantry divisions, not counting numerous replacements required to put the first 20 infantry divisions in order. Such a large regrouping for an army having a total of 60–65 infantry divisions is complicated to a great degree. This cannot be done using free reserves. These new infantry divisions must be taken from other sectors of the front.

FORMS OF THE BLOW

Given modern frontages, when the flanks of the belligerents are secured by allies or abut neutral states and the sea, the first, the initial, operations will always involve *frontal blows*. The German plan for war with France that Schlieffen developed envisaged a deep turning of the left flank of the entire French Army. However, at the same time, the plan counted upon presence of the Belgian Army and Belgian fortresses. Therefore, initial German Army operations were purely a frontal blow where the entire French-Belgian Front was concerned. Only after the Belgian Army was routed and pushed back to Antwerp did the blow take on the form of a turning of the French Army's left flank. The offensive of the Western *Front* in 1920 was planned as a turning of the left flank of the Polish front. But, since this flank abutted neutral Lithuania, those units that covered the Polotsk–Vil'no sector initially had to be crushed and pushed back in a frontal offensive and a frontal blow was required to expose the Polish Front's left flank.

The inevitability of frontal blows will have to be considered in the future as well. Frontages are enormous. They will be partitioned off by forces from sea to sea. Here, there will be no breakout to the flank, let alone to the enemy rear area, without frontal blows.

A breakthrough in its pure form cannot promise a rich operational harvest given the contemporary stability and tenacity of the defense. A breakthrough, even when undertaken with an enormous superiority of forces and with a shock grouping, which, like a heavy hammer, breaks everything in its path, cannot count upon serious destruction of the enemy, on annihilation of a *large* number of his forces. Under modern conditions, the defender has the capability easily to remove the main mass of his forces out from under such a blow and, therefore, the results of a frontal offensive cannot be great. One will not gain an extraordinary victory in such an operation.

Moreover, a series of successive operations designed to a great depth requires that the damage inflicted on opposing forces in the first (initial) operation be such that it will free the attacker's hand relative to the remaining enemy front. Hence the great significance of combinations of blows directed from both sides, on intersecting axes, against the enemy group of forces we have selected as the object of actions in order to seize in a double envelopment, encircle, capture, and destroy this portion of the enemy forces. Such a combination of blows is possible not only when the front is broken, but when it is rectilinear as well. In 1920, the commander of the Western Front intended to employ such a combination of blows to encircle and liquidate enemy units defending the Germanovichi–Glubokoye area and this would have been possible as well, given the actual targetting the 4th and 3rd Armies received: the 4th via Sharkovshchizna to Postavy, the 3rd to Dokshitsy–Lake Madzoil'. But this required having powerful flanks (4th and 3rd Armies) and a weak center (15th Army). In actuality, it turned out just the opposite – weak flanks and a powerful center. As a result, the enemy was pinched, but was not enveloped and not bypassed. A blow on intersecting axes promises the greatest success when the front has a concave configuration.

Given the modern army's depth of operational disposition, a turning movement and envelopment of a front must be targetted deeply enough so that it does not lead to a simple bending of the defensive flank. The operational disposition in a defense reaches a minimum depth of 20–35 kilometers. A large-scale turning movement must not only overwhelm the enemy tactical defensive zone directly, but the entire front with its army reserves as well in order to tie down all the enemy forces disposed on a given front. This requires that the depth of the swing of the flank being turned must reach 35–50 kilometers. Turning movements of such scope require that forces comprising several corps (four to five), with sufficient cavalry and motorized forces, be assigned to carry them out.

But even given such a deep turning movement, forces cannot avoid conducting purely frontal combat during a clash with the enemy. Thus, the forces making the turning movement must possess sufficient shock power and the artillery and tank composition must take into account a swift surmounting of the resistance of an enemy attempting to restructure his front. In any event, corps must have artillery assets permitting them to roll over any enemy opposition in a meeting clash with his reserves, that is, be in a position to deploy at least 30 pieces per kilometer of front, given presence of another two–four battalions of tanks for each corps carrying out the turning movement.

OFFENSIVE ON A WIDE FRONT

In a major *front* operation, at the same time shock armies advance with a large number of suppressive assets in a dense grouping, a whole series of other armies must accomplish auxiliary missions. Due to a shortage of assets, they will be forced to advance on a less dense front and with lower artillery support norms. One should consider that, normally, armies acting in secondary sectors will not have additional suppressive assets (neither artillery nor tanks) and, therefore, must be limited to their own organic assets. Besides all that, despite their constrained resources, these armies will be tasked to advance on wider sectors than shock armies.

But it would be a mistake to convert the offensive actions of these armies into a simple "feint," without chances of success, because of this. One should recall that shock armies can count upon a large "operational harvest" only if the enemy is constrained on the entire remaining front, when the pressure on the entire front is so great that the enemy will not only be in no position to pull reserves from secondary sectors, but will also not be able to withdraw without cost, will be unable to slip out from under the blow. Thus, an offensive in secondary sectors must also be organized so that it will have *positive* results in those instances when the situation demands. But this requires that the offensive also be undertaken with the forces and the grouping that make success probable, given the known circumstances.

It is natural that an offensive in secondary sectors cannot be supported by the same distribution of forces and the same suppressive assets that support an offensive in main sectors. Therefore, armies accomplishing these secondary missions in a majority of cases cannot count on independent *initial* success, especially if the enemy has succeeded in forming a continuous and sufficiently dense and fortified front. In this case, success in the actions of these armies will depend upon success in the main sectors, but beginning when the combat actions take on a mobile character along the entire front and armies acting in secondary sectors can and must achieve independent success. Secondary armies can count upon independent success from the very outset of an operation if the enemy is weak and the front extended and unfortified.

In either event, a secondary army must be provided with the forces that will permit it to create offensive groupings in individual sectors of its front.

One rifle division per every two kilometers of front and up to 60 pieces per kilometer of front are required in shock armies for a main attack, but these norms may be reduced significantly in armies accomplishing secondary missions. Rifle divisions in these secondary armies may be assigned sectors corresponding to their maximum infantry capabilities (up to three–four kilometers), but the number of suppressive assets may be reduced to norms required for an offensive against a weakly fortified enemy lacking artificial obstacles, that is, up to 21–24 and a maximum of 30 pieces per kilometer of main attack.

Depending on situational conditions, one or several sectors may be selected for the main attack. One may be constrained when defining the frontages of these sectors by the requirement that attacking forces cannot be exposed to machine gun cross fire (such conditions will be established relative to artillery fire in sectors of the main blow). Attack sector frontage for this must not be less than five–six kilometers.

Such an attack by a rifle corps is feasible. Even if the corps will be able to allocate only two divisions for the main attack, then up to 120 pieces can be concentrated for its support, which provides 20–24 pieces per kilometer of front. This artillery may be strengthened a bit more at the expense of the corps' third division and second-echelon regiments formed. The overall offensive frontage for the corps can be raised to 12 kilometers, of which five–six kilometers is the main attack sector and six–seven kilometers is the holding force (one to two rifle regiments with one to two artillery battalions, not counting regimental artillery).

An army comprising three to four rifle corps advancing on a front of 60–80 kilometers can form one or two shock groups acting next to one another or across a known interval of a passive sector. Corps normally will be assigned sectors with a frontage of 20–25 kilometers, with that of corps accomplishing shock missions being up to 10–12 kilometers.

Such an army will be allocated a strip up to 100 kilometers wide for movement. Under these conditions, each of the main attack divisions may usually move via one road. The remaining divisions may follow via two and some even three roads. Naturally, the main blow divisions may also have two roads if a dense network of dirt roads exists. But, even in this case, it is useful for the army commander to retain in the second echelon one or two divisions from the composition of corps in secondary sectors.

DEFENSIVE OPERATIONS

The limited forces at the disposal of modern armies make it necessary very widely to resort to a defensive means of actions for the duration of an entire war. We noted earlier that a major offensive operation requires the inclusion of 50 or more divisions in the first echelon alone and that such an operation can encompass a front of no more than 120–150 kilometers. If the overall frontage is 1,000 or more kilometers and modern armies comprise no more than 60–80 infantry divisions, a partial transition to defensive actions on the remaining enormous frontage is unavoidable.

The defense has received very powerful assets in modern infantry weapons. The stability of a front saturated with automatic weapons has risen to a great degree. Therefore, at present, speaking in the abstract, it is easier to achieve a stable front in the defense than was previously the case. But the misfortune of the defense is that its assets are always constrained, that, as is known, it controls small forces and thus cannot always provide the density of front that would insure that combat formations have the requisite ability to resist.

Given existing divisional fire weapons, a sufficiently stable position results when a division occupies a sector of from four to eight kilometers (defense in "normal sectors"). The stability of a defense decreases by a factor of two if sector frontage increases to 12 kilometers, while a rather sparse disposition easy to penetrate results in a 20-kilometer sector.

Defense on a large scale will have sectors of completely different density, beginning with normal divisional sectors on vital axes and ending with disposition on an extended front on secondary axes. Given the limited forces modern armies have, a defense primarily will be extended. The density of front may be increased through more uniform distribution among its various axes only during those periods when one side or the other is forced to shift to a prolonged lull (to accumulate new resources, let us say).

Nonetheless, the enormous number of automatic weapons gives the infantry great prerequisites for a prolonged and stubborn defense, even given an extended disposition.

A division occupying a 20-kilometer sector can assign up to six battalions to the holding force, two battalions from each regiment. Having allowed 1.5–two kilometers between battalions, we will still have a sector no more than two kilometers in width. A battalion in such a sector can provide a quite sufficient density of fire. The problem of defending the gaps remains. With dimensions of 1–2 kilometers, effective machine gun flanking fire and oblique artillery fire can defend these gaps. They must be covered by an artificial obstacle for greater reliability.

In general, given modern weapons, efforts spent on organization of the terrain by engineer work pay off better and provide a greater tactical effect than in the old organization of the forces. It is no more difficult to construct a modern company position with its six light machine guns, nine rifle squads, and two heavy machine guns than it was the one for the old company comprising four platoons of 45–50 people each. Moreover, the fire weapons that will defend the new position are more powerful by a factor of two than the assets defending the old position. The difference in fire power within a battalion is greater by a factor of three.

The advantages of today's defense are also increased thanks to the peculiarities of modern combat formations, which are more dispersed, better adapted to the terrain, and require individual registration of each machine gun, each squad, for their suppression.

It is impossible to pass an effective machine gun that has not been suppressed or neutralized. Suppression of a well-fortified, well dug-in machine gun requires up to 75 76mm shells and from 40 to 100 howitzer bombs[24] at ranges of 2.5 to 4 kilometers. Neutralization of a well dug-in machine gun using the assets of the advancing infantry alone will almost always require a 2:1 or 3:1 superiority to allow this machine gun to be taken under fire from different directions.

The power of the defense lies in machine gun fire. Therefore, the most important task of the command element in defense is not only to select the area for the defense and to distribute forces correctly and advisably, but also to give them the capability to dig in rapidly, to fashion natural obstacles swiftly, to construct in a short period of time shelters for machine guns that will not be subject to destruction by light artillery calibers (especially gun calibers), but whose suppression will require heavy howitzer artillery. Since the density of fire in front of the position's forward edge is sufficient given extended disposition as well, the stability of the defense will be dependent entirely on the tempo and scale of the organization of the ground by engineer work.

For solid efforts, one must not base calculations solely on

"local resources" or on supplies shipped to parks. A major defensive operation requires supply of dozens of trains of materials from warehouses deeper in the rear. Not only iron, wire, prefabricated concrete slabs, quick-set concrete, and gravel, but often lumber and also workers, must be brought in from the rear area. Along with trains carrying artillery shells, which are usually dispatched to shock army areas, trains carrying engineer equipment and construction materials will be dispatched to a defensive area. It would be erroneous to think that the railroads in defensive sectors will be idle.[25]

Antitank obstacles are of great significance in the engineer preparation of a position under modern conditions. Digging ditches requires much time and involves major excavation work. For this reason alone, they cannot be considered the *main measure* for countering tanks. Natural obstacles extant in the defensive zone and inaccessible to tanks (deep, wide ditches, the same type of rivers, and so on) in a modern defense are of more significance than was the previous case thanks to this alone. The antitank mine should be highlighted as one modern asset to be employed widely. All the position sectors vulnerable to tank attack must be absolutely equipped with antitank minefields.

Certain sectors representing choke points are contaminated with persistent toxic agents at the first signs the enemy is preparing an offensive.

Although in a tactical disposition where there is a shortage of forces, one must take all measures to reduce second echelons and provide a stable fire system, moving maximum forces into the holding force, it is impossible at the army level to defend oneself without large reserves.

If he has decided to do so, the enemy will always surmount a defensive zone, regardless of how it has been fortified. The whole problem boils down to time. Henceforth, banking mainly on his reserves, an army commander can conduct an operation.

Army reserves must be disposed approximately one day's march (25–35 kilometers) from threatened sectors of the front. This will permit them to support the forces of the combat line promptly. The disposition of the reserves may be moved back to the depth of a vehicle trip (80–100 kilometers) and they may serve a broader front if a vehicle park adapted for mass movement of forces is available. Preparation of all roads for a rapid lateral movement of reserves is of enormous significance.

At the moment the enemy breaks through the defense zone,

forces must break off from the enemy and assemble in a new area for new resistance. It is usually difficult to determine the results of the damage at the front immediately and, in this connection, the scale of the measures that are required to reestablish the position. Very often, especially in those instances when the enemy offensive is undertaken with not especially large forces, immediate reserves will suffice for formation of a new stable front around the attacker's forces that have broken through.

The *rate* of concentration in the breakthrough area of reserves sent there is of decisive significance. The period required to concentrate the units tasked to liquidate the breakthrough determines the magnitude of the rearward bound. We showed that, in future operations, periods of concentration of new forces significantly decreases as the numerical size of vehicle and rail transport increases. Over a period of three–four days, reserves can be brought up from areas at least 50–100 kilometers from the penetration point. Therefore, the first rearward bound may be no deeper than 30–40 kilometers, that is, half way between the edge of the defense zone and the area of disposition of deep reserves. The enemy will be unable to move in contact more than 8–10 kilometers per day if any of the divisions in the penetrated sector are replaced by new units or supported by machine gun units transferred by vehicle. The main mass of arriving reserves will be brought to the flanks of the enemy units that have broken through in order to organize a counterblow against them or at least force the enemy to roll up or splinter his basic grouping against the new targets of actions.

If the scope of the breakthrough is great and the matter cannot be corrected by employing local reserves, a major decision on lateral movement of forces must be made. We pointed out that the conditions for a lateral movement in the existing East European Theater of Military Actions, especially in its Polish sector, are incomparably higher than in 1914–17 and 1920, that they make it possible over a period of two weeks to shift the center of effort of an army like the Polish Army from one axis to another.

The degree of organizational preparation of the railroads, the art of command and control on these railroads, the way military railroad authorities operate, how fast the requisite schedules and plans for mass movements are compiled are of enormous significance here. The rate at which these railroads themselves operate is of decisive significance. In any event, the modern rail network represents a mighty resource for maneuver.

The entire defensive operation takes on new planning from the moment the major decision is made to move forces laterally. The time needed to accomplish the intended lateral movement determines the nature of the actions and the rate of withdrawal of forces pulling back from the front. These same data define the areas and directions of withdrawal. From that time, the new operation is prepared as a purely offensive operation, for which forces are assembled partially by rail from other sectors of the front, partially from withdrawing divisions brought up to strength by means of filler replacements. It will be erroneous to rush into a transition to a counteroffensive without waiting for a full concentration of forces and their sufficient support from suppressive assets (artillery, tanks). A counteroffensive undertaken with insufficient forces can lead only to the rout of these forces and may play into the hands of the enemy.

On the other hand, a defender may not always have sufficient space for a withdrawal. Hence, the *tempo* of measures regarding lateral movement is of enormous significance. From the very outset, the defense must restructure its entire air defense – regroup antiaircraft assets, employing them to secure rail junctions and stations on those axes to which streams of forces are headed, and moving the main mass of its combat aviation to the assembly and deployment area of these forces – so the enemy will be unable to employ air strikes to disrupt or prolong the concentration of reserves. Vigorous actions in the air by the defense will begin before ground forces are prepared for a counteroffensive.

COSTS OF THE MODERN OPERATION

Development of automatic weapons, rates of fire, the range of artillery, and appearance of new weapons (chemistry, aviation) have increased to a great degree the duration of engagements, having imparted to them a character that is prolonged, that wears down the strength and nerves of the troops. Conducting a modern operation involves great costs, both in personnel and in various kinds of combat equipment, accessories, and especially ammunition. During the German offensive in 1914, comparatively rare engagements, large peacetime cadres (up to 33 per cent), and the selective composition of reserves taken into the ranks of the army at the outset of the war allowed the attacker to reach the Marne with comparatively minor losses. But already by 1915 Mackensen's offensive at Gorlice–Tarnow, even in a struggle against a Russian Army that had experienced great difficulties owing to a shortage of ammunition, cost the Germans 20 per cent losses during a month-long operation. The March 1918 offensive (overall duration of 10 days, albeit under the conditions of static warfare) cost the Germans 20 per cent of their men. Fewer men were killed and wounded in the Civil War, where the combat intensity generally was lower (less dense front, less enemy ability to resist), but the number lost due to illness was high. During the offensive to the Vistula, the Red Army lost up to 40 per cent of its composition in a 1.5–month period. Of this total, 12 per cent were lost due to illness.

One must anticipate a further increase in losses in the future. In this regard, the maneuvering period of the World War cannot be considered characteristic of future operations. On the contrary, the nature of future combat will be more akin to the combat that stemmed from the 1918 operations on the Western Front where saturation with automatic weapons, where the ratio between offensive and defensive resources, where the scale at which aviation and chemical weapons were employed are concerned. A wealth of data exists, which increases the weight of offensive conditions, even compared with the static position of the World War. First, there are the new achievements in aviation regarding *precision* aerial bombing and firing machine guns. Second, there is the broader use of chemical weapons, especially the completely new ways of employing these weapons such as free spraying of toxic agents, which makes it possible to contaminate large expanses of terrain in a comparatively short time, and dumping them from aircraft, which provides the capability to contaminate entire organic columns in several minutes.

Conditions under which a battle and operations are conducted are incomparably more difficult and complex. The bounds of fields of battle have increased to thresholds equal to the radius of actions of modern aircraft, the infantry's ability to resist has increased, aerial gunnery and bombing are more precise, and new obstacles in the paths of the attacker have multiplied (strips of contaminated terrain). All this has a tendency towards further quantitative and qualitative increase. And, given all of this, development of suppressive assets *clearly lags behind* the rate of development of defensive resources. In addition, if you also consider that chemical defense resources are lagging both qualitatively and quantitatively behind the development of means of attack, it would be erroneous to look upon the experience of 1914 and even 1918 as indicative of future operations. In the future, the same results, the same goals, will be more costly, will be achieved with losses of great energy, great resources, and many men.

Operations in a main theater, where the density of fronts, both rifle and aviation, is anticipated to be high will undoubtedly involve losses significantly exceeding those during the World War. One must consider that an operation lasting five–six days will involve personnel losses ranging from 12 to 20 per cent for a first-echelon division based upon the nature of the clash (meeting clash, offensive against an enemy who has fortified himself ahead of time). The lower the percentage of suppressive assets (artillery, tanks) supporting an attack, the higher the percentage of losses.

Losses of 20 and even 30 per cent during the World War, especially during its first period, still did not put units out of action. They led only to a simple reduction in the number of "bayonets" in the companies. Some 130–150 rather than the TO&E strength of 200–250 men remained in the companies and we know that they fought on with these and even smaller companies, without disrupting the organization of the forces.

The company as constituted at present in all armies does not exceed 150–180 men. A company of this composition serves from nine to 12 light and two heavy machine guns. The loss of 50–60 men from a company will lead to an inevitable reduction in the number of automatic weapons, and, since it comprises the foundation of the infantry organization, also to a considerable breaking of the organization of forces, and, hence, of the tactical actions. The organization of forces today is more ponderous and more fragile, than the 1914–16 organization. The percentage of losses endured rather harmlessly then can now disrupt the organization of forces and put them out of action. At a time when many Russian Army units lacking a light automatic weapon and having a limited number of heavy machine guns endured 20–25 per cent losses quite easily, the 20 per cent losses the German infantry suffered in the 1918 offensive led to the complete disruption of the majority of divisions.[26]

Therefore, the problem of the replacement of personnel losses in future operations will be more acute than previously.

In the future, it will be normal and neccessary that each division have a reserve comprising 15–20 percent of TO&E strength immediately available right at the start of an operation, that is, have a reserve regiment with a trained complement of reservists available. Only the presence of reserve forces directly in the organic rear area (divisional or corps) makes it possible to replace losses in first-echelon divisions fast enough to insure employment of these divisions in further operations.

The logistical supplies the forces will require will also increase to a great degree.

The daily food and forage requirement of one rifle corps comprises of 280 tons, requiring 22 boxcars to deliver it. This rises to 30 cars if the corps is reinforced by one division of additional artillery. This is the rail transport requirement of one shock army comprising five rifle corps reinforced by four–five artillery divisions (16–20 artillery regiments) and 16–20 tank battalions: four trains to supply food and forage,[27] 18 to supply one unit of fire,[28] and a minimum of one train supplying fuel for tanks, aviation, and vehicle transport. Thus, the army rail transport requirement for a day of intense combat will be 23 trains, not counting the requirement for medical trains, to supply engineer and communications equipment, the requirements of the military transport troops restoring the railroads, and, finally, the requirements of the railroad itself. Medical evacuation at the front may be based mainly on temporary medical trains (deadheading), but three–five trains will still have to be added to the remaining requirements, that is, *in toto*, an army will require 25–28 trains per day.

Of course, all this cargo need not be supplied *regularly* to the front every day. Just the food and forage will be supplied in the same quantity each day. The requirement for ammunition, fuel, medical trains, and railroad construction materials will change, depending on the nature of the combat actions.

We pointed out earlier that five–seven days are required to conduct an operation designed to a depth of 30–50 kilometers. The number of shells required per weapons unit on the first day of the operation is somewhat greater than one unit of fire. Based on the nature of the combat, the second day of the operation will differ little from the first, so the second day's requirement roughly will equal one unit of fire. Over a two-day period, the efforts of the first-echelon enemy forces and immediate reserves will be surmounted and, from the third day on, combat will take on a more mobile character. The number of forces in combat simultaneously will drop radically. A deeper and more echeloned disposition will manifest itself. Therefore, on subsequent days, looking at corps level, ammunition expenditure will drop initially to half and then to one-third of a unit of fire. Rounding off, one must consider that an operation designed to a depth of 30–50 kilometers (five–seven days of combat) will require at least four units of fire per corps.

If the norm for artillery support to an attack is low (below normal), the basic load *will increase*. Naturally, this also entails a high percentage of guns put out of action.

An operation designed only to 30–50 kilometers can be based almost exclusively on the transport of the forces themselves. Only individual corps, predominantly flank corps, will have a longer line of communications and will require the army link in the supply chain. But in such a limited amount, vehicle assets can meet this requirement, even in armies with little vehicle transport.

It is different when the problem involves supplying subsequent operations, when forces are cut off from the railroads, when the traffic capacity of newly restored rail sectors will be constrained, when all corps will require the army link in the supply chain. In this case, the supply organization will be more complex, but we will return to an examination of this in the next chapter.

Successive Operations

PREMISES

The largest operation modern armies are capable of conducting may be undertaken only with forces comprising some 50 divisions. These forces suffice for a decisive attack on a front on only 120–150 kilometers. Just in the Soviet–Polish sector of the front, these 120–150 kilometers comprise only one-sixth of the front. Five-sixths of the entire remaining Soviet–Polish Front remains unaffected by this blow. The initial blow, even if it is undertaken on the front where the main enemy forces are disposed, may engage no more than 12–15 infantry divisions. An additional three to five divisions may reach the combat area during the first operation. Thus, under the most favorable conditions, one operation will engage from 15 to 20 enemy divisions. In the majority of cases, far fewer enemy forces will be engaged. Thus, the amount of damage done to the enemy in the first operation and, thereby, the amount of influence it has on the course of the war, will be extremely limited.

If the mission with which the army is tasked has no local

significance, but pursues a decisive goal, if the combat actions contemplated at a given time have in mind achievement of such results as a rout of the enemy that might be reflected decisively during the further course of the war, then a significant penetration into the depth of the enemy disposition, immediate infliction of a second, third, and subsequent blows on the heels of the first must be envisioned to bring the enemy to complete defeat. The ideal would have to be to plan the actions of friendly armed forces in such a way that, employing a series of crushing blows carried to their conclusion, they would lead to complete defeat of the enemy, to his complete capitulation.

Unfortunately, the capabilities of modern armies to inflict a series of deep blows are limited. We already have presented figures characterizing the costs involved in the conduct of one operation. These costs are great, both in personnel and in materiel, mainly the ammunition required to sustain prolonged combat actions. Not only artillery equipment, but food and forage as well, for million-man armies must be transported from the rear area and regular supply is dependent completely on the condition of the railroads, the rate of their restoration, their traffic capacity in newly-reconstituted sectors, the amount of vehicle transportation available to the army,[29] and the condition of dirt roads remaining after an enemy withdrawal.

Ammunition comprises the greater portion of the supplies an army conducting vigorous actions requires. It constitutes 75 per cent of the items supplied per day of intense combat. Since not all days of an operation are days of intense combat and since there will be days during a prolonged operation when combat actions will encompass a very small area and the troops will be capable of moving, just remaining in contact with the enemy or even having lost this contact, the amount of ammunition that must be supplied per day of an operation generally will be below the norm set for a day of intense combat. This amount depends upon the nature of the combat, its frequency, its intensity; it depends upon how rapidly the enemy takes measures to establish the disrupted balance at the front, on how rapidly he dispatches replacements, new units from the rear area, new divisions from other sectors of the front, to the area of the operation. The rate at which the defender restores stability on the front will mainly depend on the rate of arrival of these forces. From this stems the solution of the problem of whether or not the enemy will bound rearwards deeply without serious combat or will he attempt to halt the advance of the attacker, will he stem the course of events without a great rearwards bound? Thus, the scope of the required supply of ammunition per day of the operation is directly dependent upon the conditions under which major forces are moved laterally in modern theaters of military actions.

HOW TO MOVE LARGE FORCES LATERALLY IN THE EASTERN EUROPEAN THEATER OF MILITARY ACTIONS

In Eastern European armies, owing to a limited amount of vehicle transport, the lateral movement of large forces during combat actions is possible predominantly by means of railroads or a march. Conditions for the lateral movement of forces, let us say in the Polish Theater of Military Actions, will boil down predominantly to the conditions under which forces are redistributed between the Ukrainian and Belorussian fronts. Distances here are so vast that redistributing forces by means of a march requires a great deal of time, and use of vehicles is unsuitable. It is 250–300 kilometers by air from the area of Rovno and Kremenets to Brest-Litovsk. The distance between the Baranovichi–Molodechno area and Brest-Litovsk is about the same. Only the railroads can support the lateral movement of large forces over such distances.

These distances are covered by rail in less than a day, but the number of troops transferred by rail depends completely upon railroad traffic capacity. The Polish rail network has rather solid lateral rail lines permitting rapid lateral movement of forces from south to north or vice versa. Four or five lateral rail lines link the Belorussian and Ukrainian fronts: (1) Rovno– Sarny–Baranovichi; (2) Rovno–Kovel'–Brest; (3) Zdolbunovo–L'vov–Kholm–Brest; (4) Volochinsk–L'vov–Peremyshl'–Lublin–Sedlets; (5) Kopychintsy–Stanislawow–Krakow–Warsaw (the longest). The first has little operational significance due to its proximity to the border and the other four will provide a strong link between the northern and southern fronts. The distance along all axes except the fifth, via Warsaw, can be covered in a day. A transfer via Warsaw requires two days. The traffic capacity of the first three lines permits one infantry division to be transferred via each line daily. The Stanislawow–Krakow–Warsaw axis can support only about one-half a division per day,[30] that is, up to three and one-half divisions per day can be supplied simultaneously via all axes, or, rounded off, three infantry divisions per day.

Major lateral movement including transfer of 20 infantry divisions from one front to the other will require about one week's time. Figuring that preparations for such a major shift by rail (preparation of rolling stock, of entraining and detraining stations) also requires another five–seven days, one must recognize that it is entirely possible in 12–14 days to shift by railroad the center of gravity of the efforts of an army like the Polish Army from the Ukrainian to the Belorussian theater and back. The entire problem boils down to how fast the corresponding units, in consonance with the course of military actions, can be withdrawn from combat and concentrated at entraining stations and the degree to which these movements are protected against both land-based blows and air strikes.

In 1914 during the whole German invasion of Belgium to the end of the Battle of the Marne (from 23 August to 15 September, some 24 days), the French were able to shift a total of about 11 infantry and six cavalry divisions to their left flank by rail and march. More decisive reinforcement could not be undertaken since all the French Army's forces turned out to be tied down in operations in Alsace-Lorraine in the center of the French Front.[31]

On the other hand, in 1918 when the Allies had up to 61 infantry divisions in reserve in the rear area of their front concentration, it only took about 10 days to concentrate 40 infantry divisions, three cavalry divisions, and 20 artillery regiments. Transfer of Austro-German reserves in 1916 against the Russian Southwestern Front also occurred quite swiftly. At that time, up to 48 infantry divisions (10 Austrian, 36 German, and two Turkish) were sent to Galicia in a period of 2.5–3 weeks.

A Polish Army regrouping took place under difficult conditions in July and August of 1920. In late July, Pilsudski was unable to accomplish his intended lateral movement of several divisions from the Ukrainian *Front* to the Brest area since the divisions he had earmarked for the move, being tied down in vigorous actions by our Cavalry and 12th armies, could not be withdrawn from the front for a long time. Brest fell before that lateral movement could be completed.

At present, such a lateral movement may be accomplished more rapidly than was the case not only in 1920 (there can be no comparison here), but even during the World War as well, in the same theater. In 1914–17, the railroads of Galicia were not linked with the roads of the former Kingdom of Poland as is now the case. On the Lublin, Kholm, and Vladimir–Volynskiy axes on the

Russo-Austrian border, the link between the Russian and Austrian roads was very poor, with some (Kholm-Zamost'ye) lacking even a junction between them. All these roads have now been upgraded to mainlines and prepared for mass military movements. That is why the tempo and the gradual and steady increase of forces in the breakthrough area in any of the sectors of the aforementioned front will be greater than previously in this theater. Conditions for a lateral movement have also been facilitated for the simple reason that it is now easier to withdraw units from combat than was the case during the World and Civil wars. The increasing defensive capability of the infantry now permits wider employment of the defense with insignificant forces on a wide frontage than in 1914–1917 on the Russian Front. True, in some respects, these conditions have deteriorated. At present, it is more difficult to conceal withdrawal of major organic entities from the front and major rail movements than previously was the case. Given the systematic efforts of aviation, such regroupings may be more easily detected than during the World War. But, in the final analysis, since defensive resources are more powerful than those of attackers and since a major offensive even against an extended defense is impossible without the concentration of additional artillery assets, the defender has greater capabilities to conduct such a regrouping without serious interference from the attacker. We should keep in mind that the defender withdraws his forces to a location where the enemy has no main forces. Thus, the railroads and the conditions for the conduct of defensive actions now support a higher rate of supply of fresh forces from other sections of the front than previously. Therefore, one must count on more frequent combat and, besides, the intervals between successively developing operations will be shorter than during the first period of the World War and, where the Civil War is concerned, these periods of time are not even comparable. Present conditions for the lateral movement of large forces in the Eastern Theater of Military Operations approximate to those extant in the Western Theater in 1918, when the rate of accumulation of reserves at the breakthrough point was so high that there was no interval at all between the operation to break through the Allied defensive zone and operations against arriving new forces, when the initial and subsequent operations melded into one uninterrupted prolonged operation.

Of course, conditions for a lateral movement by rail in the east at present are very different from those in the Western Theater.

But, based on the existing state of affairs, in the east as well we are closer to the conditions in 1918 on the Franco-German Front than to those at the end of the World War on the Russo-German Front. The maneuver in 1920 that required the Polish Army to fall back behind the Vistula River in order to accomplish it, may in the future be accomplished even prior to having to withdraw to the Western Bug River under less stress than was the case previously, given million-man armies larger by a factor of four or five, Acceleration greater by a factor of two has been achieved in a lateral movement just where space is concerned. If we also consider the number of troops able to be transferred within the same period of time, then the factor of the improvements in the conditions for conducting major defensive operations within the Poland of today must be considered to have increased by a factor of 8–10 compared with the 1920 Civil War period.

One must anticipate even greater complexity of such conditions in the future.

PACE OF ADVANCING ARMIES

The speed of an offensive, its pace, depends wholly on the frequency of the combat the attacker must conduct *en route* to the assigned target. If a first echelon of the defense is so structured that it cannot independently offer new resistance to an attacker and new defensive forces are late reaching the area where combat has been joined, an offensive will then proceed with no serious combat of any kind. In this event, the pace of the offensive will differ little from a conventional march with security measures in proximity to the enemy. Individual corps may move up to 20–25 kilometers, some divisions even farther, and the army as a whole up to 15–20 kilometers. If a first echelon of the defense retains some capability for independent resistance, the superiority of forces on the side of the attacker is not so great, and his operational posture as a result of the first operation is not as advantageous, the attacker will have to move in contact in more dispersed formations. Forces will often have to deploy for combat and again roll up for the march and the pace of the offensive naturally will decrease. The daily advance during successive operations may vary greatly. Depending on the degree of enemy resistance, this advance may fluctuate from three–five (serious enemy resistance) to 8–12 kilometers[32] if his resistance is weaker. Thus, the overall pace of an army offensive between two operations, one following the other, depends upon the rate of the possible gradual and steady increase of forces in the breakthrough area. If these forces arrive in small contingents and are committed successively, the defender will be in no condition to achieve any kind of turning point in the combat actions in his favor, but he will slow the enemy pace. That was the nature of the Russian Army's defense in the 1915 Galicia Campaign. The decision was made as early as 3 May to send up to six infantry and three to four cavalry divisions to assist the 3rd Army in liquidating Mackensen's breakthrough. The Austro-German attack frontage at the onset of the operation (2 May) did not exceed 35 kilometers. Had these new forces been committed simultaneously, they would have sufficed to liquidate the breakthrough. But, the units reached the area of the operation at different times and in too small contingents. Of the two divisons (lead) that were dispatched by rail on 6 May, only six battalions from the first (13th Siberian) and two battalions from the second (composite) division arrived.[33] The decision was made on 7 May to dispatch an additional three corps to the area of the operation.[34] But, these forces were concentrated so slowly that the arriving forces turned out to be absorbed into the combat actions in packets and were unable to halt the Austro-German offensive. Arrival of fresh troops forced Mackensen to proceed more carefully and slowed the rate of development of the entire operation. The Austro-Germans lost 13 days surmounting the expanse from Gorlice to Sarny, which equates to an average of only seven–eight kilometers per day.

In a case where the defender has made up his mind to achieve a turning point by employing more decisive measures during combat actions, he sacrifices territory, refrains from daily engagements when a given balance and grouping of forces are disadvantageous to him, and organizes deeper leapfrogs to withdraw forces that have been defeated in order to meet the enemy on terrain advantageous and prepared for a defense. These rearward bounds continue until completion of the main regrouping of forces permitting the course of events to be changed by going over to a counteroffensive.

Such was the nature of the 1914 French defense during the withdrawal to the Marne. Pilsudski followed such a method of actions in 1920 during the Red Army offensive to the Vistula.

Following the frontier operational engagement that ended on 25 August, Joffre made up his mind to initiate the withdrawal of the center and left flank of the Allied armies in order to assemble a new shock group on his left flank. The central armies were instructed to withdraw slowly to the Verdun–Reims Front. The left-flank armies (5th French and British) had to withdraw to the Laon–Amiens area. A new, 6th, Army had to be assembled in the suburbs of Amiens. The deadline was 2 September (six days for the regrouping). They did not fully succeed in accomplishing this maneuver. Only the central armies, which essentially had forces equal to the enemy and which were conducting frontal combat, succeeded in breaking out to their assigned area. The 5th French Army, faced with making an oblique movement to shift to the left, was attacked under disadvantageous conditions at St. Quentin–Guise and was forced to continue a further rearward bound to the south. The British Army did not accomplish its mission at all. It made a large bound directly to the south instead of a planned withdrawal to the southwest, having disrupted the left flank of the Allied front. And, finally, such a short period of time (five–six days to prepare and accomplish transfers) turned out to be insufficient for concentration of the 6th Army near Amiens. The situation for the French following this first attempt at changing the course of military events became such that Joffre was forced to make a second, deeper, rearward bound to the Seine River.

This nature of defensive actions led to the fact that the 2d German Army, most indicative regarding what is of interest to us, moved 40–43 kilometers (virtually a full two days' march) the first 2 days after the frontier operational engagement. During the subsequent three days, from 28 to 30 August during the period of combat at St. Quentin–Guise, it moved only 30 kilometers (10 kilometers per day) and on subsequent days the rate of movement again reached 18–20 kilometers per day. The average rate of movement again dropped to 10–11 kilometers during the new operation on the Marne.

The small number of forces in the 1920 Polish Army, the vigorous actions the Southwestern *Front* conducted simultaneously with the offensive of Comrade Tukhachevskiy's armies towards the Vistula, and destroyed rail transport, did not permit Pilsudski to accomplish a rapid flow of forces to the northern axis. Therefore, the Polish Army's rearward bound was of great scope. The army withdrew with great bounds, attempting to hold only on such lines as the Neman, Narev, Bug, and Vistula.[35] Accordingly, the Red Army's pace was comparatively great. Individual armies moved at a speed of 20–22 kilometers during the intervals between operations, but the pace fell to 7–10 kilometers per day when they had to move in contact.

Naturally, it is difficult, it is simply impossible, to perform any kind of specific calculations on the pace on a particular front in a future war. This would require having the specific data on the situation of future operations that one cannot now possibly have. But there is no doubt that there is a wealth of data defining the *general* nature of the development of successive operations in the future.

Rail transportation conditions improved since 1920, larger armies, and conditions facilitating a tactical defense (superiority of defensive resources over offensive resources) make a more rapid rate of gradual and steady increase of defensive forces in the area of an operation possible in the future. This signifies that the defender will be in a position to attempt to halt the advance of an attacker, that intervals between individual operations may be shorter, and that an operational engagement with an enemy that has completed a regrouping may occur earlier than happened in France in 1914 or in Poland in 1920. In the future, if one cannot anticipate the rate of the gradual and steady increase of forces such as occurred in 1918 with the Allies that resulted in no interval whatsoever between the initial operation and subsequent actions, then a rate of gradual and steady increase of forces permitting the organization of counteraction and shorter rearward bounds is possible in any event. We have already indicated that conditions under which future operations will be conducted, even in the Eastern Theater, will be closer to the 1918 conditions on the French Front than was the case in 1914, 1915, 1917, and 1920 (World and Civil Wars). We pointed out that Pilsudski's maneuver in 1920 with an army larger by a factor of four or five might be carried out in the future even before the withdrawal to the Bug. That is why, for future operations, one must anticipate, as a rule, a greater number of days in contact than in 1914 and in 1920.

For the aforementioned reasons, the overall rate of development of an offensive prior to the clash with the main enemy forces will be *slower* than previously. Only conditions especially favorable for the attacker, to wit, presence of superior forces permitting an advance simultaneously in different sectors of the front in order to engage all enemy forces and to complicate conditions for rapid lateral movement, general moral decay in the defense debilitating the stability of the forces, or any kind of major errors by the defender may create for an attacker conditions reminiscent of the 1914 and 1920 operations.

It will be correct if, for our calculations regarding future offensive operations, we adopt a slower pace for the forces than that in the 1914 and 1920 offensives. One must consider that, until the enemy has reserves or capabilities to shift forces from other sectors of the front, that is, until the main enemy forces have been routed, from one-third to a half of all the days of an operation will be days in contact. Given these conditions, the average daily advance cannot exceed 8–10 kilometers per day.

Meanwhile, *such mobility is absolutely insufficient* for achievement of decisive successes. The rate of advance not only must not be less than, *must exceed*, the possible rate of enemy withdrawal in order to achieve encirclement of the enemy, to deprive him of the chance to slip out from under the blow. Otherwise, any operation (more correctly, a series of successive operations) designed to envelop, turn the flank of, or encircle the enemy very rapidly will lead to a frontal blow. Normally, an attacker must retain the capability for an offensive with his main forces at an average speed equal to the average rate of movement of the organic masses, that is, less than 20–25 kilometers per day. Here, individual army units (cavalry and mechanized units) must make up to 35–50 kilometers in order to retain a position enveloping or threatening the enemy deep rear area, to provide the capability for a breakout to his rear areas and a denial of his planned withdrawal. Accomplishment of that mission depends upon solution of the problem of high-speed tanks with a large radius of action (quality and quantity) and creation of mechanized units of sufficient size. Motorization of the strategic cavalry must also be added to these measures.

Given the contemporary state of affairs, a rapid rate of advance is possible *after* a clash with an enemy that has regrouped, after his main forces have been routed. Success in such an operation opens broad perspectives for a more rapid further pace, it creates conditions for development of true pursuit at the maximum rapidity and tempo the physical condition of the troops will allow. At this time, one must anticipate a daily advance of up to 20–25 and 30 kilometers.

SHOCK ARMY REQUIREMENTS DURING PROLONGED OPERATIONS

Operations more saturated with skirmishes, a defense more stubborn than was the case in 1914 and 1920, are also linked with greater personnel and materiel costs. Any reduction here in the requirements of troops engaged in combat will inevitably cause their rapid attrition and the foundering of combat actions. Combat actions require personnel replacements, ammunition, and fuel. An absolutely uninterrupted and accelerated supply of men and horses during an entire operation is necessary to maintain the physical strength of the troops at the requisite level.

Food and forage requirements are identical for every day of an operation. As we have already indicated, they comprise four trains for an army of five rifle corps. If strategic cavalry is also attached to the army, this requirement increases to 4.5–5 trains per day. The fuel requirement is comparatively low. One train per day will satisfy this requirement, including other aviation and vehicle transport needs as well.

The daily ammunition requirement is much more difficult to define since it is impossible to foresee ahead of time the nature of the combat actions each day of operations designed to a great depth and for a prolonged period. Therefore, the calculation must be based upon certain other prerequisites.

The complete ammunition norm calculated per full day of intensive combat for an entire army will be required probably only for the period of a decisive operation, which may last 5–6 days, just as for an initial operation. On the remaining days, even during a period of intervening operations, the ammunition requirement will be less than the norm established for intensive combat. Based on the nature of the combat actions (enemy stability, results of the initial operation, rate at which defensive reserves arrive), this requirement on a day of combat must be considered to be from 50 to 100 per cent of the norm for intensive combat. The requirement on other days must be considered to be no more than one-eighth to one-tenth of the aforementioned norm.

If one takes a series of successive operations intended all in all for one month, then, stemming from the aforementioned initial data, the following figures may express the ammunition requirement (overall ammunition budget). Initial and decisive operations with a duration of five–six days each will require four to five units of fire each. Of the remaining 18–20 days, up to 6–10 will be combat days. Figuring half to two-thirds of a unit per day, we will get an additional three to six units of fire. An additional one to two units will be required for the remaining non-combat days. All told, a minimum of 12, maximum of 18, and an average of 15 units of fire must be supplied per month. There must be at least four to five units of fire in the immediate tactical rear area at the beginning of a decisive operation. If you figure that about five units of fire required for an initial operation can be brought up before combat actions, then, from the day the initial operation ends, about one-third unit of fire, which comprises six ammunition trains per day, must be supplied daily. Thus, the army requirement for supply of food and forage, fuel, and ammunition is expressed in 11 trains per day (four food, six artillery, and one with fuel and other materiel). Having added one–two medical trains for the seriously wounded (lightly wounded are moved via temporary medical trains) and one–two for other random (or sporadic) needs, we will get an overall requirement of 13–16 trains daily.

The aforementioned nature of combat actions, which involve a large number of combat days, large ammunition expenditures, and great intensity for the advancing troops, also entails significant personnel losses. In the previous chapter, we determined that the personnel losses during the initial operation alone may equal 12–20 per cent of a first-echelon division.

For successive operations that include up to an additional 11–16 days, one must figure on at least an additional 20–30 per cent loss of the combat composition of all army units, that is, from 10,000 to 15,000 new replacements per corps, this figure including the replacements for the additional artillery. Of this number of losses, approximately half are from combat actions prior to the decisive skirmish with a regrouped enemy. Thus, if the losses divisions suffer in the initial operation are not replaced on the spot, immediately upon the conclusion of this operation, shortages in the forces at the onset of the decisive operation will reach 10–15 per cent. In the event losses in the initial operation are not replaced, the personnel shortage at the onset of the decisive operation will increase to 27–35 per cent. This degree of shortage will lower the fighting efficiency of the forces to such an extent that there is a high degree of risk associated with embarking on a decisive operation with them. A significant percentage of divisions may turn out to lack fighting efficiency altogether.

RAILROAD RESTORATION RATE

An inevitable part of an operation plan now is the destruction of roads during a retreat. At the start of the war, railroads were destroyed on a very limited scale, but in 1918, the Germans had already begun to do this more thoroughly. During their July–September 1918 withdrawal, they radically destroyed everything, especially the rail bed, stations, bridges and highways. All bridges were turned into piles of rubble onto which locomotives were driven to delay repairs. The bases of abutments were loosened and embankments on approaches were destroyed in some places. Tunnels were destroyed using charges of enormous power, with the blasts causing the soil on the tops of the hills being crossed to shake. Tunnel restoration turned out to be more difficult than construction of new ones in virgin soil.

Track was destroyed, almost as a rule, by using explosive cartridges to break the joints, thus rendering all the rails unusable. During the later months (August–September), track was blown up by special track busters. Rail stations were put to the torch or blown up, telephone and telegraph equipment removed, and communication lines destroyed completely. The Germans left behind them on the railroads and in the stations mine obstacles that detonated when trains approached or during restoration work. Roye Station blew up 75 days after the German withdrawal. Explosions occurred even after the armistice.[36]

The French advanced extremely slowly owing to the destruction of the railroads, locally having lost contact with the withdrawing German Army. They spent four months restoring several roads leading to the front.

The Germans began the withdrawal from the Ypres–Amiens–Compiegne–Epernay line in late July. Four months later (11 November), when the front ran from Ghent to Mons and further along the Meuse River (a stretch of 130–140 kilometers), the roads were restored only along the Courtry–Le Cateau–St. Quentin–Reims–Verdun line (restoration of 50–60 kilometers). The entire network on the remainder of the route (depth to 50–80 kilometers) remained destroyed. The railroads were restored at a rate of one kilometer per day (not counting tunnels) on several lines containing many artificial structures and where the destruction was thorough (Compiegne–Roye, Chaulnes–Montdidier, Villers–Cotterets–Soissons, and others). The Peronne–Strasburg mainline, damaged by high-explosive shells, was restored at a rate of two kilometers per day. The Amiens–Tergnier line, on which several undamaged stations remained, was restored between 8 and 15 August, with an average advance of 3,200 meters per day. The

Soissons–Reims rail line, which suffered even less destruction, was restored between 10 and 20 September at a rate of six kilometers per day.[37]

Thus, the 1918 railroad restoration rate fluctuated from 900 meters to six kilometers per day (not counting time required to restore tunnels). It depended upon the degree of destruction of the rail bed, station structures, water supply, and the number of artificial structures, bridges mostly. The rate of restoration was one–two kilometers per day where restoration required supply of large quantities of construction materials. The pace rose to five–six kilometers per day on lines whose restoration required supply of less construction materials. But, generally speaking, the destruction was vast even in the latter case. All were prepared ahead of time, within several weeks. The Germans were fully capable of carrying out such destruction since they withdrew slowly and according to plan.[38]

There was less destruction at the outset of the World War. Thus, during the First Marne in 1914, all Belgian and the northwestern French railroads were destroyed to such a small extent that traffic restoration on them went swiftly. Sections remained intact (Linden–Charleville) or were damaged very little. The mainline from Aachen to Liège–Brussels–Mons–Valenciennes–Cambria–Compiegne was restored at an average rate of 18 kilometers per day. The stations at Tam and St. Quentin on this railroad were opened by 4 September (beginning of the Battle of the Marne).

But restoration proceeded at a rate of only eight–nine kilometers per day on the central axis, where the French withdrew more methodically than on their left flank, and where the destruction was more thorough (bridges across the Meuse, tunnels).

In essence, the Germans did not deal with the bridges across the Meuse until the end of the Battle of the Marne and, therefore, the 2d Army was forced to break off contact 150 kilometers from the railheads (Fourmies and Honoré were opened 30 August). Restoration from Charlesville to Honoré (60 kilometers) took seven days or eight–nine kilometers per day.

The railroad restoration norms on the Eastern Front in 1914 were essentially the same, both for the Russian Army during its offensive in Galicia and for the Germans in 1915 during their offensive deep into Russia.

We find the identical railroad restoration rate also during the Red Army offensive to the Wisla in 1920.

From 4 to 23 July, by the time the Red Army had broken out along the Newman and Shchara rivers, restoration had reached the Vil'no–Vileyka–Stolbtsy line or a restoration rate of 7–10 kilometers per day.

Later, restoration on the former Aleksandrovka railroad proceeded at a faster pace. By 10 August, 280 kilometers of track (Stolbtsy–Brest, Stolbtsy–Belostok) had been restored in 19 days or a rate of 14–15 kilometers per day. The restoration rate on subsequent days remained 9–10 kilometers per day on the remaining lines.

After the war, railroad destruction and restoration problems occupied a rightful place in a country's system of defense preparedness. At present, even given a rapid withdrawal, destruction on railroads will be more considerable than in 1914–15 and 1920. In maneuver warfare, it is difficult to count upon the destruction that was wrought in 1918, but there is no doubt that bridges, station structures and the water supply will be destroyed thoroughly. The rail bed will also be more thoroughly destroyed because all armies now do this mechanically using special locomotive-borne devices. Telegraph, telephone, and other valuable equipment will be removed to a significant degree. Employment of delayed-action mines permitting destruction even after forces have withdrawn is absolutely inevitable.

All this signifies that, to a much greater degree than before, railroad restoration must now be based upon the *supply* of construction materials, down to ties, rails, and station equipment, inclusively, from the rear area, not to mention bridge girders and water supply equipment.

Based on the study of the technical state of the railroads in the enemy rear area, this circumstance impels one to prepare and to concentrate all required construction materials and station equipment at stations closest to the front even before major operations are initiated.[39] Nonetheless, since all this equipment and materials must be supplied from the rear area, the amount of restoration work has risen sharply, and, in this connection, the requirement for laborers, technical personnel and special transport to supply materials via dirt roads to the work area has increased incredibly, in future wars one cannot count upon the railroad restoration rate achieved in the 1914 and 1920 campaigns.

There are three types of railroad destruction: capital, when all artificial structures, station structures and their equipment, the water supply, communications, and the rail bed (ties and rails) are virtually 50 per cent destroyed; medium, when there is analogous destruction, but the supports and some bridge spans remain intact, water towers in the water supply are intact (only the reservoirs in the water towers are destroyed), and only the rail bed is dismantled; minor, when only individual structures are destroyed, delaying traffic for one–two days.

Given that the stability of the defense has increased, one must mainly count on capital destruction on railroads in the future, even for maneuver warfare. A daily withdrawal rate of 8–12 kilometers provides the full capability to prepare for and to carry out all the destruction on railroads envisioned for capital destruction.

Much also has changed in the railroad restoration system since the World and Civil Wars. An entire series of measures has technically been worked out allowing railroad bridges and the water supply to be restored more rapidly, road bed repair has been mechanized, and measures have been developed permitting initiation of traffic on railroads before capital buildings and the water supply are restored.[40] At present the authorities, the repair organizations that will do the restoration work are being trained more widely and thoroughly. Therefore, where railroad restoration is concerned, one must anticipate considerable facilitation compared with the period of the World and Civil Wars.

Nonetheless, there remains the great dependence on the supply of an enormous quantity of construction materials from the rear area, the large requirement for laborers and special transport for delivery of materials via dirt roads to the work site, the comparatively long periods needed for restoration of railroad bridges. All this will place definite technical constraints on embarking on the efforts, thus constraining the railroad restoration rate in the future.

Given the most favorable conditions, that is, provision of a full work force and motor transport for supply of materials to a work site, calculations show that the railroad restoration rate may not exceed five–six kilometers per day when railroads are destroyed to such an extent that their restoration requires supply not only of station and other equipment, and materials for bridges, but rails and ties as well. The restoration norm may reach 8–10 kilometers per day in those instances when the supply of rails and ties is not so great, when there is no need for such a supply (for instance, when restoration work on double-track lines involves only one rather than both lines). Given so-called partial destruction, when many railroad structural elements (water towers, bridge supports and so on) remain intact, the daily restoration norm reaches 15–20 kilometers per day.[41] Restoration of lightly damaged rail lines cannot delay traffic for more than two–three days.

One must take into account massive destruction on railroads during major operations and, consequently, given extant technical resources, the following restoration rate: either five–six kilometers per day on single-track lines always and on double-track lines when restoration is in progress on both lines simultaneously or 8–10 kilometers per day when only one track of a double-track line is being restored. One can count upon so-called partial destruction of railroads only on secondary axes and when conditions are especially favorable and, in this connection, the daily restoration norm is 15–20 kilometers per day.[42] But what is of interest to us is not only the railroad restoration rate, but also the rate at which the traffic capacity of the newly-restored rail sections is returned to the level that meets army requirements. It is a case where, owing to extant technical capabilities, the traffic capacity of newly-restored sections in the *first week* cannot exceed three to four, a maximum of five, pairs of trains per day. The railroad fully employs this number of trains to supply construction materials and laborers, work train operations, and so forth.

The sticking point reducing the lead sector's traffic capacity is water supply. It takes a great deal of time to restore water towers (which are not too hard to destroy). The consideration is that only at the end of the first week can the maximum traffic capacity of newly restored rail sections be increased to 15–17 pairs of trains, and this figure is the maximum for newly restored single-track lines. Only restoration of a second line or introduction of a block signalling system on single-track lines can provide a further increase in rail capacity.

The aforementioned railroad restoration capabilities do not satisfy operational requirements at all. These capabilities are less by a factor of two than the probable traffic norms even of modern armies lacking sufficient tanks and assets to accompany the infantry into combat and sufficient vehicle transport. These norms are less by a factor of four or five than the possible rate of advance of armies with a large number of mechanized troops.

That is why railroad technology is tasked with absolutely vital missions:

1. Insure that railroads that have suffered capital destruction

are restored at a rate of 12–15 kilometers per day, the minimum being 10 kilometers per day, including the time required to restore bridges;
2. Provide railroad traffic capacity of at least 17–21 pairs of trains on single track and 35–45 pairs of trains on double-track lines within the first two days following restoration. Such requirements are neither fantastic nor unattainable.

The only things preventing achievement of these norms now are:

1. Water supply, which constrains the traffic capacity of the lead sections and, in this connection, supply of materials for railroad restoration;
2. Constrained amount of motor transport required to supply construction materials to a work site. In view of the wide practice of erecting railroad bridges at a low level and timely preparation of prefabricated forms, there should be no major difficulties in restoring such bridges.

The water supply problem will be solved technically in the near years by use of pneumatic stations and diesel locomotives. It is inevitable that motor transportation will develop for purely economic considerations. Satisfaction of the aforementioned requirements of operational art is just a question of time.

SCALE OF SUCCESSIVE OPERATIONS

The rate of railroad restoration and the nature of the transport (vehicle or horse) on dirt supply roads to a significant degree determine the scale (depth) of successive operations. Earlier, we determined the scope of the normal daily (regular) supply for a shock army comprising five rifle corps with additional artillery to be 13–16 trains, with no consideration at all given to the supply of personnel replacements. If repair trains (at least three per day), service (one train), and a mandatory option of at least three–four pairs are added, then the maximum traffic capacity of a railroad where one shock army is based must equal 20–24 pairs per day at a time when the maximum traffic capacity of newly restored single-track lines does not exceed 15–17 pairs of trains, given extant realistic capabilities. *Hence, we conclude that, at present, an army comprising no more than three rifle corps or an army assigned auxiliary missions can be based on a single-track railway.* The daily requirements of these armies in a prolonged operation are from 10 to 13 pairs of trains, but a *more powerful army* (five rifle corps with additional suppressive assets) *requires either two single-track or one double-track railroad.*

There is no capability to assign two railroads to one army in the East European Theater of Military Actions (sparse railroad network). Therefore, if the necessity arises to have an army comprising five rifle corps in a particular sector and, additionally, corps comprising second and third echelons are in the same sector (something absolutely unavoidable in some sectors), then such an army must be based unavoidably on a double-track railroad. Moreover, the density of the railroad network in the East European Theater of Military Actions is so sparse that two armies inevitably must be based on several railroads to obtain the requisite offensive grouping.[43]

Hence, it follows that, as a rule, both tracks on all double-track lines must be restored immediately in offensive operations in our theater and, consequently, at present one must consider a restoration rate of about five–six kilometers per day.[44]

Given a daily advance of 8–12 kilometers (average of 10 kilometers) by our forces, the railroad restoration rate will be less by a factor of two than the pace of the forces.

During successive operations calculated to last one month and, consequently, to a depth of 300—350 kilometers, the troops will be up to 150 kilometers from restored railroad sections. However, since the final 50 kilometers of restored railroads, given today's means of traction (steam locomotives) and water supply and employing water towers, will have a traffic capacity not exceeding five pairs of trains, the actual separation from *railheads* will reach 200 kilometers. Vehicle and animal transport must serve this distance. Unit trains can serve only 50–60 kilometers so, consequently, the army link in the supply chain must be introduced for the remaining 140 kilometers. Even if the army link in the supply chain is served by motor transport exclusively, supply depth cannot exceed 80 kilometers (limit of efficient vehicle exploitation). Thus, based upon supply conditions, one must consider that maximum separation from railheads must not exceed 140 kilometers, figuring in the organic link in the supply chain as well. Given the present state of affairs, this denotes that supply conditions do not support successive operations to a depth of 300 kilometers. Rail restoration assets and supply via dirt roads limit this maximum depth to 200–250 kilometers. In this event, railroads will be restored 100–125 kilometers out, those with a full maximum traffic capacity only 60–80 kilometers out. Supply via dirt roads will service the remaining 140–165 kilometers.

Of the overall amount of cargo delivered by rail to an army, a minimum of 13 trains of cargo is dispatched to the forces. Moving this cargo requires either 2,000 three-ton trucks (100 motor transport companies) or 11,000 double wagons (55 army trains).[45]

A day's run for motor transport on our roads cannot exceed 80–100 kilometers, that is, 100 motor transport companies can make a round-trip supply run of 40–50 kilometers (1.5–2 days' march). The same number of vehicles will be required for the next 40–50 kilometers.

A day's run for animal transport is 25–30 kilometers. Thus, up to 130 army trains per army are required for a round-trip supply run to a distance of one day's march.

Servicing the link in the supply chain for every corps will require either 20 transport companies (per 40–50 kilometers) or 22 army trains (per 25–30 kilometers).

Each corps moving via two roads will require an average of up to 10 transportation companies or up to 11 army trains. A transport detachment column is one kilometer long. A transport detachment column should average three kilometers in length when the intervals between vehicles and between detachments are considered. The length of an army train column is two kilometers, also being three kilometers when intervals are considered. Based on these calculations, the length of the column of army supply assets will be up to 30 kilometers for a 40-kilometer link in the supply chain, given motor transport; given horse transport, it will be up to 33 kilometers for a 25–30 kilometer link in the supply chain.

Thus, it is difficult to service the forces if the number of railroads is limited. However, it is still possible using motor transport, but absolutely impossible using horse transport alone. In the latter case, every road in the sector the horse transport is servicing will literally be filled with wagons and, in some instances, they will not even be able to fit on the section of road assigned to them.

Hence the first major conclusion is that a *shock army* (*having in its composition additional artillery from the calculation we are using*) *cannot structure its army link in the supply chain on horse transport.* This link in the supply chain must inevitably be transferred to motor transport. Since the same difficult picture involving horse transport can also crop up at the corps link in the supply chain, it is absolutely necessary that servicing of all additional artillery at the corps link in the supply chain also be transferred to *vehicle traction.* The army will then have a normal supply capability and minimal conditions for freedom of maneuver.

Naturally, the problem of dirt roads, their quality, how they are maintained, how transport of supplies is organized via dirt roads in general arises in all its magnitude. Uninterrupted work in the army rear area cannot be considered insured without appropriate organization of dirt roads (about analogous to organization of railroads). Are the aforementioned transport resource norms new, fantastic? We calculated that one shock army requires 2,000 vehicles per 40–50 kilometers. This number increases to 4,000 when the army link in the supply chain is 100 kilometers (maximum area for operation of a vehicle). If four to five shock armies are present, the number of required vehicles jumps to 20,000. Back in 1918, the French Army had a vehicle park of 100,000 vehicles, with up to 24,000 alone in the reserve of the commander-in-chief. This means that the requirements we calculated are not extraordinary. This is the minimum, without which a modern mechanized army cannot consider decisive and deep operations.

Thus, the depth of successive operations where supply conditions are concerned (railroad restoration rate, distance of profitable motor transport operation given extant technical capabilities) is limited to 250 kilometers and only in the event an army has absolutely no constraints on vehicle assets, when it can allocate up to 40 motor transport companies with a capacity of 50 tons each to supply each corps. The depth of these operations will drop radically if sufficient vehicle resources are lacking. And such operations are out of the question if the foundation is horse transport exclusively. Only corps acting on a wide front and having at least three or four roads for supply can be based on horse transport. In this case, the maximum separation from railheads cannot exceed 75–100 kilometres (one to two links in the army supply chain), that is, the overall depth of successive operations given horse transport may reach 135–150 kilometers. Meanwhile, the depth of operations stemming therefrom is absolutely insufficient for decisive and crushing blows. It will be possible at such depth (150–250 kilometers) to achieve finite success only against an enemy occupying a front approximately equal to this depth, that is, a front of 150–250 kilometers. In this case, an attacker with a rate of advance not much less than the rate of withdrawal will have the capability to envelop and cut off routes of withdrawal of the main mass of enemy forces occupying a given front, and destroy them.

Such a depth is clearly insufficient against an enemy occupying a front more than 150–250 kilometers long (for instance, the Ukrainian or Belorussian sector of the Soviet–Polish Theater of Military Actions). It is simpler under these conditions for the defender to slip his forces out from under the blow. The broad front provides him with numerous withdrawal routes, while the attacker is involved with a slower pace than the defender, and the attacker's offensive is very rapidly forced to break off owing to lack of supply.

One must assume that a powerful crushing blow normally requires, first, that the attacker's pace does not lag behind the rate of withdrawal of the defender's main forces and, second, that the attacker has been provided with the capability to penetrate into the depth of enemy territory to a distance equal to the length of the enemy front under attack. Operations designed against an enemy occupying a front of 350–400 kilometers require a depth of at least these 350–400 kilometers of accelerated pace.

The extant state of railroad technology still does not support these norms. But all the prerequisites now exist so that this technology in the near years will be able to provide operational art the capability to inflict deep and crushing blows against the enemy.

The problem of replacing personnel losses in operations designed to a depth of 350–400 kilometers presents no special difficulties. It requires only a special system of organizing reserve units.

Losses linked with conduct of an initial operation may be replaced now immediately upon its conclusion. This requires that every corps have a reserve unit comprising 20–25 per of the total corps complement. This reserve unit (reserve regiments) at the outset of an operation must have a full complement of *trained* Red Army soldiers. During the operation, they follow the corps ahead of the second-echelon divisions and corps and provide replacements to divisions as required. Replacement of possible losses in successive operations requires having a second set of army reserve units of the same size (20–25 per cent of the complement of the combat units in the army) in the immediate rear area (on the line of the second-echelon corps). These units advance simultaneously with the offensive of the forces (movement one–two days later depending on the pace of the offensive) exclusively by a march. Moving them up to the front line will require no more than two–three days. Replacements are fed into the divisions as the latter are assigned to the second echelon.

NATURE OF SHOCK GROUPING ACTIONS

Despite modern armies being significantly heavier, despite the relatively limited scale of some successive operations under modern conditions, despite the enormous intensity with which vigorous, courageous, and crushing blows are linked, nonetheless, these deep and crushing blows remain the most decisive weapon in a strategy to achieve the goals a war assigns.

It would be an irreparable error due to the difficulties in the conduct of deep (offensive) operations arising in connection with the development of military technology to fall into a unique kind of "opportunism" negating vigorous and deep blows and advocating the tactic of staying put, of inflicting blows at close range, actions characterized by the stylish word "starvation." Such a view towards modern operational art provides no evidence of profound understanding of the peculiarities of modern warfare, but is a result of decadent feelings, a result of capitulation to those difficulties linked with temporary lagging of suppressive assets, of resources to accompany the infantry into combat, and of rail and vehicle transportation resources behind the requirements that organization of deep blows levy.

Therefore, the desire "voluntarily" to constrain the depth of successive operations, tendencies toward self-restraint in the planning of combat actions, that will elevate a system of close-range blows to the highest achievement of military thought, these tendencies toward "starvation" cannot be considered the proper path of development for operational art. The correct path of development of operational art must follow the line of *full* employment of all capabilities for rapid and true infliction of the greatest losses, of the most telling blows, on the enemy. The proper solution to this problem unavoidably will be linked with full employment of all capabilities to develop decisive blows to the maximum depth permitted by the physical and moral condition of the troops, by road restoration and supply conditions. Of course, this absolutely necessary desire for full employment of the power of the troops and the capabilities of the rear area must not lead to the overtaxing and rupture of the physical and moral strength of the troops.

The art of the strategist and the operator is correctly to sense that limit in pushing personnel and material resources which might lead to a sharp deterioration in the psychologial state of the troops, which might bring with it not victory, but defeat. More properly, *progressive* paths to the development of operational art require that lagging sectors of military art now be elevated, errors in the organizational development of the armed forces be corrected, the quantity and quality of suppressive assets be improved, transportation assets and technology (rail and motor) be elevated to the requisite level – as a result, all this creates conditions under which it will be simpler and more probable for operational art to achieve the goals war assigns.

Relatively major missions to rout an enemy may also be achieved at the depth to which successive operations are designed under modern conditions.

The Balkanization of Europe following the Versailles Peace Treaty led to the founding of an entire series of small states, the depth of the territory of which covers the aforementioned distance (250 kilometers), with a bit over.

Where the larger states are concerned, the distance equals virtually half the entire depth of their territory. This means that, given skillful conduct of combat actions, operations at that depth will essentially engage all the armed forces of the minor Lilliputian states and at least half or, in an extreme case, one-third, those of the larger countries. And, in turn, this denotes that the minor Lilliputian states may be destroyed with one blow. As far as the larger states are concerned, it is possible to employ a series of successive operations to achieve such a rout of their armed forces, which, given a favorable confluence of other conditions, may create the prerequisite for true strategic pursuit or, at the least, lead to a significant weakening of their armed might.

Deep and crushing blows may put entire state organisms out of the game quite rapidly. Where the large states are concerned, these blows may lead to the rout of their armed forces piecemeal, in large packets. These blows are a truer means of rapid attrition of enemy personnel and material resources, of creation of objectively favorable conditions for sociopolitical upheavals in the enemy country.

Deep and crushing blows may create a situation close to that in Poland in 1920, when, in Pilsudski's own words, due to the successes of the Red cavalry in Galicia and the unstoppable Red Army offensive north of the Pripyat' Marshes, "*the work of the state began to collapse, panic erupted in locales situated even hundreds of kilometers from the front, the most dangerous internal front began to be organized.*"[46] Deep and crushing blows remain one of the truest means of converting war into civil war.

That is why modern operational art cannot abandon deep crushing blows. A correct and wise policy toward organizational development of the armed forces must insure conditions favorable for the conduct of war using this method.

The form of the blow is of great significance in the conduct of operations.

It is difficult to count on an expansive "operational harvest" from a unilaterial ram, a blow directed against one enemy flank when the enemy is occuping a broad front and has a completely exposed rear area (French in 1914, Poles in 1920). Such a ram, even if it is on the correctly selected operational axis, cannot provide major results at the rate of development of combat actions inherent in modern weapons. Given such a blow, the enemy main forces, if they consider combat disadvantageous for them, will always be able to avoid combat, to slip out from under the blow. A ram acting only on one axis is unable to force an enemy maintaining an exposed flank, free routes of withdrawal, to engage in combat with his main forces where combat is advantageous to the attacker and disadvantageous for a defense. Sacrificing space, the enemy may withdraw from under the blow; he is capable of moving rapidly, of making 25–30 kilometers per day, even of using the railroads to withdraw his forces at a time when the attacker must move in contact and is constrained by a maximum rate of advance of 8–12 kilometers per day. This property inherent in a unilateral ram to a significant degree explains why neither the Germans in 1914 nor the Red Army in 1920 were able to achieve the decisive rout of enemy personnel despite a deep intrusion into enemy territory. Every time the attacker brandished his "battering-ram grouping" to deliver a blow against the main forces of the enemy, the latter dodged the blow and withdrew if he considered combat under the given conditions disadvantageous.

In fact, let us take a 400-kilometer front with an exposed rear area and repeat the blow against it by the Germans in 1914 or the Red Army in 1920.

Following the initial operation, one still cannot count upon decisive results if the "battering-ram grouping" will even outdistance the flank of the remaining sector of front. The enemy has free routes of withdrawal and, for that reason, the capability to encircle and rout even part of the enemy forces is ruled out. Only encirclements of small enemy units on a narrowly tactical scale are possible when this form of blow is employed. A major success can only be achieved against an engaged enemy with a narrow front and disadvantageous withdrawal route axis.

It is possible to achieve greater results employing actions on intersecting axes against an enemy occupying a wide front and having an exposed rear area. This form of blow promises the greatest success if undertaken with sufficient forces. It may also lead to complete encirclement of a significant portion of the enemy armed forces under modern conditions.

Naturally, this form of blow requires more forces. Here, we are dealing in essence with two blows and each must be organized on a wide enough front so that the troops carrying it out cannot be enveloped rapidly from the flanks and parried. Each blow must be undertaken with sufficient forces so that shock groups will be able without delay to move forward towards one another, trapping the enemy in pincers. Moreover, securing the flanks with one shock grouping requires less forces than such support in the form of two groups acting on different axes. But nonetheless, it will be better in many instances to have two shock groups advancing, one on an 80-kilometer front (two shock armies) and the other on a front of 40–50 kilometers (one shock army), rather than one shock group advancing on 120 kilometers of continuous front. A unilateral ram is advisable only in those cases when there is the possibility of employing a blow along one axis to press the enemy against an impassable area (neutral border, sea, impassable mountain chain).

Actions on intersecting axes are advantageous not only because of the results that such an operation provides, but also because of the sustainment and basing of the armies conducting the operation. This form of operation makes basing on a broader railroad network possible, it provides broader enveloping basing less sensitive to fluctuations of the front line. And it is easier and more flexible to maneuver two groups than to maneuver one battering-ram mass that must be based on one or two rail lines.

In both forms of blow, the unilateral ram or actions on intersecting axes, enemy personnel remain the main target of the actions. The area where the main enemy forces operating in a given theater are located or are assembling at a given time not only defines the axis of the flow and a successive change in this axis, but the pace of the attacker's actions also depends entirely on the nature of the actions of the enemy forces. The norms of advance in an offensive operation presented above are not an order for the actions of the forces. These norms only orient the commander-in-chief's operational planning and support measures. Forces must attain maximum successes, maximum movement forward. The enemy will attempt especially strongly to defend vital axes, vital points, which cover his withdrawal routes, or a concentration of fresh forces. The art of the attacker is to determine these axes and these points and to unleash the entire mass of forces quickly enough to break out to the flank and rear area of the enemy forces, to cut his withdrawal routes and disrupt any new grouping of forces the enemy is preparing. Combat actions during this period require an incredibly fast pace, the maximum possible intensity, great flexibility, and maneuverability.

Despite forces being heavier, such mobility within the framework of specific operational norms is fully possible even now. If forces are not overly ponderous in individual sectors, if there is no disorder and chaos in their rear areas, if both the forces themselves and their trains and support institutions are sufficiently trained, if they are prepared for rapid and deep advances, if the leadership (command element) is on top of the situation, then high tactical mobility is also possible with the current force organization, with existing growing trains, and with the numerous logistics.

Cavalry and mechanized units must have especially high mobility and maneuverability. At present, the cavalry must take into account the growing stability of the defense, and the higher density of fire. But this does not signify that it is removed from the field of operation, or that it must press itself against or be covered by the infantry. On the contrary, these conditions require the cavalry to appear on the field of a modern operation with new resources and new methods of combat. It must have resources sufficient to suppress the fire of infantry that hurriedly has gone over to the defense, and be able to operate dismounted at least as well as that infantry. Cavalry, reinforced by sufficient artillery (including howitzer artillery), light high-speed tanks, and machine gun units, and mounted in vehicles (off-road vehicles best of all), must operate on the exposed moving flanks of shock groups that have moved far foward (up to 75–100 kilometers), successively cutting off enemy routes of withdrawal and accomplishing the tactical encirclement of his main forces operating on a given front. This vigorous work by strategic cavalry that has moved far forward simultaneously must also insure the conduct of ground-based reconnaissance for the *front* and army command elements.

Aviation must manifest enormous intensity during prolonged operations. A great deal of systematic work (reconnaissance and combat) simultaneously with movement forward of its airfields are required here.

Following the initial operation, during which a major part of aviation operated over the field of battle, it again expands the zone of its actions. Fresh enemy forces arriving in the area of the operation by rail, march, or in vehicles will become the targets of its observations and attacks. Fresh forces detected at detraining stations or on the march must be kept under regular observation from the air to provide the command element timely data establishing the area of their assembly and, consequently, new targets for further actions by ground and air forces. But enemy units making a withdrawal cannot be ignored. The secret of an enemy decision may be uncovered by comparing two sets of data, that is, where newly arrived forces are heading, and where, in what direction and formation will troops at the front withdraw. These data will outline an area that must also become a target of aviation's daily observation.

Aviation again disperses its efforts when an enemy withdrawal begins. Organic aviation is tasked entirely to observe the withdrawing enemy, while army aviation is tasked to monitor newly arriving enemy forces.

The focus of the work of bomber aviation also gradually shifts following the initial operation. In the early days of pursuit, the withdrawing enemy forces are the object of its actions. Along with the ground forces, bomber aviation finds the enemy beaten on the front, attacking him on the march, at crossing sites, at points where forces accumulate. When the arrival of new waves of reserves is detected, bomber aviation shifts its efforts to these forces, railroads, systematically destroying or employing toxic agents to contaminate enemy detraining stations. Aviation's mission is to move stations where reserves are detrained farther back, to delay the concentration of reserves, and from the very beginning to employ powerful air strikes to destroy the morale of the newly arriving enemy units.

New enemy aviation formations will also appear in the area of the operation at the same time as new ground units. Enemy fighter aviation will be reinforced, new bomber units will gradually appear. The airfields for these new aviation units will naturally become a target of actions for the attacker's bomber aviation. The attacker will again be confronted with the problem of defending vital targets in his rear area, especially areas where railroad and railhead restoration work are underway. But fighter aviation's basic mission will remain air support for the main groupings of advancing troops and friendly airfields. Antiaircraft assets protect logistics targets exclusively. All these missions must be accomplished at the same time friendly airfields are systematically moved forward.

Aviation must move its airfields forward in accordance with the overall rate of advance. If one stems from the fact that reliable communications with staffs (organic and army) are possible when corps aviation's airfields are within 25–30 kilometers and army aviation's airfields are within 50–75 kilometers of the front, then corps aviation must change its airfields every third day and army aviation every fifth day. As a rule, there will be periods here when army airfields settle on organic airfields in order, immediately thereafter, to leave them gradually behind.

This work tempo requires enormous intensity from all aviation. Any regular rest during an operation, even one designed to last one month, is out of the question. Individual aircraft, individual detachments, entire squadrons are either at work accomplishing regular missions to reconnoiter, bomb, or cover a particular sector or are transferring to new airfields. As a rule, only non-flying days will serve as days of rest and, at most, short rests are possible on flying days.

A month of intense work will involve great costs to aviation. War experience demonstrates that these costs can reach 30–40 and even 60 per cent of the equipment and 20–30 per cent of the flying personnel. These figures define the equipment and personnel reserve that must be prepared at the outset of operations and gradually fed forward so that organic units are not attrited completely.

Successive operations designed for the depth indicated and encompassing a front of 250–400 kilometers engage not only the enemy armed forces disposed on this front or those that may arrive at the field of battle during combat actions. These operations also engage and inevitably spur into movement the enormous mass of the enemy population. In some states, these operations will engage the entire population of their country with its entire economy. In others, they will engage a *significant* portion of both the population and the economy of the country. For these reasons, the results of such operations grow from purely military factors to those of a political significance. Hence both the decisive significance of politics in the initial selection of the target and axis of the blow and the assistance politics renders to military actions during the operations themselves. Correctly placed political work among the population that the combat actions engulf can facilitate the outcome of combat actions to a significant degree.

To a great degree, major regroupings are difficult for an attacker during an operation. He will be 100–150 kilometers from the rail stations from which operational regroupings via rail can begin. At this time, motor transport will be involved entirely in supply efforts.

In a zone comprising four to six days' march, all regroupings must be done exclusively in march formation. Of course, this circumstance will impact only the *speed* of the regroupings. Technically, one cannot rule out the possibility that such courageous lateral movements as the one Kluck's army, comprising four corps, made in early September on the Marne can be completed. At present, highly trained troops will be able to complete such regroupings as an alteration of an army's front, requiring up to 50–70 kilometers of march movements in a period of one, maximum two, days.

Any operational transfers entailing the dispatch of forces to other fronts (sectors) require preliminary withdrawal of forces up to 100–150 kilometers to rail stations, that is, up to a week will be required for concentration at rail stations alone. Railroads can be prepared for such transfers before the troops arrive at entraining stations.

The beginning of new operations depends on how long it takes to bring forces up to strength, replace equipment losses, accumulate new ammunition reserves, and complete the restoration of railroads and dirt roads.

Railroads are the greatest choke point requiring the greatest amount of time and the element upon which all remaining problems depend.

The railroad situation in the rear area at the moment of a break in operations will be as follows. On double-track lines on which simultaneous railroad restoration was in progress, there will be a sector of up to 90–155 kilometers yet to be restored and, further to the rear, 40–50 kilometers of restored track with a traffic capacity of no more than four to five pairs of trains. And only further to the rear will the railroads have a normal traffic capacity. Restoration of the final 90–100 kilometers will require up to three weeks. Moreover, up to an additional week will be required to bring the traffic capacity on the entire length of the railroad to normal levels. Thus, overall, a one-month break is required for complete restoration of the railroads, after which new operations can be initiated. The situation will be approximately the same when only one line of a double-track line is restored initially, followed by restoration of the second line. At the end of the third week, there will be up to 50 kilometers of unrestored line, 50 kilometers of line with a traffic capacity of five pairs of trains, and an additional 50 kilometers of single-track line with a traffic capacity of 17 pairs of trains on these lines.

Under the most favorable conditions, it will take up to one week to restore the last 50 kilometers of destroyed line. It will take an additional week to bring this sector's traffic capacity up to 17 pairs of trains and at least another week to restore the second line. The second line in the entire remaining sector can also be restored during this time, that is, a total of three weeks will be required in this instance to restore the railroads.

During this period, of course, all preparatory work can be completed, replacements brought up and fed into the forces, equipment shipped in (in combination via rail and via dirt roads as well), and ammunition and remaining equipment replaced. Thus, new operations can be initiated at a minimum two–three weeks (if the single-track railroad can meet the army's requirements) and at a maximum one month if restoration of second lines is mandatory.

Such a break is undesirable, of course. If broad perspectives for a further rout of enemy personnel are revealed following one successful operation, these perspectives will be even broader after a series of successive operations. The temptation not to interrupt combat actions, to embark at once on inflicting successive blows, is enormous in the majority of cases. But calculations show that courageous and vigorous operations predominantly require people and ammunition. There is a high degree of risk involved with initiation of new operations if the railroads do not support the regular supply of the appropriate amount of ammunition.

Therefore, it is more advisable either to await restoration of the railroads or to initiate new operations on another axis. In both instances, these operations will require a new operational deployment.

POLITICAL SUPPORT TASKS

Successive operations under the conditions outlined above place in motion enormous masses of people numbering millions. Significant areas of a theater of military actions with dimensions of up to 120–150 kilometers in frontage and depth will be flooded with forces, trains, and logistics institutions. All populated points in these areas will overflow either with the forces or with the institutions serving them. The local population will be crowded to the utmost and a significant portion of the forces will be forced to sleep under the stars, using natural cover (forests near populated points, gardens, straw, and so forth), continually for several weeks. The travails and deprivations of the local population will be increased due to unavoidable requisitions and deliveries of cattle, vegetables, oats, and other food to the troops. The able-bodied population and transport assets periodically and very often will be called upon to help haul logistical supplies and for defensive efforts. A significant part of the fields will be dug up or trampled down. Entire villages, cultural institutions, will be burned down or destroyed in the battle areas. Many areas will be contaminated by chemical weapons. Populated points occupied by the forces or logistics institutions will be subjected to shelling by enemy long-range artillery and attack by bomber aviation. The populace must suffer losses equal to those of the forces.

The great accumulation of forces will unavoidably complicate life in military units. It will be difficult to maintain cleanliness and internal order, sanitary conditions will become difficult, there may even be a shortage of potable water.

It is absolutely inevitable that there will be disruptions in supplies and shortages of certain food items during operations, even given conditions most favorable for railroad restoration and organization of supply. Some units accomplishing responsible missions may go several days without a hot meal. Individual regiments and entire divisions and corps will have to fight under difficult conditions for weeks, cut off from their logistics, without regular supply, banking entirely on the reserves they carry with them. Nor is the possibility excluded that formations will be completely cut off both from their own logistics, and from other friendly troops, not only during defensive actions, but also during major offensive operations. They will be called upon to fight for days in encirclement with an inverted front and against superior enemy forces. The troops will often be called upon to fight for several hours in a contaminated atmosphere while wearing gas masks.

At times, the difficulties and deprivations of combat will be enormous. But despite this, enormous intensity and unbelievable energy will be required from the troops. Success in forthcoming operations can be achieved only when the troops enter combat with verve and enthusiasm, despite the deprivations and difficulties.

Only an army that knows what it is fighting for, and that it is defending its vital interests, is capable of this.

The Soviet state will never assign goals and missions that will contradict the interests of the working class and the broad toiling masses. The war of the Soviet state against any capitalist power will have a class, a revolutionary, nature. It will be directed in the final analysis at defense of the factories and plants taken from the capitalists against their old "masters," of the land against the landowners, the defense of the socalist society against the possibility of restoration.

These missions cannot but be understood by the broadest strata of the toiling population of the country. Nonetheless, they require very clear formulation, explanations and introduction into the consciousness of the masses. The situation in wartime is difficult. Deprivations at both the front and in the rear area are enormous. Under the effect of today's trials and tribulations, people may lose sight of the final mission, the final goal. We observe this among the most fluctuating and unstable elements even now, in peacetime, regarding our socialist organizational development. This will be the case even more so during wartime, when the difficulties will multiply.

The most basic and fundamental mission of political work during wartime is to maintain the army at the level of those missions the war assigns, to maintain the army in a position whereby, despite difficulties, it will know what it is fighting for, why it is suffering deprivations and difficulties what it is struggling for.

This work, which goes on during peacetime as well, cannot cease even for a minute during wartime. Only the forms of this work change in a combat situation. The range of forms this work takes during wartime includes extended and regular assigned political lessons among reserve forces and field units in the deep reserve, sporadic and random chats during a march, the personal example of the commander, political staff, and individual communists in combat.

The basic work in this vital problem of our agitation and propaganda must be done even prior to the onset of an operation, as preparations are being made for it. The question of the class nature of war, the goals we and our enemy are pursuing, proper representation of the internal state of our country, the balance of class forces in our society and the enemy's society, all this must be assimilated before combat actions begin, before forces set out on a march. We saw from previous chapters that successive operations designed to a depth of 200–250 kilometers require up to three–four weeks and, during that time, troops as a rule are in continuous action. They are either moving forward or they are holding. In direct skirmishes, the troops during the day conduct combat and, during the night, regroup, occupy new initial positions for subsequent combat. Rest will be possible at different times of the day only to receive food and take a quick nap. There will be no time during this period for regular and systematic agitation and propaganda. Therefore, all the basics, everything the situation, exercises, allow must be done before the operation starts. For a significant number of Red Army soldiers, this work must be done when they are in reserve units.

Agitation and propaganda of general political questions do not end with the beginning of the operation or when the troops set off on a march. They take on different forms. During this time, those questions that were brought to the consciousness of Red Army soldiers by means of systematic work during the preparatory period find new substantiation, new confirmation in new facts taken from the situation at the front or in more evident examples from the international situation. Concise information on these facts compared with what is already known, very brief commentaries on them, suffice to support, develop, and inculcate a representation of the class nature of ensuing events in the consciousness.

The focus of political work during operations themselves shifts to direct servicing of the troops. As indicated above, the situation for the combat activity of the troops is so complicated that suitable working conditions, a concerned attitude towards the needs of the troops, prevention of everything that unnerves, that weakens, the troops can be provided through attentive and continuous direction by the supervisory staff. Red Army soldiers and all commanders must be convinced that any deprivations result from an objective cause, the peculiarities of a combat situation, and are not the result of the inefficiency, the slovenliness of the control apparatus, or a lack of attention and lack of concern for their responsibilities on the part of the corresponding chiefs. Hence the task of the entire command and political staff, all leaders, and the entire control apparatus is to create in the area where forces are disposed and moving a situation whereby the troops will be convinced that everything has been done, that the deprivations and difficulties of life in the field have been reduced to a minimum.

If this task is accomplished, it will greatly facilitate purely political work among the troops. Then, agitation and propaganda, even in the abbreviated forms already discussed, will find a favorable climate. At the same time, political work must provide the troops with high-quality exhaustive information on what is going on in our country, in the enemy's country, what is new at the front, what major new events have occurred on the international scene. Technical accomplishment of this mission, as experience shows, encounters great difficulties. As troops are on the move, newspapers are late arriving from the rear area, they barely keep up with the forces. Military presses cannot operate regularly because they must follow the troops. The same is true of radio stations. Therefore, there is an absolute requirement that mail be delivered by vehicle or aircraft (using civil aviation), that military presses be mechanized. Presses must be mounted so they can operate aboard vehicles, in large barns, in special tents.

When the operational engagement begins, political work is even more differentiated, problems of the political effect on Red Army soldiers fall almost completely on the shoulders of the lower cells in the political apparatus, on commanders, on individual political workers. A personal example, a reminder of the goals the war is pursuing, short slogans inspire and call to combat. The least-stable formations most needing direct servicing are placed in the center of attention of the political apparatus. Problems of the ammunition supply, the efforts of the rear area, the supply of food, particularly for units accomplishing the main mission, those acting in the sectors of the main blow, require uninterrupted attention.

Operations will run successively for several weeks. During that time, an enormous distance will be travelled, huge territories with a massive population will be taken from the enemy. As a result, many *new facts* illustrating the class nature of the war, the attitude of enemy government organs towards different strata of the population, economic interrelationships among various classes, and so forth will become known. All of these facts, or the clearest ones, must be used for political agitation. Since the troops will be on the move continuously, all of this work must be done *en route*, its forms must be adapted to life on the march. A well-prepared military newspaper briefly expounding events again has enormous significance. *Front* and central newspapers will describe the events of life in combat with an unavoidable delay, so the regular work of organic newspapers must be supported properly.

A second group of problems comprising a subject of political work is work among enemy forces. This does not take a back seat to work among our own forces where scale and significance are concerned. Agitation and propaganda done correctly among enemy troops, when done regularly and tenaciously, can provide major results for final winning of the war. In the second chapter, we discussed a whole series of moments that characterize force quality problems. We pointed out at that time the *inevitable* class, national, and other contradictions that will be found in the armies of our enemies. We indicated the degree to which these contradictions will be exacerbated during the war itself. The enemy through his own agitation and propaganda will attempt to smooth over these contradictions, not permit them to manifest themselves; he will strive in various ways to preserve civil peace in the country and among his armed forces. The missions of our agitation and propaganda are to unmask the true goals of the war the enemy is pursuing, to reveal to his soldiers its real nature, to use specific examples to show in whose interests the war is being conducted. Our agitation and propaganda must give the enemy troops correct information about what is going on in their country, how in actuality the deprivations of war are being distributed between the propertied and the poor classes, unmask the individual measures of the government aimed at maintaining civil peace in the country, at "duping" the mass of the people.

This enormous task requires organization on a national scale. There are various way to penetrate the strata of enemy forces. Correct arrangement of efforts on a mass scale requires systematic and continuous reconnaissance of the deep rear area of the enemy country itself. Technical dissemination of propaganda will require many resources (literature in the enemy's language, compilation and duplication of this literature, its delivery to enemy territory, its distribution). Therefore, this work is organized as a rule by the state authority directly.

Against this general background, the *front* political apparatus concentrates its efforts on those enemy forces directly opposing it. To do so, it must study as completely as possible the class and national composition of individual enemy units and formations, monitor their morale, political moods, and, regarding them, in more specific form assign identical missions of illumination of the class struggle and national policy in the countries of our enemies.

Successful conduct of this political work among enemy troops can, along with other situational data, create conditions favorable for deep crushing blows. Major offensives with relatively small forces, with lower suppressive asset norms, can also be undertaken against morally unstable and politically vacillating enemy troops. On the other hand, each major success by our forces may create identical conditions favorable for further political work, for our further agitation and propaganda.

Therefore, the *front* and army command and control apparatus must use the results of our successful operations to the maximum possible extent for the purposes of political work among enemy forces. Enemy soldiers must learn of these successes as soon as possible, they must be told of the futile policy contradictory to the interests of their class their government is conducting, their will to fight on must be weakened, they must be entreated to surrender voluntarily and given a guarantee of immunity. Only in this way, properly using political agitation to prepare the prerequisites of a military blow, the results of these blows for further political agitation and propaganda, is it possible to achieve the successive physical and moral rout of the enemy, gradually to create an internal front in the rear area, to convert the war into a civil war.

Finally, work among the population comprises the third group of problems in political work. In content, it does not differ from the work done among friendly and enemy forces. Its focus is directed identically – to show the true concept of the ongoing war, to show its class nature, to unmask the true intentions of the enemy. Print and oral agitation must be employed widely here. The job is facilitated by the fact that, in the majority of cases, the population can see or experience for itself the *difference* between the Soviet and capitalist forms of state structure, the difference in economic policy, the difference in the policy on national and other problems. The political apparatus need only be able to illuminate, to explain, these facts.

Special attention must be devoted to the mutual relations of the troops and the population, to prevention of any rapacious constraints on the local populace not caused by the conditions of the combat situation, to correct class-consistent distribution of labor and livestock obligations among the various strata of the population. Agitation must be the result not only of words, but deeds as well.

Enormous work involving Sovietization of regions captured from the enemy will fall to the political apparatus. Major successive operations, given favorable conditions, may over a period of three–four weeks lead to liberation of territory with frontage and depth of 200–250 kilometers. If small states are involved, this signifies that one must cope in a short time (two–three weeks) with Sovietization of entire states. This could mean three–four weeks of Sovietization of extremely large areas if larger countries are involved. Of course, complete Sovietization of such territories is a long-term concern, but deployment of a Soviet apparatus must take place within the aforementioned periods. Here, from the very outset, one must achieve a high-quality and reliable apparatus dedicated to the ideals of Soviet power, people capable in deeds of demonstrating to the population of newly captured areas the difference between the Soviet and the capitalist system must be put in place.

It will be very hard to count upon local assets when organizing revolutionary committees because the enemy will undoubtedly destroy all local revolutionary organizations in the area of the front. Only part of the technical apparatus and the most-responsible workers will be found locally. All responsible workers and even some of the technical personnel must be brought in. Of course, they will and, if the capability exists, must be taken from among the local workers, who fled from the Whites. The number of these workers required to carry out the Sovietization of newly captured areas will be enormous. There are five provinces and up to 90–100 districts in Polish territory from the border to the San. The picture in Western Belorussia is essentially the same. Creation of the required number of adminitrative organs will require up to 500–1,000 people, figuring 5–10 people per unit. The Sovietization mission, of course, cannot be handled without wide use of local workers, local revolutionary organizations. Strengthening the Soviet system and the Soviet apparatus wholly depends on the rate of reestablishment of revolutionary social organizations, such as labor unions, poor peasant committees in villages, and so forth.

The Soviet system in captured areas will be finally strengthened only when their own peaceful Communist Party is created.

COMMAND AND CONTROL PROBLEMS

Decision. "Military actions will be conducted not by lyricism and not with declamations, but with specific materiel. If the goal will not accord with extant materiel, then the idea, incorporated in our concept, will become just phrases and will manifest itself as fruitless shaking of fists. There will be no blow capable of pushing the enemy back and leading us to a crowning operation, to an operational victory."[47] If tactical art is regulated and placed in blinkers by the normal organization of tactical formations (divisions and corps) and by the regulation norms developed for their actions, then no norms or initial data, which a commander must use for guidance in decision-making, have been established or are recognized for operational art. This field falls entirely to the "talents" of the commander, his "intuition," his "feel." Based on the experience of the old Russian Army, one can see all the futile results of making the question of leading troops dependent on the commander's "intuition" and "feel." Numerous fruitless decisions unsupported by materiel and linked with a great deal of blood and few victories characterized the activity of Russian generals. Meanwhile, operational art not only must, it also can, be subjected to known rational substantiation. The specific combat actions that comprise operations require very specific materiel and personnel efforts. All real effort is directed towards establishment of the initial data that must correctly orient operational thought when the materiel and personnel resources required for a given operation are being defined.

But it would also be erroneous to look upon operational art as some sort of bookkeeping effort; it would be incorrect to convert operational decisions into simple arithmetic multiplication. The materiel required for every specific case depends not only on the properties of the weapons and arithmetic figures characterizing the length of the front, on the operational and tactical density of the enemy front, how well his positions are fortified, the quality of both the resources and the enemy troops and commanders. These latter data change too much. The art of the leader is to calculate the operational significance of these changing situational elements correctly and to determine the correct material and personnel resources required to accomplish a given specific mission.

An operational decision entails not only correct selection of the axis and form of the blow, but also proper organization of the instrument, the army formations, which the commander will employ to accomplish the mission. One must define the quantity of the different combat arms (artillery, tanks, and aviation in particular) that must be included in the composition of the army, distribute them among the rifle corps to insure both the dependability of the action of the first blow and continuous reinforcement of the troops on those axes where this will become necessary during combat actions.

Degree of command and control centralization. Command and control of armed forces numbering 2–3 million men and deployed on a front with an overall length of 1,000–1,500 kilometers requires three degrees of operational direction on the hierarchical ladder: Headquarters, *front*, and army.

Even at the onset of the World War, the experience of the German Army demonstrated that, without *front*-level command and control, it is impossible to control armies that include a total of 70 infantry divisions and are deployed on a front of only 340–400 kilometers. The German Headquarters lost firm direction of operations during the offensive to the Marne, resorted to a surrogate *front* authority with subordination of one army to the commander of another, and was forced at a decisive moment to leave the decision-making on the further conduct of operations to Colonel Hensch, in essence an irresponsible General Staff officer. The further course of events forced both sides, the German and the French armies, to shift to *front* (army group) command and control. Faced with two different enemies and two theaters separated from one another (Eastern Prussia and Galicia), the Russian Army introduced *front* command and control authorities from the very outset.

Armies such as the French, our Red Army, and even the Polish, in the future will be unable to do without the *front* command and control apparatus. Large armies and broad fronts will not permit direct Headquarters-Army command and control. Under these conditions, Headquarters will be unable to accomplish the firm direction without which coordination of the actions of a large number of army formations is senseless. On the other hand, such small armies as that of Romania, of course, will have only Headquarters-Army command and control.

In major operations, direction of all army formations accomplishing the main blow can be entrusted to one *front* command element (for example, when these armies are deployed in the form of a battering ram side by side on a comparatively small front). In this case, as far as major operations are concerned, Headquarters defines their immediate and subsequent targets, allocates the requisite resources for their conduct, but operational direction itself, in the exact sense of the word, is entirely the task of the commander of a given *front*.

Headquarters' direction of the conduct of major operations decreases and it retains only overall direction of the actions of the *fronts* accomplishing *different* missions, as occurred in 1914 in the Russian Northwestern *Front*'s offensive into East Prussia and the Southernwestern *Front*'s offensive into Galicia or the 1920 offensive by different *fronts* to Warsaw and L'vov.

But command and control may also be organized so that Headquarters will retain not only direction of the *fronts* that, in essence, are accomplishing different missions, but also directly of those forces that, at a given time, conduct *major* operations linked where the goal of the actions and axis of the blow are concerned. For example, command and control of the 1918 German Army offensive, when the blow was inflicted at the point at which the flanks of adjacent fronts met, was organized that way and Ludendorff retained immediate direction (coordination) of their actions.

Command and control is organized based upon the number of forces conducting major operations, the frontage of their deployment, and the form of the blow. It is advisable to concentrate direction of the operations in hands of the *front* commander alone if few forces have been allocated for vigorous actions, deployment frontage is slight, and the battering ram form of the blow is planned. But, on the other hand, it will be useful to have two *fronts* and to retain immediate operational direction of operations in the main theater of military actions directly in the hands of the commander-in-chief if many divisions have been assigned for vigorous actions, deployment is on a broad front, and the axis of the blow is via intersecting operational axes.

How often does a particular authority have to intervene in the conduct of combat actions? This question must depend on the periods of time during which it is possible, given modern weapons, to accomplish tactical and operational missions.

In fact, we saw that a tactical mission (surmounting the depth of the modern defense zone) normally requires one–two days.

During this period, tactical authorities, the division and corps, are in charge. The army commander will be required to intervene during that period only in the event tactical actions are bottled up, forces turn out to be insufficient, and new artillery or rifle troops have to be committed. Normally, the army commander, having deployed forces for the operational engagement and having assigned them their tactical missions, may later on, until these missions are accomplished, limit himself to monitoring the course of the combat actions and intervening in the business of the corps commanders only if the latter deviate from his instructions or events take a course that does not correspond to his intentions. The army commander will indicate a subsequent general goal of the actions and will assign immediate missions to the corps only when accomplishment of the tactical missions is drawing to a close.

The *front* commander (the commander-in-chief when Headquarters is exercising immediate direction of the operations) will be required to intervene after additional prolonged periods of time.

It is usually necessary immediately to assign armies missions that entail surmounting the entire enemy operational disposition, that is, designed to a depth of 30–50 kilometers and requiring four–five days. The army commander himself regulates the course of the combat actions within the framework of these missions and deadlines. The *front* commander will be required to intervene during this period only in those instances when the situation requires a change in the initial missions assigned to the armies. He will normally be able to await resolution of the results of the initial operation. After that, he will assign the armies the goals for further actions and immediate missions entailing actions up to deployment for a new operation. These rather long stages during which a particular authority intrudes into the course of combat actions should not be confused with provision of information, or orientation as to the actions of friendly forces.

Normally, one must insure that, by the end of the day, the *front* commander (or Headquarters) has complete information on the course of the previous days' combat actions and the points (lines) *each divison* has attained. During these periods, all new orders that will be issued to the armies to develop or to change previous combat orders and directives must be available at the *front* staff (or at Headquarters). Information processing and communications capabilities make this fully possible.

Timely intervention of a senior chief during combat actions is possible only if such orientation is provided about the actions of friendly forces and, consequently, about the enemy, hence the degree of firmness of direction as well. Only then will there be fewer lost opportunities and uncoordinated actions.

Location of staffs. The chief in whose hands direction of the operations will be concentrated (be it the commander-in-chief himself or the *front* commander) must select the location for his own disposition so that, during the day, he will be able to have exhaustive data on the course of combat actions at the front, even in a case where technical communications refuse to operate for some reason or another. The daily round-trip operation of the modern vehicle which must exceed 100–150 kilometers from the front line (figuring from the location of the staff not only to the center of the *front*, but to the flank corps as well), defines the distance of the staff from the front. Both the staff and the entire *front* administration initially will be located with the commander. Modern communications (telephone, telegraph, vehicles) also fully justify a staff being separated from the front administration. The staff must move in full complement, having the chiefs or responsible representatives of the services with it. There is no necessity to assign any field staffs, as they destroy the natural structure of the command and control apparatus.

Identical data regarding army units define the disposition of the army staff. The army staff must normally remain within 20–50 kilometers of the front line if the offensive frontage is 40–50 kilometers. Army directorates are completely with the army staff. Given these distances, there is again no necessity to assign field staffs. The army staff (*in toto*) is separated from army services only in extreme cases, when movement forward is required and the situation makes it inadvisable to move all army directorates forward. In this case, service representatives also move forward with the staff. This includes the chiefs of artillery, communications, engineers, technical services, and the air forces, who are continually with the army staff. This determines the nature of the communications network and these chiefs must be provided with reliable communications with their units. This particularly applies to the communications of the chief of the air forces with airfields.

The staff will have to be relocated at least twice during a series of successive operations designed to a depth of front of 180–200 kilometers. It is advisable at the beginning of the operation to move the *front* staff about 50–70 kilometers closer to the front to avoid frequent relocations. A staff can remain in the same place for 7–10 days (70–100 kilometers of advance).

Army staffs will have to relocate more often, about every 25–30 kilometers of advance, that is, every three, maximum four, days. The communications configuration fully permits this.

Tactics, operational art and strategy as a whole stem from the materiel and personnel that a state allocates for the conduct of warfare. Military art, torn away from this foundation, is inevitably converted into adventurism and fantasy and can lead to nothing good. But all this has a reverse influence as well. Tactics, operational art and all strategy not only consider the materiel base and flow from this, but, in turn, indicate and map out the paths of further development and expansion of this materiel base. They solve problems such as which branches of military and overall civilian technology must be developed in the future, the trend this should follow, the combat arms that require further alteration, and what improvements and upgrades must be carried out within the armed forces system.

Our study in the main has been built on a modern materiel base. It considers possible changes in this base. But, in addition, it poses a whole series of problems concerning further development and construction of the armed forces. Categorically, it poses the question of suppressive assets, of assets accompanying the infantry into combat, of tanks in particular. In all its magnitude, it poses questions about the significance of transport assets for modern armed forces, problems of rail technology, and introduction of vehicles into the army. And, given all of this, it places questions of force quality in the forefront. All this technology that is or will be in the inventory may fall into enemy hands if proper skills and combat training, a proper command element and command and control, proper moral and political state of the army, and proper force quality are not insured.

Notes

PART ONE

1. The Maxim M1908 heavy machine gun with water and mount weighs 64kg; the Browning M1918 machine gun with water and mount weighs 33kg; the German M1908-1918 and Italian 1A M1918 weigh 16–16.4kg; the American Browning M1918 rifle-machine gun weighs a total of 7kg.
2. See Burov's Foreword to Shvarte's [Max Schwarte] book *Tekhnika v mirovoy voyne* [Technology in the World War], p. 17.
3. In Britain, £54,000 (1921), £103,000 (1923), £115,000 (1925), and £132,000 (1926) were spent on chemical experimental work at the military installation at Porton. In America, $720,000 (1925) and $904,000 (1926) was spent at Edgewood Arsenal. Last year, the Japanese spent 5 million yen on military chemical affairs.
4. Svechin, *Strategiya* [Strategy], 1st edn., p. 172.
5. Abroad, Fuller, Seeckt, Zol'dan, and others. Here, A. I. Verkhovskiy has adopted that point of view. In his latest book, *Osnovy nashey taktiki. Ogon' i maskirovka* [Fundamentals of Our Tactics. Fire and Camouflage], he writes (p. 231): "It is clear that, when an armed force is organized in this manner, the massive army will disappear, a small army of knights, which can be structured according to the classic principle, will replace it. Structured in this manner were units of knights, where only one knight participated in a joust and was armed, with the entire remaining group having to accept the result of the joust and obey unconditionally."
6. Svechin, *Strategiya* [Strategy], p. 170.
7. According to certain data, France alone retained 10,000 light field guns, 6,000 heavy guns, about 3 million rifles and carbines, 25,000 heavy machine guns, 140,000 light machine guns, 3,000 tanks, 600 million rifle cartridges, 60 millon light shells, and 10 million heavy shells.
8. Concerning peacetime cadres, see Zayonchkovskiy, *Podgotovka Rossii k mirovoy voyne* [Russia's Preparation for the World War], p. 93; Novitskiy, *Mirovaya voyna* 1914–1918 [The 1914–1918 World War], Vol 1, pp. 55, 56.
9. Here, all 29 new reserve divisions entered the war without machine guns and with weak artillery (each first-line division had 72 pieces, while each reserve division had 36).
10. The strength of the French reserve divisions is identical to that of the cadre field divisions.
11. There is the view that peacetime cadres in the 1914 mobilization were employed irrationally, that there was a requirement to employ them more decisively for second-line formations as well. We do not agree with this viewpoint. Vigorous actions at the outset of the war required high-quality forces. Given strong diminution of cadres, the Germans could in no way count upon the tempo of combat work, the maneuverability, and the persistence they displayed in the 1914 campaign.
12. In particular, the Poles resorted to this often, the last time in connection with the Lithuanian revolution.
13. See Novitskiy, *Mirovaya voyna na Zapadnom fronte* [The World War on the Western Front], Vol I, pp. 78, 79.

14. Novitskiy, ibid.
15. Second-line division infantry had no machine guns.
16. Svechin, *Strategiya* [Strategy].
17. Germany had a total of 242 infantry divisions at the end of the war. The remaining 33 were disbanded at different times due to enormous combat losses.
18. Triandafillov, *Vozmozhnaya chislennost' budushchikh armiy* [Possible Numerical Strength of Future Armies], *Voyna i revolyutsiya*, 1927, Book 3.
19. Ibid.
20. Lapchinskiy's foreword to Gopper's book *Voyna Germanii v vozdukhe* [Germany's War in the Air], Gviz, 1924 edition.
21. *Kak vooruzhayutsya imperialisty* [How the Imperialists Arm Themselves], 4th edition, RKKA Staff Directorate, 1926, pp. 74 and 76.
22. *Frantsuzskiy voyennyy vozdushnyy flot* [The French Air Fleet], translation from the French, 1925 edition.
23. The annual German requirement in 1917 for a 5 million man army was 2.34 billion cartridges and 100 million shells. For the French in 1917, this was 2 billion and 90 million, respectively. The numerical strength and armament of the mobilization first echelon of future armies are essentially the same as those of the 1917 French and German armies. This means the first year of a future war will require the identical intensity that the World War required in the third year of combat actions.
24. According to the 1921 census, which to a significant degree underestimated the numerical strength of the national minorities, Belorussia comprised 35.3 per cent Belorussians, 5.9 per cent Ukrainians, and 8.4 per cent Jews. Volynia comprised 68.4 per cent Ukrainians and 10.5 per cent Jews. The Western Ukraine was 52 per cent Ukrainians and 6.2 per cent Jews. After 1921, when the refugees returned, the percentage of national minorities in the regions increased another 5 per cent.
25. Shvarte, *Tekhnika v mirovoy voyne* [Technology in the World War].
26. Err, *Artilleriya proshedshego, nastoyashchego i budushchego* [Artillery of the Past, Present, and Future].
27. Manchikovskiy, *Artilleriyskoye snabzheniye russkoy armii* [Russian Army Artillery Supply].
28. *Vozhdeniye i boy soyedinennykh rodov voysk* [Leadership and Combat of Combined Combat Arms].
29. A division in the defense normally occupies up to 8 kilometers, which, if the division has 72 pieces, provides 9 pieces per kilometer of front. When corps artillery is figured in, this number of pieces will increase to 10–11. Countering the enemy artillery requires twice the number of pieces, i.e., 20–22 (rounded off to 20 pieces per kilometer of front).
30. An example is Russia in the World War. At a time when the Germans and French during the war increased their artillery by a factor of 2.5–3, the Russians, banking on all their allies, including America and Japan, were only able to increase all their artillery by a factor of 1.5.
31. The French Army had eight cavalry divisions in 1914 and now has five. Prior to the war, Tsarist Russia had 24 cavalry divisions. The Soviet Army has only 13. The Polish Army has only 4 cavalry divisions and 5 separate cavalry brigades for 30 infantry divisions. The Romanian Army has 2 cavalry divisions for 15 infantry divisions.
32. The number of tank organizational formations in peacetime in France alone will reach 23 regiments. The other countries each have only several battalions, such as eight in Britain and three in Poland. The chemical troops are even weaker.

NOTES

PART TWO

1. One 30-aircraft squadron can simultaneously cover a 12-kilometer front (see Mezheninov, *Vozdushnyye sily v voyne i operatsii* [Air Forces in a War and an Operation], p. 66).
2. The Polish Field Service Regulations (p. 269) consider that, in cases when the overall front with respect to extant forces is marked by a very great expanse, a division can defend on a front of 30 and even 40–50 kilometers. According to the calculation presented above, given this disposition, the density of fire and disposition depth are so insignificant that, in this case, we will be dealing not with a defense, but with a screening force accomplishing a cover and reconnaissance mission.
3. Grendal', *Ogon' artillerii* [Artillery Fire].
4. *Boyevoy ustav artillerii 1927 g.* [1927 Artillery Field Manual], Section 229.
5. Kyul'man, *Obshchaya taktika* [General Tactics], Gosizdat, 1928, p. 319.
6. *Boyevoy ustav artillerii 1927*, Section 207.
7. *Pols'kiy ustav* [Polish Regulations], p. 301.
8. Ibid. pp. 303, 304.
9. Moreover, another hour is required for registration and preliminary suppression of defensive artillery. Some 5–6 hours are devoted to artillery preparation, i.e., it takes up the entire first half of the day. The second half of the day, with difficulty, will suffice for carrying out the attack and its development until there is a complete breakthrough of the defense zone (8–12 kilometers).
10. Kyul'man provides the following norms for a corps in maneuver warfare: from 2.5 to 4 kilometers for a main attack, up to 8 kilometers for auxiliary attacks. The offensive zone in static warfare is compressed to 1,200 and 2,000 meters, respectively.
11. Kyul'man, *Obshchaya taktika* [General Tactics], p. 320.
12. In a 100-kilogram aviation bomb, which corresponds to a 21 cm artillery shell, the weight of the charge is 58 per cent of the weight of the bomb, while the corresponding figure for an artillery shell is only 6.8 per cent.
13. Lapchinskiy, *Taktika aviatsii* [Aviation Tactics], Moscow, 1926.
14. In our opinion, preparatory work requires less time, necessitating only minutes for many railroad stations.
15. The Germans had even concentrated an enormous amount of aviation in the area of a future operation, but, for camouflage, aviation began flights immediately before onset of combat actions. Thus, Allied aviation had the capability to operate virtually on a daily basis. See Bazarevskiy, *Kampaniya 1918* [The 1918 Campaign].
16. One fighter squadron supports a 12-kilometer front (see Mezheninov, *Vozdushnyye sily v voyne i operatsii* [Air Forces in a War and an Operation], p. 66). A shock army's offensive frontage is 50–75 kilometers. One must assume that, for some corps moving through a forested region, their own antiaircraft artillery will suffice.
17. The depth of the combat units of a column of a rifle division with one regiment of additional artillery, figuring from the head of the security units, will reach 25 kilometers. The depth of a corps or fourth artillery regiment of a division will reach 3 kilometers. Divisional logistics have a depth of about 15 kilometers. All told, the depth of the combat units and divisional logistics is some 38 kilometers, all corps logistics having a depth of 35 kilometers. Given the distribution among the three divisions, one should consider another 12 kilometers per road. This totals 50 kilometers. The intervals between column units has been included throughout the entire calculation.
18. Our *Boyevoy ustav konnitsy* [Cavalry Field Manual], Part 3, 1927, envisions the army cavalry moving up to 100 kilometers forward.

19. A column with additional artillery will be 23–26 kilometers long. Given high-quality forces, the deployment rate is 5 kilometers per hour (1 kilometer every 12 minutes). If they are poorly trained, this drops to 3 kilometers per hour (i.e., 1 kilometer every 20 minutes). Along with combat unit training, the level of training of organic trains is of great significance here.
20. The length of a column comprising two divisions along one road is 60–70 kilometers. Second-echelon divisions normally will need 3 days to move up to the line of lead units. This deployment may also be concluded in 2 days if personnel are speeded up.
21. Surmounting the enemy tactical disposition (8–10 kilometers) will require 2 days, considering deployment (1 day under favorable conditions). During this time, reserves 25–40 kilometers from the point of penetration will reach the combat area. Reserves 100 kilometers away will make it there if vehicle transport is available. These forces, along with those that have withdrawn, form a new front with a depth again of 6–8 kilometers. Along with the depth of withdrawal of the first echelon (to the range of artillery fire – 10–15 kilometers), the overall depth of the "battlefield" is formed to 25–35 kilometers.
22. This, of course, does not denote that all forces achieve only 5–6 kilometers per day. On the contrary, the majority of divisions and even corps will be forced to make 30–40 kilometers to achieve those points from which they will go directly into combat. We will not forget that the depth of the area that a modern army occupies for movement will reach 60–70 kilometers. The figure indicated (5–6-kilometer daily advance) applies to the rate of development of the operation as a whole during a frontal clash.
23. Le-Enaph and Boranek, *French Railroads and War*.
24. *Boyevoy ustav artillerii* [Artillery Field Manual], 1927, p. 72.
25. According to our reference data, fortification of 1 kilometer of position in maneuver warfare requires up to 165 tons of materials for a hastily fortified position. A division defending 20 kilometers will require 3,300 tons of materials, the shipment of which will require 5 trains. The amount of materials required per kilometer of front for more solid fortifications, even without concrete structures, increases to 500 tons, 3,400 tons with concrete works, i.e., the supply of construction materials for a 20-kilometer divisional sector, judging from the nature of the work, will already require from 15 to 100 trains.

    The German Army recognizes four variants of the construction of protective works. The first variant envisions erection of light shrapnel shelters, a light type of wire, and fire points by the forces themselves and requires 260 rail cars (5 trains) of materials for a divisional sector. The second variant envisages erection of shelters to protect against 15-centimeter shells and requires 1,600 rail cars (40 trains) of materials for a divisional sector. In the third variant, the number of shelters rises to 220 and the number of rail cars of construction materials to 2,900 (up to 58 trains). Finally, the fourth variant includes erection of shelters for half of all reserves (400 shelters) and then the number of rail cars rises to 5,200 (100 trains). Thus, more or less solid fortifications will require the supply of at least 40–60 trains of construction materials per divisional sector.
26. The rate at which men are put out of action has great significance here. Identical losses can completely disrupt an organic unit if they are suffered in a brief but intense skirmish, but they may go virtually unnoticed if the people are put out of action over a long period of time.
27. Of this number, three trains for the rifle corps and additional artillery and one for army units and institutions.
28. Figuring that an ammunition train comprises 30 cars.
29. It was already indicated that basing a shock army on horse traction is

essentially ruled out. The army link in the supply chain for a shock army must be structured predominantly on vehicle transportation.

30. The maximum mainline traffic capacity on the first three railroads is 36 pairs of trains, of which 28 may be used for military movements (75 per cent of total traffic capacity). A Polish division with limited artillery can be moved by this many trains and especially if you consider the inevitable shortages in troop units during combat actions. The last axis, via Warsaw, has a maximum traffic capacity of only 22 pairs of trains in its initial sector (Kopchintsy–Stanislawow), i.e., it can move only about half a division per day.
31. At the outset of the deployment, the French left wing (3rd, 4th, and 5th Armies) comprised 11 corps, 3 cavalry divisions, and 9 reserve divisions. During the frontier operational engagement, the composition of these armies increased to 14 corps, 6 cavalry divisions, and 9 reserve divisions. In the Battle of the Marne, a new army, the 6th, participated on the left flank and a new 9th Army was formed in the center. In the five left-flank armies, the French had 15 corps, 9 cavalry divisions, and 12 reserve divisions. The overall reinforcement over the 24-day period was 11 infantry and 6 cavalry divisions. The French railroads could have coped with much larger transfers.
32. A divisional column requires 4–5 hours to deploy. Enemy artillery fire has a range of up to 12 kilometers (most enemy artillery). Surmounting that depth under artillery fire will require 4–5 hours, i.e., up to 8–10 hours will be spent on deployment and closing. Another 2–3 hours of march prior to deployment must be added, i.e., the troops will have a 10–12 hour workday. One cannot demand more of them. Movement forward on days of direct combat cannot exceed 6–8 kilometers (2.5–3 hours of artillery preparation and 4–5 hours of combat) or, figuring both closing and the attack, an average of 8–10 kilometers per day.
33. Bonch-Bruyevich, *Poterya nami Galitsii* [Our Loss of Galicia], p. 96.
34. One from the Northwestern *Front*, a second from the 4th Army, and a third from the 3rd Army's left flank. Along with the XXIX Corps that had begun to detrain, that provided four German corps.
35. In the Red Army's 42-day offensive from the Western Dvina and Wisla, no more than 8–9 days total were devoted to combat.
36. Le-Enaph and Bornek, *Frantsuzskiye zheleznyye dorogi v mirovuyu voynu* [French Railroads in the World War]. See also Norman, *Razrusheniye i vosstanovleniye putey soobshcheniya* [Railroad Destruction and Restoration].
37. Norman, ibid.
38. From 8 August to 11 November (about 90 days), the 18th Army moved 190 kilometers (Montdidier–Chimay) and the 7th Army just 170 kilometers (Chateau–Thierry–Revin) from 18 July to 11 November (about 110 days).
39. Restoration of thoroughly destroyed railroads requires 24 rails, each 12.5 meters long, and 200 ties per kilometer of front. Along with the other materials (spikes, covers, bolts, cushions), this comprises cargo requiring two rail cars to move it (some 14 rail cars of construction materials are needed per kilometer of track for newly laid track).
40. One should note the following from these technical data: use of longer rails (60 meters), which means fewer joints and less shaking of the bed; replacement of wooden ties by pig-iron ties, special machines for preparation of ballast (crushers); light steel for bridges, making lighter girders possible and facilitating restoration of large bridges; temporary replacement of bridges by ferries and approach roads at a low level, and so forth.
41. Restoration of railroads that have suffered capital destruction requires: on single-track lines being restored at a daily rate of 5–6 kilometers – three trains of construction materials, four vehicle companies, six transport (horse) companies, eight labor companies, two regiments with carpenter battalions, and two to three advance mobile repair shops. The lead section of a rail line,

whose traffic capacity in the first 7 days after restoration does not exceed three to four pairs of trains, can cope only with the supply of this material.

When only one track on double-track lines is being restored, up to 8–10 kilometers may be restored per day, given virtually the same amount of supplied material and labour. *Simultaneous* restoration of both lines on double-track lines at a rate of 8–10 kilometers per day requires approximately six railroad trains of construction materials, five vehicle companies, eight transport companies, and four to five advance mobile repair shops. The lead railroad section must have a traffic capacity of 8–10 pairs of trains to supply 6 trains of construction materials. At present, railroad restoration conditions (water supply) do not support such traffic capacity. Thus, the restoration rate in this case cannot exceed 5–6 kilometers per day.

Introduction of diesels and invention of light field block signalling also may support a faster double-track line restoration rate in the future.

42. These data accepted for calculations in our army coincide with official reference data in other armies. Thus, the Germans consider that the restoration on capitally-destroyed double-track railroads is 5 kilometers (considering also the time required to restore bridges), given availability of the maximum work force (eight railroad companies); the figures for medium and minor destruction are 10 and 20 kilometers, respectively.
43. Actually, the Polish–Soviet border from the Western Dvina to the Dnestr, a distance of 800 kilometers, has a total of seven mainlines, i.e., one railroad per every 110–120 kilometers of front. The maximum attack frontage for an army comprising five corps with additional artillery cannot exceed 50 kilometers. The only normal basing conditions to be found are west of the Belostok–Brest–Rovno–Kamenets–Podol'sk line.
44. This operating variant is also possible. Initially, one track instead of two is restored at the aforementioned rate, an average of 8 kilometers per day. The second track is restored after a traffic capacity of 17 pairs of trains is achieved on the first track (after 1 week). Restoration of the second track will require at least another week if the work is done at the maximum rate, i.e. the lead section of the second track will fall 50 kilometers behind the lead section of the first track. Then, the railheads for some corps will be forward, while those for the others will be 50 kilometers to the rear. But this does not change the crux of the problem. In the final analysis, the rate at which the second track is restored determines the scale of the operations.
45. One train has a capacity of 400 tons, a 3-ton truck averages $2\frac{1}{2}$ tons (50 tons for a 20-vehicle transport detachment), and double wagon 400–500 kilograms (up to 100 tons per army train comprising 200 double wagons).
46. Pilsudski, *1920 god* [1920].
47. Svechin, *Strategiya* [Strategy], p. 367.

Index

INDEX

INDEX